Praise from Job Seekers for the *Knock 'em Dead* Books

"I got the position! I was interviewed by three people and the third person asked me all the questions in *Knock 'em Dead*. I had all the right answers!"
— **D.J., Scottsdale, Arizona**

"I just finished writing the letter I have dreamed of writing for three years: my letter of resignation from the Company from Hell. Thanks to you and the book, *Knock 'em Dead*, I have been offered and have accepted an excellent position with a major international service corporation."
— **C.C., Atlanta, Georgia**

"Thank you for your wonderful book! I read it before attempting to secure a position in an industry that I had been out of for fourteen years. The first company I interviewed with made me an offer for more money than I had expected."
— **K.T., Houston, Texas**

"My previous employer asked me to resign. Your book got me through my depression, and in only four weeks, got me four job offers. This is the first time in my career I have this many options to choose from."
— **D.H., North Canton, Ohio**

"I credit you as being the number one source of information on this issue, and recommend you every time I hear that someone is in the job market. The cost of the book is the best money I've ever spent."
— **T.S., Atlanta, Georgia**

"After college graduation, I searched and searched for a job, and ended up taking a few low-paying ones I was overqualified for. Finally, I read your book and have been offered *every* job I have applied for since."
— **L.E. (no address given)**

"I followed the advice in *Knock 'em Dead* religiously and got more money, less hours, a better hospital plan, and negotiated to keep my three weeks vacation. I start my new job immediately!"

— A.B., St. Louis, Missouri

"My job search began a few months ago when I found out that I would be laid off because of a corporate buyout. By following your advice, I have had dozens of interviews and have received three very good job offers. Your excellent advice made my job hunt much easier."

— K.C., St. Louis, Missouri

"I found your book to be absolutely invaluable during my recent job search. Since then I have had a chance to speak with my interviewer, who informed me that it was my strong interview that landed me my job offer. He went on to outline what had turned him off about other candidates, and it was some of the very same mistakes I used to make before reading your book!"

— D.D., Houlton, Maine

"Every time I've used your book, I've gotten an offer! This book is incredible. Thanks for publishing such a great tool."

— W.Z., Columbia, Maryland

"Just a quick note to let you know how much your book has helped me. I was chosen for my job out of over one hundred applicants! I later loaned the book to a friend and circled the things that had helped me. She interviewed on a Thursday, and she was offered the position that Thursday night! Thanks for writing such a helpful book."

— S.G., Sacramento, California

"Your book is simply fantastic. This one book improved my yearly income by several thousand dollars, and my future income by untold amounts. Your work has made my family and myself very happy."

— M.Z., St. Clair Shores, Michigan

"Thank you for all the wonderfully helpful information you provided in your book. I lost my job almost one year ago. I spent almost eight months looking for a comparable position. Then I had the good sense to buy your book. Two months later, I accepted a new position. You helped me turn one of the worst experiences of my life into a blessing in disguise."
— **L.G., Watervliet, New York**

"I was out of work for four months—within five weeks of reading your book, I had four job offers."
— **S.K., Dallas, Texas**

"Yesterday I received two job offers in the space of fifteen minutes. I am now using the 'Negotiating the Offer' chapter to evaluate these positions."
— **W.B., Thornhill, Ontario**

"I read every page in the book and, after a two-month search, got ten interviews with top-performing companies and six offers (five of which I declined)."
— **M.V., Millington, Tennessee**

"I was sending out hordes of resumes and hardly getting a nibble—and I have top-notch skills and experience in my field. I wasn't prepared for this tough job market. When I read your book, however, I immediately began applying some of your techniques. My few nibbles increased to so many job interviews I could hardly keep up with them!"
— **C.S., Chicago, Illinois**

"I read the book, cover-to-cover, and then flew to California to complete fourteen intense interviews in a two-day period. Although I was interviewing for an entry-level position with a high-tech firm, I faced few technical questions. Most of them were behavioral questions, exactly the types your book prepared me for. I had the enviable position for making a choice of which job to take!"
— **S.T., San Jose, California**

"I got two job offers within a twenty-four-hour period. The information you've provided is as valuable as the air you breathe."

— J.M., Greensboro, North Carolina

"I will always remain a student of yours. Since the first edition to the last, I got every copy, and with each I learn more. I have had several interviews, all of which were generated by the tactics of your book."

— M.R., Beaumont, Texas

"It was as if the interviewer had just put the same book down! After being unemployed for more than a year, I am grateful to say that I've landed the best job I've ever had."

— E.M., Honolulu, Hawaii

"I read and used your book, *Resumes That Knock 'em Dead,* as I searched for a job. I was called for an interview and was up against ten applicants. To make a long story short, I interviewed on Monday morning, and by Monday afternoon knew I had the job."

— E.H. (no address given)

"I just received the offer of my dreams with an outstanding company. Thank you for your insight. I was prepared!"

— T.C., San Francisco, California

"After reading your book, *Resumes That Knock 'em Dead,* I rewrote my resume and mailed it to about eight companies. The results were beyond belief. I was employed by one of the companies that got my new resume, and received offers of employment or requests for interviews from every company. The entire job search took only five weeks."

— J.V., Dayton, Ohio

COVER LETTERS

THAT KnOCK 'em DEaD

COVER LETTERS THAT KnOCK 'em DEaD

Martin Yate

Adams Media Corporation
Holbrook, Massachusetts

Acknowledgments

Knock 'em Dead is now in its 15th year of publication, and has become a staple for job hunters around the world. This is due to the ongoing support of my publisher Bob Adams, and the tireless encouragement of the Adams Media sales team headed by Wayne Jackson. This, and the other *Knock 'em Dead* books, are kept fresh and vibrant thanks to the ministrations of my editor, Ed Walters, the Associate Publisher of Adams Media. Finally, this year I am indebted to Jennifer Lantagne for her indefatigable work on three simultaneous sets of galleys.

Published by Adams Media Corporation
260 Center Street, Holbrook, MA 02343
www.adamsmedia.com

ISBN: 1-58062-423-5

Printed in the United States of America.

J I H G F E D C B A

**Library of Congress Cataloging-in-Publication Data
available from publisher.**

This publication is designed to provide accurate and authoritative information with regard to the subject matter covered. It is sold with the understanding that the publisher is not engaged in rendering legal, accounting, or other professional advice. If legal advice or other expert assistance is required, the services of a qualified professional person should be sought.
—From a *Declaration of Principles* jointly adopted by a Committee of the American Bar Association and a Committee of Publishers and Associations

Rear cover author photo by Ariel Jones

This book is available at quantity discounts for bulk purchases.
For information, call 1-800-872-5627.

Visit our home page at www.careercity.com

*To good fortune,
the intersection of opportunity,
preparation, and effort.*

Read This First

There's a cruel paradox at work when it comes to writing cover letters.

We strive to excel in our professions, spending our energies to become top-notch accountants, truck drivers, brain surgeons . . . and we spend little or no time learning to promote ourselves on the printed page. When suddenly our livelihood depends on our ability to compose a compelling written summary of the advantages of working with us, we find ourselves in dire straits.

If we ever developed the necessary skills in school, we find they have long since rusted. Writing it all down for review by others in a position to hire us has simply never made it onto the daily to-do list. Many professionals create the thoughts behind their business communications, but hire others to craft (and not always well) the messages themselves.

If you find yourself in this situation at the most inopportune time imaginable—during your job search—take heart. This book will solve your problem quickly. Use it exactly as I recommend in the pages that follow. If you do, you will reap a number of benefits, the most important of which is this:

- Your job hunt and ensuing career will benefit tremendously, because your letters will look great, pack a punch, get read, and position you as a mover and shaker worth interviewing.

There are other advantages:

- You won't waste a moment of precious time.
- You'll have the satisfaction of having made a tough, intricate, and vitally important professional challenge a little easier and more enjoyable than it is for most people in your shoes (your competitors, for example).
- You might even have some fun.

Employers go through four distinct stages in reaching a hiring decision.

1. Long-list development. Advertising and other sources develop the biggest possible field of qualified candidates.
2. Short-list development. The long list is screened to rule out also-rans. Those who make the cut are invited in for an interview.
3. Short-list prioritization. Through a series of two or three interviews, candidates are weeded out. Those still standing are ranked according to various criteria.
4. Short-list review. After the dust settles, each candidate's strengths and weaknesses are reviewed for one last time before the final decision. The information in the dossier created for every short-list candidate plays a key role here. This dossier will contain all the knowledge the company has about you. This will include your resume, cover letter, and any follow-up letters you have been smart enough to send during the interview process.

In each of these steps, letters have a role to play in taking you to the next level. For example, a resume without a cover letter rarely gets any further than the trash can. A "To Whom It May Concern" letter fares little better. A letter with a salutation by names gets read and kept. As will follow-up letters on meetings that make comments on the discussions and issues addressed.

It's estimated that the average piece of business correspondence gets less than thirty seconds of the reader's attention. Even a truly great cover letter will not get much more. In crafting your cover letter, you are not aiming to win a place next to a favorite novel on the reader's bedside table. A powerful cover letter will win that momentary flash of genuine interest and get your resume read with serious attention. Once that's accomplished, you can use the models for the follow-up letters in this book to help you step upward on the four-tiered ladder to the job offer.

Letters help you move through each phase of the hiring cycle and on to the offer in ways most people have never understood. In the fourth step (the short-list review) the interviewer recalls what happened in each phase of the interview cycle. All notes and documentation in the applicant dossier are reviewed on each candidate. This means that as you pass through each step of the cycle, you are presented with a heaven-sent opportunity to advance your candidacy when The Moment of Truth finally arrives. You can forward all manner of pertinent information that will identify you as the unquestioned prime choice when that last, most critical evaluation is taking place.

◆ ◆ ◆

I took a common-sense approach to putting this book together: I collected over four thousand successful job-hunting letters from the most cynical professionals in the country, corporate human resources people and professional headhunters. I approached over a thousand of these people and asked them to provide the truly impressive letters they came across—the letters that made a difference, grabbed attention, and advanced someone's candidacy against tough competition. The cream of the crop can be found within these covers.

From these letters, and from my discussions with professionals in the field, I learned about certain things that work and don't work when putting together a cover letter. These are explored in detail later on in the book, but there is one overriding factor that virtually all the successful letters shared. It's worth exploring here.

All but a handful of the letters were only one page long. Yours probably should be too. Why is brevity so important? My sources feel that:

1. They don't have time to wade through dense patches of text, and they view those who can't get to the point in a dim light.
2. Second pages get detached and often lack sufficient contact information. (For that matter, first pages often fall short in the same category.)

Perhaps the most overlooked benefit of a comprehensive mail dimension to your job-hunting campaign is that the letters can be working for you while you are investing your time and energy elsewhere. A strong mail dimension to your plan can double and triple your effectiveness. Throughout the book whenever you read the word "mail" it has a double meaning—regular mail and e-mail. The most effective job hunting campaign will always use the two mediums in tandem.

If you use the letters simply as noncustomized templates, you may open a few doors. But the "real" you will be so different from the letters that the interviewers will eventually be left with a nagging doubt that you aren't all you appear to be.

Browse through the letters in the second half of this book. Not all of them will fit your needs at this moment, but take a look anyway. You will see, on every page, proven methods of getting the good word across to potential employers.

This book will also highlight key phrases and wording techniques that caught the eyes of people whose eyes are usually tough to catch. You will discover a "rhythm" to the words and phrases that have real impact. Then you'll be able to incorporate them into your own original work.

In choosing the examples for this book, I was pleased to see that the ones that rose to the top were all businesslike, with no gimmickry or cuteness. Some may even seem a little dry to you, but remember: They worked. This collection of successful job-hunting letters includes the best of the best as determined by corporate gatekeepers and captains of industry who know a winner when they see one. It is just such people who will be evaluating your efforts, and the drawbridge of opportunity will be raised (or lowered) for you depending on their evaluation.

Now let's learn how to put together some jigsaw puzzles. I suggest that you read this book with a highlighter in hand, so you can flag appropriate sections for later reference. That way you'll have a wealth of good ideas you can use after just one read. Then you'll be ready to create your own unique job-hunting letters that will knock 'em dead.

Table of Contents

Broadcast

Networking

1 | What Is a Cover Letter?

Junk mail never gets the attention a personal letter does. You junk it—either without reading it, or after a quick glance.

Too many employment queries end up being treated as junk mail—and if a piece of correspondence is treated like junk mail, that's what it is. Your cover letter is the personalized factor in the presentation of an otherwise essentially impersonal document, your resume. A good cover letter sets the stage for the reader to accept your resume as something special. Only if your cover letter and resume do their job will interviews and employment offers result.

When the envelope is opened, your cover letter is the first thing seen. It can make an indelible first impression. Of course, I'm not saying that the letter alone will get you the job, or even land you the interview, but the letter will help you along the way by getting that resume read with something like serious attention.

The higher up the professional ladder you climb, the more important cover letters and job-hunting letters become. For the candidate who must demonstrate written communication skills in the execution of daily duties (and that's just about all of us), these letters become a valuable vehicle for demonstrating critical job skills. Mess up here and the door to opportunity could well slam shut.

Step One

Grab your reader's ATTENTION. Do this by using quality stationery, and envelopes. Use the same paper your resume is printed on. This way your letter and resume will match and give an impression of balance and continuity. See chapter 5, "The Final Product," for details.

Step Two

Generate INTEREST with the content. Do this by addressing the letter to someone by name and quickly explaining what you have to offer. The first sentence grabs attention, the rest of the paragraph gives the reader the old one-two punch. The rule is: Say it strong, say it straight and don't pussy-foot.

Do some research. Even a little can get your letter off to a fast start. A case in point is:

> *"I came across the enclosed article in* Newsweek *magazine and thought it might interest you. It encouraged me to do a little research on your company. I am now convinced of two things: You are the kind of people I want to be associated with, and I have the kind of qualifications you can use."*

Check out a company's Web site; you will find lots of eye-opening data, including news and press clippings. You can also use search engines, to find interesting info about the company, by typing in the company name as a keyword.

Of course, in the real world, we can't all apply for jobs with companies that are featured in the big magazines. Here are some more everyday examples.

> *"I have been following the performance of your fund in* Mutual Funds Newsletter. *The record over the last three years shows strong portfolio management. With my experience working for one of your competitors, I know I could make significant contributions . . ."*

> *"Recently I have been researching the local _____ industry. My search has been for companies that are respected in the field and that provide ongoing training programs. The name _____ keeps coming up as a top company."*

> *"With the scarcity of qualified and motivated (your desired job title) that exists today, I feel sure that it would be valuable for us to talk."*

"Within the next few weeks I will be moving from New York to _____ . Having researched the companies in my field in my new home town, I know that you are the people I want to talk to . . ."

"The state of the art in _____ changes so rapidly that it is tough for most professionals to keep up. I am the exception. I am eager to bring my experience to bear for your company."

Step Three

Now turn that INTEREST into DESIRE. First, tie yourself to a specific job category or work area. Use phrases like:

"I am writing because . . ." or "My reason for contacting you . . ."

". . . should this be the case, you may be interested to know . . ."

"If you are seeking a _____, you will be interested to know . . ."

"I would like to talk to you about your personnel needs and how I am able to contribute to your department's goals."

"If you have an opening for someone in this area, you will see that my resume demonstrates a person of unusual dedication, efficiency and drive."

Next, call attention to your merits with a short paragraph that highlights one or two of your special contributions or achievements:

"I have an economics background from Columbia and a quantitative analysis approach to market fluctuations. This combination has enabled me consistently to pick the new technology flotations that are the backbone of the growth-oriented mutual fund."

Similar statements applicable to your area of expertise will give your letter more personal punch. Include any qualifications, contributions, and attributes that prove you are someone with plenty of talent to offer. If an advertisement (or a conversation with a potential employer) reveals an aspect of a particular job opening that is not addressed in your resume, it should be included in your cover letter:

> *"I notice from your advertisement that audio- and video-training experience would be a plus. In addition to the qualifications stated in my enclosed resume, I have over five years of experience writing and producing sales and management training materials in both these media."*

Whether you decide to use bullets or list your achievements in short staccato sentences will be determined in part by the amount of space available on the page.

Step Four

Here's where your letter turns that DESIRE into ACTION. The action you're shooting for is that the reader will dash straight on to your resume, then call you in for an interview. You achieve this action with brevity—leave the reader wanting more.

Make it clear to the reader that you want to talk. Explain when, where, and how you can be contacted. You can now be *proactive* by telling the reader that you intend to follow up at a certain point in time if contact has not been established by then. The reader may then want to initiate action.

Just as you worked to get the opening right, labor over the closing. It is the reader's last impression of you; make it strong, make it tight, and make it obvious that you are serious about entering into meaningful conversation.

Useful phrases include:

> *"It would be a pleasure to give you more information about my qualifications and experience . . ."*

"I look forward to discussing our mutual interests further . . ."

"While I prefer not to use my employer's time taking personal calls at work, with discretion I can be reached at _____ . . ."

"I will be in your area around the 20th, and will call you prior to that date. I would like to arrange . . ."

"I hope to speak with you further and will call the week of _____ to follow up."

"The chance to meet with you would be a privilege and a pleasure, so to this end I shall call you on _____."

"I look forward to speaking with you further and will call in the next few days to see when our schedules will permit a face-to-face meeting."

"May I suggest a personal meeting where you can have the opportunity to examine the person behind the resume."

"My credentials and achievements are a matter of record that I hope you will examine in depth when we meet . . ."

"I look forward to examining any of the ways you feel my background and skills would benefit (name of organization). I look forward to hearing from you."

"Resumes help you sort out the probables from the possibles, but they are no way to judge the caliber of an individual. I would like to meet you and demonstrate that I have the personality that makes for a successful _____."

"I expect to be in your area on Tuesday and Wednesday of next week and wonder which day would be best for you. I will call to determine." (Because many employed people are concerned about their resumes going astray, you may wish to add: *"In the meantime, I would appreciate your treating my application as confidential, since I am currently employed."*)

"With my training and hands-on experience, I know I can contribute to _____, and want to talk to you about it in person. When may we meet?"

"After reading my resume, you will know something about my background. Yet, you will still need to determine whether I am the one to help you with current problems and challenges. I would like an interview to discuss my ability to contribute."

"You can reach me at _____ to arrange an interview. I know that your time investment in meeting with me will be repaid amply."

"Thank you for your time and consideration; I hope to hear from you shortly."

"May I call you for an interview in the next few days?"

"A brief phone call will establish whether or not we have mutual interest. Recognizing the demands of your schedule, I will make that call within the week."

As we have noted, some people feel it is powerful in the closing to state a date—"I'll call you on Friday if we don't speak before"—or a date and time—"I'll call you on Friday morning at 10 A.M. if we don't speak before." The logic is that you demonstrate that your intent is serious, that you are organized, and that you plan your time effectively (all desirable behavioral traits).

On the other hand, at least one "authority" has said that the reader would be offended by being "forced" to sit and await your call. Frankly, in twenty years of being involved in the hiring process, I have never felt constrained by such statements; I guess I'm just not the sensitive type. What I look for is the person who doesn't follow through on commitments as promised. Therefore, if you use this approach, keep your promises.

2 | Four Types of Cover Letters

There are four types of cover letters. The examples that follow will show you which fits your situation.

The General Cover Letter

Here is an example of a general cover letter. It has been created using the sample phrases listed earlier in this book (note the highlighted text). You, too, can write a dynamite cover letter by using these phrases. Then all you have to do is make the minor adjustments necessary to personalize each document. (This letter should be sent as a result of direct research.)

JAMES SHARPE

18 Central Park Street ◆ Anytown, NY 14788
(516) 555-1212

October 2, 20—

Jackson Bethell, V.P. Operations
DataLink Products
621 Miller Drive
Anytown, CA 01234

Dear Jackson Bethell,

Recently I have been researching the leading local companies in data communications. My search has been for companies that are respected in the field and who provide ongoing training programs. The name of DataLink Products keeps coming up as a top company.

I am an experienced voice and data communications specialist with a substantial background in IBM environments. If you have an opening for someone in this area, you will see that my resume demonstrates a person of unusual dedication, efficiency, and drive. My experience and achievements include:

- The complete redesign of a data communications network, projected to increase efficiency company-wide some 12 percent.
- The installation and troubleshooting of a Defender II call-back security system for a dial-up network.

I enclose a copy of my resume, and look forward to examining any of the ways you feel my background and skills would benefit DataLink Products. While I prefer not to use my employer's time taking personal calls at work, with discretion I can be reached at (516) 555-1212 to initiate contact. Let's talk!

Yours truly,

James Sharpe

James Sharpe

JANE SWIFT

18 Central Park Street, Anytown, NY 14788
(516) 555-1212

David Doors, Director of Marketing   January 14, 20—
Martin Financial Group
1642 Rhode Island Way
Anytown, NY 01234

Dear David Doors,

I have always followed the performance of your fund in *Mutual Funds Newsletter.*

Recently your notice regarding a Market Analyst in INVESTORS DAILY caught my eye—and your company name caught my attention—because your record over the last three years shows exceptional portfolio management. Because of my experience with one of your competitors, I know I could make significant contributions.

I would like to talk to you about your personnel needs and how I am able to contribute to your department's goals.

An experienced market analyst, I have an economics background (M.S. Purdue) and a strong quantitative analysis approach to market fluctuations. This combination has enabled me to consistently pick the new technology flotations that are the backbone of the growth-oriented mutual fund. For example:

I first recommended ABC Fund six years ago. More recently my clients have been strongly invested in Atlantic Horizon Growth (in the high-risk category), and ABC Growth and Income (for the cautious investor). Those following my advice over the last six years have consistently outperformed the market.

I know that resumes help you sort out the probables from the possibles, but they are no way to judge the personal caliber of an individual. I would like to meet with you and demonstrate that along with the credentials, I have the personality that makes for a successful team player.

Yours truly,

Jane Swift

Jane Swift

The Executive Briefing

The executive briefing is a different and very effective form of cover letter. You can use it whenever you have some information about a job opening from a help wanted ad, an online job posting, or a prior conversation. This kind of letter gets right to the point and makes life easy for the corporate recruiter. Only those who read the *Knock 'em Dead* books know about this technique.

Why send an executive briefing? It's often the weapon of choice because:

1. The initial resume screener might have little understanding of the job or its requirements.
2. Your general resume invariably needs customizing for any specific job. (Overly broad resumes are like "one-size-fits-all" clothes—one size usually fits none.)
3. Your resume is somewhat (or more than somewhat) out of date and you have to send something out immediately to take advantage of the opportunity of a lifetime.

Also worth considering: resume screeners like people who make life a little easier for them.

Based on my extensive experience on both sides of the desk, I developed the executive briefing to increase the odds of your resume getting through to the right people.

How can the executive briefing help you through the screening and multiple interview cycle? To answer this we must begin by acknowledging a painful fact. Your resume, by definition, has drawbacks. It is usually too general to relate your qualifications to each specific job. More than one person will probably be interviewing you, and when this happens, the problems begin.

A manager says, "Spend a few minutes with this candidate and tell me what you think." Your general resume may be impressive, but the manager rarely adequately outlines the job being filled or the specific qualifications he or she is looking for. This means that other interviewers do not have any way to qualify you fairly and specifically. While the manager will be looking for specific skills relating to projects at hand, the personnel department will be trying to match your skills to the vagaries of the job-description manual, and

The executive briefing, which supplements the resume, solves this problem with its layout. It looks like the following:

JAMES SHARPE

18 Central Park Street ◆ *Anytown, NY 14788*
(516) 555-1212

October 2, 20—

Dear Sir/Madam:

While my resume will provide you with a general outline of my work history, my problem-solving abilities, and some achievements, I have taken the time to list your current specific requirements and my applicable skills in those areas.

Your Requirements	My Skills
1. Management of public reference, etc.	1. Experience as head reference librarian at University of Smithtown.
2. Supervision of 14 full-time support employees.	2. Supervised support staff of 17.
3. Ability to work with larger supervisory team in planning, budgeting, and policy formation.	3. During my last year I was responsible for budget and reformation of circulation rules.
4. ALA-accredited MLS.	4. ALA-accredited MLS.
5. 3 years' experience.	5. 1 year with public library; 2 with University of Smithtown.

You will see that my attached resume provides further in-depth background. I hope this will enable you to use your time effectively today.

Sincerely,

James Sharpe

James Sharpe

---

the other interviewers will flounder because no one told them what to look for. A chain of events like this, naturally, could reduce your chances of landing a job offer.

An executive briefing sent with a resume provides a comprehensive picture of a thorough professional, plus a personalized, fast, and easy-to-read synopsis that details exactly how you can help with an employer's current batch of problems.

The executive briefing assures that each resume you send out addresses the job's specific needs and that every interviewer at that company will be interviewing you for the same job.

The use of an executive briefing is naturally restricted to jobs you have discovered through your own efforts or seen advertised. It is obviously not appropriate when the requirements of a specific job are unavailable.

The Broadcast Letter

The broadcast letter is a simple but effective variation on the cover letter. Much of the information will be culled from your resume, because the intent of the broadcast letter is to *replace* the resume. You would be well advised here to conduct an in-depth analysis of your background in much the same way you would for a resume (see chapter 4). A broadcast letter can often get you into a telephone conversation with a potential employer, but that employer is usually likely to request a proper resume before seeing you anyway.

You should also know that broadcast letters are most frequently used by mature, successfully established professionals.

Beware: if you don't *have* a resume, you might well have to fill out one of those dreadful application forms. This requires putting your background in the format the employer wants—not the package of your choice. Consequently, I do not advise using this kind of letter as the spearhead or sole thrust of your campaign. Rather, you should use it as an integral part of the campaign in one of these ways:

- For small, highly targeted mailings to specific high-interest companies, where it works as an effective customizing technique.
- For small, highly targeted mailings to specific high-interest jobs about which you have enough detailed knowledge that such a letter would supersede the effectiveness of your resume.

- As an initial thrust, but with the more traditional cover letter and resume already in place for a back-up second mailing. In practice, the cold-mailed broadcast letter often results in a request for a resume, and other times results in a telephone interview and subsequent invitation to a face-to-face interview—with the request that you bring a resume.
- As part of a multiple-contact approach where you are approaching a number of people within a company with personalized letters (see chapter 6).
- As a back-up approach when your cover letter and resume don't generate the response you want from individual target companies.
- To headhunters. Broadcast letters rarely get passed on to employers without your permission.

Here is what a typical broadcast letter might look like:

JANE SWIFT

18 Central Park Street, Anytown, NY 14788
(516) 555-1212

October 2, 20—

Dear Employer,

For the past seven years I have pursued an increasingly successful career in the sales profession. Among my accomplishments I include:

SALES
As a regional representative, I contributed $1,500,000, or 16 percent, of my company's annual sales.

MARKETING
My marketing skills (based on a B.S. in marketing) enabled me to increase sales 25 percent in my economically stressed territory, at a time when colleagues were striving to maintain flat sales. Repeat business reached an all-time high.

PROJECT MANAGEMENT
Following the above successes, my regional model was adopted by the company. I trained and provided project supervision to the entire sales force. The following year, company sales showed a sales increase 12 percent above projections.

The above was based on my firmly held zero price discounting philosophy. It is difficult to summarize my work in a letter. The only way I can imagine providing you the opportunity to examine my credentials is for us to talk with each other. I look forward to hearing from you.

Yours sincerely,

Jane Swift

Jane Swift

Employment Agencies and Executive Recruiters

You might as well know something about headhunters right from the onset. The best way to get the attention of headhunters is to give them the respect they deserve. They are, after all, the most sophisticated salespeople in the world—they and they alone sell products that talk back!

A headhunter will be only faintly amused by your exhortations "to accept the challenge" or "test your skills by finding me a job" in the moments before he or she practices hoops with the remains of your letter and the trash can. They don't have the time or inclination to indulge such whimsical ideas. So with headhunters—whether they are working for the local employment agency, contingency, or retained search firm—bear in mind these two rules and you won't go far wrong:

1. Cut to the chase.
2. Tell the truth. Answer questions truthfully and you will likely receive help. Get caught in a lie and you will have established a career-long distrust with someone who possesses a very diverse and influential list of contacts.

   "I am forwarding my resume, because I understand you specialize in representing clients in the _____ field."

   "Please find the enclosed resume. As a specialist in the _____ field, I felt you might be interested in the skills of a _____."

   "Among your many clients there may be one or two who are seeking a person for a position as a _____."

Remember that in a cover letter sent to executive search firms and employment agencies, you should mention your salary and, if appropriate, your willingness to relocate.

Here is an example of a cover letter you might send to a corporate headhunter:

JAMES SHARPE

18 Central Park Street ◆ *Anytown, NY 14788*
(516) 555-1212

December 2, 20—

Dear Mr. O'Flynn:

As you may be aware, the management structure at _____ will be reorganized in the near future. While I am enthusiastic about the future of the agency under its new leadership, I have elected to make this an opportunity for change and professional growth.

My many years of experience lend themselves to a management position in any medium-sized service firm, but I am open to other opportunities. Although I would prefer to remain in New York, I would entertain other areas of the country, if the opportunity warrants it. I am currently earning $65,000 a year.

I have enclosed my resume for your review. Should you be conducting a search for someone with my background at the present time or in the near future, I would greatly appreciate your consideration. I would be happy to discuss my background more fully with you on the phone or in a personal interview.

Very truly yours,

James Sharpe

James Sharpe

JS
enclosures

3 | What Goes In, What Stays Out

Once upon a time, there were just a few set rules for writing a great job-hunting letter.

Everything was black and white—you did this, you didn't do that. The rules of the game have changed; now more than ever, communication is a prerequisite for any job.

Saying "I'm a great engineer. Give me a chance and I'll prove it to you" just doesn't cut it any more. It is no longer economically feasible to take employees on approval. Today job skills and behavioral traits are under close scrutiny throughout the entire selection process. Make no mistake; the process starts the moment you make contact—and that means the content and style of your cover letter had better be up to snuff.

If there is one overriding objective for your cover and follow-up letters, it is to demonstrate your awareness and possession of the learned behavioral traits that make for successful professionals and good hires.

Developing Personal, Professional, Achievement, and Business Profiles

There are twenty universally admired key personality or behavioral traits; they are your passport to success in all aspects of your job hunt. When reading your letter, the interviewer will search for clues to determine what kind of person you really are. The presence of positive clues in your letter tells the company representative how you feel about yourself and your chosen career, and what you will be like to work with.

Personal Profile

Use these words and phrases to project a successful, healthy personal profile.

Drive:
A desire to get things done. Goal-oriented.

Motivation:
Enthusiasm and a willingness to ask questions. A company realizes a motivated person accepts added challenges and does that little bit extra on every job.

Communication Skills:
More than ever, the ability to talk and write effectively to people at all levels in a company is a key to success.

Chemistry:
The company representative is looking for someone who does not get rattled, wears a smile, is confident without self-importance, and gets along with others—in short, a team player.

Energy:
Someone who always gives that extra effort in the little things as well as more important matters.

Determination:
Someone who does not back off when a problem or situation gets tough.

Confidence:
With every level of employee—neither intimidated by nor overly familiar with the big enchiladas.

Professional Profile

All companies seek employees who respect their profession and employer. Projecting these professional traits will identify you as loyal, reliable, and trustworthy.

Reliability:
Following up on yourself, not relying on anyone else to ensure the job is done well, and keeping management informed every step of the way.

Honesty/Integrity:
Taking responsibility for your actions, both good and bad. Always making decisions in the best interest of the company, never on whim or personal preference.

Pride:
Pride in a job well done. Always making sure the job is done to the best of your ability. Paying attention to the details.

Dedication:
Doing whatever it takes in time and effort to see a project through to completion, on deadline.

Analytical Skills:
Weighing the pros and cons. Not jumping to the first possible solution to a problem. Being able to weigh the short- and long-term benefits of a solution against all its possible negatives.

Listening Skills:
Listening and understanding, as opposed to jumping in to speak first.

Achievement Profile

Companies have very limited interests: making money, saving money (the same as making money), and saving time, which does both. Projecting your achievement profile, in however humble a fashion, is the key to winning any job.

Money Saved:
Every penny saved by your thought and efficiency is a penny earned for the company.

Time Saved:
Every moment saved by your thought and efficiency enables your company to save money and make more money in the additional time available. Double bonus.

Money Earned:
Generating revenue is the goal of every company.

Business Profile

Projecting your business profile is important on those occasions when you cannot demonstrate ways you have made money, saved money, or saved time for previous employers. These keys demonstrate you are always on the lookout for opportunities to contribute and that you keep your boss informed when an opportunity arises.

Efficiency:
Always keeping an eye open for wasted time, effort, resources, and money.

Economy:
Most problems have two solutions: an expensive one and one that the company would prefer to implement.

Procedures:
Procedures exist to keep the company profitable. Don't work around them. This means keeping your boss informed. Tell your boss about problems or good ideas, and don't go over his or her head. Follow the chain of command. Do not implement your own "improved" procedures or organize others to do so.

Profit:
The reason all the above traits are so universally admired in the business world is that they relate to profit.

Your goal is to draw attention to as many of these traits as possible by direct statement, inference, or illustration.

Writing a job-hunting letter is a bit like baking a cake. In most instances the ingredients are essentially the same—what determines the flavor is the order and quantity in which those ingredients are blended. There are certain ingredients that go into almost every letter, whether cover, broadcast, networking, follow-up, acceptance, rejection, or resignation letters. There are others that rarely or never go in, and there are those special touches (a pinch of this, a smidgen of that) that may be included, depending on your personal tastes and the need your letter will satisfy.

Brief Is Beautiful

Advertisements and job-hunting letters have a great deal in common. You will notice that the vast majority of advertisements in any media can be heard, watched, or read in under thirty seconds—the upper limit of the average consumer's attention span.

It is no coincidence that both cover letters and resumes adhere to the same rules that govern all other forms of writing. Like commercials, they need to be absorbed in less than thirty seconds. First and last, they are an urgent business communication, and business likes to get to the point.

Before getting started, good copywriters imagine themselves in the position of their target audience. They know their objective: to sell something. Then they consider what features their product possesses and what benefits it holds for the purchaser. This invariably requires some understanding of the target or targets.

For the next fifteen minutes, imagine yourself in one of your target companies. You are in the personnel department on "screening" detail. Fortunately, it is a slow morning and there are only thirty resumes and accompanying cover letters that need to be read. Go straight to the example sections of this book now and read thirty examples without a break, then return to this page. You will probably feel disoriented, as if your brain has turned to potato salad.

Now you have some idea of what it feels like, except that you had it easy. The letters you read were good, interesting ones—letters that got real people real jobs. Even so, you probably felt a little punch drunk at the end of the exercise. But I know that you learned a very valuable lesson: Brevity is beautiful. Can you imagine what it might be like to do this every day for a living?

The first thing you have to do is understand why some people get hired over others. Then look at your own background in a way that will enable you to get your point across. Every hire is made on a job applicant's ability to satisfy these five concerns of the employer:

1. Ability and suitability.
2. Willingness to go the extra yard, to take the rough with the smooth.
3. Manageability: taking direction and constructive input in a positive and professional manner.
4. Problem-solving attitude.
5. Supportive behavioral traits.

A Question of Money

Advertisements often request salary information. With the right letter you will rarely be denied at least a telephone conversation, even if you do omit your salary history. Nevertheless, there may be factors that make you feel obliged to include something. I have heard recently that some personnel people consider the word "negotiable" annoying, though perhaps not grounds for refusing to see an applicant.

If you choose to share information about salary, it must go on the cover letter or be attached to the cover letter. It should never go on the resume itself. If you choose not to include it, the contact can always ask you. When desired salary is requested, don't restrict yourself to one figure; instead, give yourself a range with a spread between the low and the high end. This dramatically increases your chances of "clicking onto" the available salary range.

When salary history is requested, the prospective employer is usually looking for a consistent career progression. Gaps or significant cuts could raise red flags. If you have nothing to hide and have a steadily progressive earnings history, spell it out on a separate sheet.

Many of us have less than perfect salary histories for any number of perfectly valid reasons. Consequently, we don't want to release these figures unless we are there in person to explain away the seeming anomalies. In these instances the matter is best skirted in the cover letter itself.

Here is one way to address the topic of money in your letters should you feel it is appropriate to do so. You will find others later in the book.

> *"My salary requirements are in the $ _____ to $ _____*
> *range, with appropriate benefits. I would be willing to relocate for*
> *the right opportunity."*

Telephone and E-mail

Once you have determined a primary contact number (and that shouldn't be too difficult) you must ensure that it will be answered at all times. There is no point in mounting a job-hunting campaign if prospective and eager employers can never reach you. Invest in an answering machine (about $50) or hire an answering service (between $30 to $75 a month). If your choice is an answering machine, keep the message businesslike. Once recorded, call the machine from another phone. Are you impressed?

You also need an alternate number; if at all possible, it should be answered by someone who is just about always there (perhaps a family member). Always list your e-mail address immediately beneath your telephone number.

Ingredients: A Basic Checklist

Skip ahead to the sample letters in chapter 7. As you read through a few of them, bear in mind that for your letters to be effective, they must:

- Address a person, not a title . . . and whenever possible, a person who is in a position to make a hiring decision.
- Be tailored to the reader as far as is practical, to show that you have done your homework.
- Show concern, interest, and pride for your profession; demonstrate energy and enthusiasm.
- Cut to the chase.
- Avoid stuffiness, and maintain a balance between professionalism and friendliness.
- Include information relevant to the job you are seeking.
- Ask for the next step in the process clearly and without either apology or arrogance.

Finally, notice the variety of letters there are for every job-hunting situation. You have many examples to help you maximize both the volume and value of your offers.

4 | Assembling Your Cover Letter

There is a fine line between pride in achievement and insufferable arrogance when listing experiences and behaviors in your work life that will help advance your candidacy.

To create the building blocks of your cover letter, complete the questionnaire on the next couple of pages. Do not skip this exercise; the self-knowledge you develop will be of real help when the time comes to sell yourself at the interview. Answer the questions for every job you held, starting with the most recent and working backward.

Take some time over this exercise and go back carefully over past jobs. Your answers to this questionnaire will form the meat and potatoes of your letters. It isn't going to be necessary to craft knock 'em dead sentences from scratch, although (believe it or not) you could, given the time and commitment. With the help of this book you'll be able to cut and paste with the best of them—your end result being a unique and arresting letter.

However, the entirely original parts of your constructed letter will be those areas that address your contributions and achievements. That means you need to spend adequate time in this period of preparation. What you jot down here will later be crafted into punchy sentences.

About the Questionnaire

This questionnaire was taken from the comprehensive "Skills Analysis" questionnaire in *Resumes That Knock 'em Dead*. Completion of this comprehensive evaluation tool will reward the prudent professional.

Questionnaire

FOR EACH OF YOUR PREVIOUS JOBS:
List three to five major duties:

_____

_____

_____

_____

_____

FOR EACH OF THESE DUTIES:
What special skills or knowledge did you need to perform these tasks
satisfactorily?

_____

_____

_____

_____

_____

What was the biggest problem you faced in this area?

_____

_____

_____

_____

_____

What was your solution, and the result of the solution?

_____

_____

_____

_____

_____

_____

_____

What was your biggest achievement in this area? Think about money made (or saved) or time saved for the employer.

_____

_____

_____

_____

_____

_____

What verbal or written comments did your peers or managers make about your contributions in this area?

_____

_____

_____

_____

_____

_____

_____

What was the greatest contribution in this area you made as a team player?

_____

_____

_____

_____

_____

_____

What desirable behavioral traits did you demonstrate in this area to get the job done?

_____

_____

_____

_____

_____

_____

Now that you've completed the questionnaire, it's time to put your responses to work for you.

Creating Punchy Sentences

Concise, punchy sentences grab attention.

The most grammatically correct sentences in the world won't get you interviews (except perhaps as a copy editor—and then not always) because such prose can read as though every breath of life has been squeezed out of it.

Sentences gain power with verbs that demonstrate an action. For example, one professional—with a number of years at the same law firm in a clerical position—had written:

> *"I learned to manage a computerized database."*

Pretty ordinary, right? Well, after discussion of the circumstances that surrounded learning how to manage the computerized database, certain exciting facts emerged. By using action verbs and an awareness of employer interests, this sentence was charged up and given more punch. Not only that, but for the first time the writer fully understood that value of her contributions, which greatly enhanced her self-image:

> *"I <u>analyzed</u> and <u>determined</u> the need for automation of an established law office. I was <u>responsible</u> for hardware and software selection, installation, and loading. Within one year, I had <u>achieved</u> a fully automated office. This <u>saved</u> forty hours a week."*

Notice how the verbs show that things happened when she was around the office. These action verbs and phrases add an air of direction, efficiency, and accomplishment to every cover letter. Succinctly, they tell the reader what you did and how well you did it.

Rewrite each of your query answers using action verbs to punch them up. To help you in the process, here are over 175 action verbs you can use. This list is just a beginning. Every word processing program has a thesaurus; type in any one of these 175 words and get ten more for each entry.

accomplished
achieved
acted
adapted
addressed
administered
advanced
advised
allocated
analyzed
appraised
approved
arranged
assembled
assigned
assisted
attained
audited
authored
automated
balanced
budgeted
built
calculated
catalogued
chaired
clarified
classified
coached
collected
compiled
completed
composed
computed
conceptualized
conducted

consolidated
contained
contracted
contributed
controlled
coordinated
corresponded
counseled
created
critiqued
cut
decreased
delegated
demonstrated
designed
developed
devised
diagnosed
directed
dispatched
distinguished
diversified
drafted
edited
educated
eliminated
enabled
encouraged
engineered
enlisted
established
evaluated
examined
executed
expanded
expedited

explained
extracted
fabricated
facilitated
familiarized
fashioned
focused
forecast
formulated
founded
generated
guided
headed up
identified
illustrated
implemented
improved
increased
indoctrinated
influenced
informed
initiated
innovated
inspected
installed
instigated
instituted
instructed
integrated
interpreted
interviewed
introduced
invented
launched
lectured
led

maintained
managed
marketed
mediated
moderated
monitored
motivated
negotiated
operated
organized
originated
overhauled
oversaw
performed
persuaded
planned
prepared
presented
prioritized
processed
produced
programmed
projected
promoted
provided
publicized
published
purchased
recommended
reconciled
recorded
recruited
reduced
referred
regulated
rehabilitated

remodeled
repaired
represented
researched
restored
restructured
retrieved
revitalized
saved
scheduled
schooled
screened
set
shaped
solidified
solved
specified
stimulated
streamlined
strengthened
summarized
supervised
surveyed
systemized
tabulated
taught
trained
translated
traveled
trimmed
upgraded
validated
worked
wrote

Varying Sentence Structure

Good writers are at their best when they write short punchy sentences. You will see that if the letters in chapter 7 have any single thing in common, it's punchy sentences. Keep your sentences under about 20 words; a good average is around 15. If your sentence is longer than the 20 mark, change it. Either shorten it by restructuring or make two sentences out of one. The reader on the receiving end has neither the time nor the inclination to read your sentences twice to get a clear understanding. However, you will want to avoid choppiness. Try to vary the length of sentences when you can.

You can also start with a short phrase ending in a colon:

- Followed by bullets of information.
- Each one supporting the original phrase.

All of these techniques are designed to enliven the reading process. An example follows.

Analyzed and determined need for automation of an established law office:

- Responsible for hardware and software selection.
- Coordinated installation of six work stations.
- Operated and maintained equipment; trained other users.
- Full automation achieved in one year.
- Savings to company: $25,000.

K.I.S.S. (Keep It Simple, Stupid)

Just as you use short sentences, use common words. They communicate quickly and are easy to understand. Stick to short, simple words whenever possible (without sounding infantile). Of course, you need action words and phrases—but the key is to stay away from obscure words.

Communicating, persuading, and motivating your readers to take action is challenging, because many people in different companies will see your letters and make judgments based on them. This means you must keep industry "jargon" to a minimum (especially in the initial contact letters—covers, broadcast, and the like). There will be those who understand the intricacies and technicalities of your profession—but unfortunately, many of the initial screeners do not. They won't know the niceties of your particular job, and you'll need to share your specialist wisdom with the non-specialists first, before you can expect to reach your professional peers.

> *Short words for short sentences help make short, gripping paragraphs: good for short attention spans!*

Within your short paragraphs and short sentences, beware of name dropping and acronyms, such as "I worked for Dr. A. Witherspoon in Sys. Gen. SNA 2.31." This is a good way to confuse (and lose) readers. Such statements are too restricted to have validity outside the small circle of specialists to whom they speak. Unless you work in a highly technical field, avoid doing this. Your letters demand the widest possible appeal, yet they need to remain personal in tone. (Of course, you don't want your letters to sound like they're from Publishers' Clearing House, either.)

Voice and Tense

The voice you develop for different letters depends on a few important factors:

- Getting a lot said in a small space.
- Being factual.
- Packaging yourself in the best way.
- Using what feels good to you.

The voice you use in your letters should be consistent throughout. There is considerable disagreement among the "experts" about the best voice, and each of the following options have both champions and detractors.

Sentences in all types of cover letters can be truncated (up to a point), by omitting pronouns and articles such as *I, you, he, she, it, they, a,* or *the*:

> *"Automated office."*

In fact, many authorities recommend the dropping of pronouns as a technique that both saves space and allows you to brag about yourself without seeming boastful. It gives the impression of another party writing about you.

Others feel that to use the personal pronoun—"I automated the office ..."— is naive, unprofessional, and smacks of boasting.

At the same time, some recommend that you write in the first person because it makes you sound more human.

"I automated the office."

In short, there are no hard and fast rules here—they can all work given the many unique circumstances you will face in any given job hunt. Use whatever style works best for you. If you do use the personal pronoun, try not to use it in every sentence—it gets a little monotonous, and with too much use, it can make you sound like an egomaniac. The mental focus is not "I" but "you," the person with whom you are trying to communicate.

A nice variation is to use a first-person voice throughout the letter and then a final few words in the third person. Make sure these final words appear in the form of an attributed quote, as an insight to your value:

"She managed the automation procedure, and we didn't experience a moment of down time."
　　　　　　　　　　　　— Jane Ross, Department Manager

Don't mistake the need for professionalism in your job hunting letters with stiff-necked formality. The most effective tone is one that mixes the conversational and the formal, just the way we do in our offices and on our jobs. The only overriding rule is to make the letter readable, so that the reader can see a human being shining through the pages. You will notice in the examples in chapter 7 that the personalities of the writers come right through.

Length

The standard length for a cover letter is usually one page, or the equivalent length for e-mails. Subsequent letters stemming from verbal communications— whether over the telephone or face-to-face—should also adhere to the one-page rule, but can run to two pages if complexity of content demands it. Generally speaking, no job-hunting letter should exceed two pages. Break this rule at your peril; to do so will brand you as a windbag incapable of getting to the point. Not the kind of person who gets a foot in the door!

Having said this, I should acknowledge that all rules are made to be broken. Occasionally a three-page letter might be required, but only in one of the following two instances:

1. You have been contacted directly by an employer about a specific position and have been asked to present data for that particular opportunity.
2. An executive recruiter who is representing you determines that the exigencies of a particular situation warrant a dossier of such length. (Often such a letter and resume will be prepared exclusively—or with considerable input—by the recruiter.)

You'll find that thinking too much about length considerations will hamper the writing process. Think instead of the story you have to tell, then layer fact upon fact until your tale is told. Use your words and the key phrases from this book to craft the message of your choice. When *that* is done you can go back and ruthlessly cut it to the bone.

Ask yourself these questions:

- Can I cut out any paragraphs?
- Can I cut out any sentences?
- Can I cut out any superfluous words?
- Where have I repeated myself?

If in doubt, cut it out—leave nothing but facts and action words! If at the end you find too much has been cut, you'll have the additional pleasure of reinstating your deathless prose.

Your Checklist

There are really two proofing steps in the creation of a polished cover letter. The first happens now. You want to make sure that all the things that should be included are—and that all the things that shouldn't, aren't. The final proofing is done before printing.

Warning: It is easy, in the heat of the creative moment, to miss crucial components or mistakenly include facts that give the wrong emphasis. Check all your letters against these points:

Contact information
- The pertinent personal data (name, address, zip code, personal telephone number, and e-mail address) is on every page.
- Your business number is omitted unless it is absolutely necessary and safe to include it.

- If your letter is more than one page long, each page is numbered "page 1 of 2," etc., and all the pages are stapled together so that they cannot get separated or mislaid. Remember the accepted way of stapling business communications: one staple in the top left-hand corner. Contact info, at least name, telephone numbers and e-mail address, should be on each page.

Objectives
- Does your letter state why you are writing—to apply for a job, follow up on an interview, etc.?
- Is the letter tied specifically to the target company and job (if you have details)?
- Does it address points of relevance, such as skills that apply from the ad or agenda items addressed at the interview?
- Does it include references to some of your personality or behavioral traits that are crucial to success in your field?
- Is your most relevant and qualifying experience prioritized to lend strength to your letter?
- Have you avoided wasting more space than required with employer names and addresses?
- Have you omitted any reference to reasons for leaving a particular job? Reasons for change might be important to the employer at the interview, but they are not relevant at this point. Use this precious space to sell, not to justify.
- Unless they have been specifically requested, have you removed all references to past, current, or desired salaries?
- Have you removed references to your date of availability? Remember, if you aren't available at their convenience, why are you wasting their time by writing?
- If your education is mentioned, is it relevant to the advertisement?
- Is your highest educational attainment the one you mention?
- Have you avoided listing irrelevant responsibilities or job titles?
- Have you mentioned your contributions, your achievements, and the problems you have successfully solved during your career?
- Have you avoided poor focus by eliminating all extraneous information? ("Extraneous" means anything that doesn't relate to your job objective, such as captaining the tiddlywinks team in kindergarten.)
- Is the whole thing long enough to whet the reader's appetite for more details, yet short enough not to satisfy that hunger?

- Have you left out lists of references and only mentioned the availability of references (if, of course, there is nothing more valuable to fill up the space)? To employers this is a given. If you aren't prepared to produce them on demand, you simply won't get the job.
- Have you let the obvious slip in, like heading your letter "Letter of Application" in big bold letters? If so, cut it out.

Writing Style

- Substitute short words for long words, and one word where previously there were two.
- Keep your average sentence to ten to twenty words. Shorten any sentence of more than twenty words or break it into two sentences.
- Keep every paragraph under five lines, with most paragraphs shorter.
- Make sure your sentences begin with or contain, wherever possible, powerful action verbs and phrases that demonstrate you as a mover and shaker.
- If you are in a technical field, don't overload with technical jargon, unless you are certain a specific reader will understand your encoded message. As we have seen, this is most important in cover letters and broadcast letters; they are likely to be screened by non-techies. Part of their job is to assist in the hiring of techies who can communicate with the rest of the human race. In subsequent letters to fellow techies, however, the technical jargon may not only be desirable but also may be mandatory to get your point across.

5 | The Final Product

Style—so easy to see but so difficult to define— usually has a distinct look and feel. Here are some of the basics you should keep in mind when creating your own stylish and professional job-hunting letters.

Layout

The average cover letter arrives on a desk along with as many as fifty or sixty others, all of which require screening. You can expect your letter to get a maximum of thirty seconds of attention, and that's only if it's accessible to the reader's eye.

The biggest complaints about job-hunting letters that nosedive into the trash can in record time are:

- They have too much information crammed into the space and are therefore hard on the eyes.
- The layout is unorganized, illogical, and uneven. (In other words, it looks shoddy and slapdash—and who wants an employee like that?)
- In the age of spell checkers, there are no excuses for misspellings, and none are accepted.

Fonts

Choose business-like fonts; stay away from script-like fonts or those that have serifs. They may sometimes look more visually exciting, but the goal is to be kind to the tired eyes of the reader who is plowing through stacks of resumes when s/he gets your message. Capitalized copy is also harder to read and causes eye strain.

How to Brighten the Page

Once you decide on a font, stick with it. More than one font on a page can look confusing. You can do plenty to liven up the visual impact of the page within the variations of the font you have chosen. You can, of course, use a different font for the contact information as you create the letterhead.

Most fonts come in a selection of regular, bold, italic, and bold italic. Good job-hunting letters will take judicious advantage of this: You can vary the impact of key words with italics, underlined phrases, and boldface or capitalized titles for additional emphasis. There are a lot of options, but these options won't work with e-mail, as the e-mail won't retain your formatting. There is a good lesson here: you can brighten the page, but the words alone must be able to carry your message!

You will notice from the occasional example in this book that letters will use more than one typographical variation of the same font. For example, a writer who wants to emphasize personality traits might italicize only those words or phrases that describe these aspects. That way the message gets a double fixing in the reader's mind. You will also notice powerful letters that employ no typographic pyrotechnics and still knock 'em dead! In the end, it's your judgment call.

If you are crafting letters that are general in content, you will need to use the mail merge feature of the word-processing program. What this does is fill in the blanks: "Dear _____" becomes "Dear Fred Jones."

> *Dear* Fred Jones:
> *Your* January 11, 2001 *ad in the* Chicago Tribune *described a need for an accountant.*

All this does is state loud and clear that this is a form letter sent, in all likelihood, to hundreds. Why needlessly detract from your chances of being taken seriously?

Another no-no is the use of "clip art" to brighten the page. Those little quill pens and scrolls may look nifty to you, but they look amateurish to the rest of the business world.

Hiring Professionals

Those who wish to hire professionals to produce their letters have more than one option to choose from.

Using a Word-Processing Service

Any reader who can use a computer can skip this paragraph; hopefully that is just about everyone. However, if you have just been returned to the earth by aliens, there are a couple of things you should know. Things have changed since you've been gone and now we all have personal computers. If you don't learn to use one right quick you are "up the creek without a paddle." That being said, if you need to use a service for any reason, here's a heads-up on what to watch out for.

Small companies come and go with great rapidity, so when your cover letter is finished, ask for three copies of it on separate disks. Why three? Funny things can happen to disks. (I once lost half a book because of disk malfunction.) Consequently, everyone with a computer should always maintain two back-up copies of the original document, *each on a separate disk*, making a total of three copies. This way, no matter where you find yourself living next time your career demands a job hunt, your letters are ready for updating. By the way, you should not be charged more than a couple of dollars for each back-up disk. Even the best-quality disks only cost about $1, and the copying process takes maybe sixty seconds to complete. Negotiate the cost of the copies before you assign the project; that way you won't have the unpleasantness of any unscrupulous operator trying to take advantage of you. (Helpful hint: Be sure the label on the disk identifies the software environment in which the letters were composed.)

Proofing

It simply isn't possible for even the most accomplished professional writer to go from draft to print, so don't try it. Your pride of authorship will hide blemishes you can't afford to miss.

You need some distance from your creative efforts to give yourself detachment and objectivity. There is no hard and fast rule about how long it should take to come up with the finished product. Nevertheless, if you think you have finished, leave it alone at least overnight. Then come back to it fresh. You'll read it almost as if it were meeting your eyes for the first time.

Before you print your letters make sure that your writing is as clear as possible. Three things guaranteed to annoy cover letter readers are incorrect spelling, poor grammar, and improper syntax. Go back and check all these areas. If you think syntax has something to do with the IRS, you'd better get a third party involved. An acquaintance of mine came up with an eminently practical solution. She went to the library, waited for a quiet moment, and got into a conversation with the librarian, who subsequently agreed to give her letter the old once-over. (Everyone loves to show off special knowledge!)

The quality of paper always makes an impression on the person holding the page. The folks receiving your letter see literally dozens of others every day, and you need every trick available to make your point. The heft of high-quality paper compared to the shining-thru copying paper sends an almost subliminal message about certain personality traits, most notably attention to detail. Another reason for using high-quality paper for your copies is that it takes the ink better, therefore giving you clean, sharp print resolution.

By the way, if an emergency demands you send a letter by fax, remember to follow it up with a copy on regular paper. This is because everything you send is likely to end up in your "candidate dossier." A fax can obliterate important parts of any communication.

Although you should not skimp on paper costs, neither should you buy or be talked into the most expensive available. Indeed, in some fields (health care and education come to mind), too ostentatious a paper can cause a negative impression. The idea is to create a feeling of understated quality. You can get 500 sheets of excellent paper for about $20 in most areas of the country.

As for color, white is considered the prime choice. Cream is also acceptable, and I'm assured that some of the pale pastel shades can be both attractive and effective. These pastel shades were originally used to make letters and resumes stand out. But now everyone is so busy standing out of the crowd in Magenta and Passionate Puce that you just might find it more original to stand out in white or cream. White and cream are straightforward, no-nonsense colors. They say BUSINESS.

It is a given that cover letter stationery should always match the color and weight of your envelopes and resume. To send a white cover letter—even if it is your personal stationery—with a cream resume is gauche and detracts from the powerful statement you are trying to make. In fact, when you print the finished letter, you should print some letterhead sheets at the same time and in the same quantity. It should be in the same font and on the same kind of paper. You don't need to get too fancy; base your design on other stationery you've been impressed with.

All subsequent letters should be on the same paper. Your written communication will be filed. Then, prior to the hiring decision, the hiring manager will review all the data on all the short-list candidates. Your coordinated written campaign will paint the picture of a thorough professional. The sum of your letters will be more powerful as a whole simply because there will be continuity of form and content.

Envelopes Send Messages Too

What goes on the envelope affects the power of the message inside. Over the last six months, I've asked a number of line managers and human resources professionals about the envelope's appearance. Did it affect the likelihood of the letter being read and if so, with what kind of anticipation? Here's what I heard:

> *"I never open letters with printed pressure-sensitive labels; I regard them as junk mail, and I simply don't have the time in my life for ill-targeted marketing attempts."*

> *"I never open anything addressed to me by title but not by name."*

> *"I will open envelopes addressed to me by misspelled name, but I am looking with a jaundiced eye already; and that eye is keen for other examples of sloppiness."*

> *"I always open correctly typed envelopes that say personal and/or confidential, but if they're not, I feel conned. I don't hire con artists."*

> *"I always open neatly handwritten envelopes. What's more, I open them first, unless there's another letter that is obviously a check."*

There are those who recommend enclosing a stamped self-addressed envelope to increase the chances of response. You can do this, but don't expect many people in the corporate world to take advantage of your munificence. I have never known this tactic to yield much in the way of results. On the whole, I think you are better advised to save the stamp money and spend it on a follow-up telephone call. Only conversations lead to interviews. I have never heard of a single interview being set up exclusively through the mail.

(*Neat trick department*: I recently received an intriguing resume and cover letter; both had attached to the top right-hand corner a circular red sticker. It worked as a major exclamation point; I was impressed. I was even more impressed when I realized that once this left my hands, no other reader would know exactly who attached the sticker, but they *would* pay special attention to the content because of it. Nice technique; don't let the whole world in on it, though.)

Appearance

Remember that the first glance and feel of your letter can make a powerful impression. Go through this checklist before you seal the envelope:

- Does the paper measure 8 1/2" by 11", and is it of good quality, between 16 and 25 pounds in weight?
- Have you used white, off-white, or cream-colored paper?
- Did you make sure to use only one side of the page?
- Are your name, address, and telephone number on every page?
- If more than one page, have you paginated your cover letter: "1 of 2" at the bottom of the page and so on?
- Are the pages stapled together? Remember, one staple in the top left-hand corner is the accepted protocol.

6 | The Plan of Attack

Great cover, broadcast, and follow-up letters won't get you a job by sitting on your desk like rare manuscripts. You have to do something with them.

Even a company with no growth rate can still be expected (based on national averages) to experience a 14 percent turnover in staff in the course of a year. In other words, every company has openings *sometimes*, and any one of those openings could have your name on it.

The problem is, you won't have the chance to pick the very best opportunity unless you check them all out. Every intelligent job hunter will use a six-tiered approach to cover all the bases, including:

- Internet job postings
- Newspaper advertisements
- Personal and professional networking
- Direct-researched opportunities
- Employment agencies and recruiters
- Business and trade publications

Online Job Postings

Here is where the Internet can play an especially useful role. There are hundreds of job banks that carry help wanted advertising, called "job postings" in Internet speak; almost every one of these sites has a resume bank. When you place your resume in a resume bank, it is available for view by any employer or headhunter. So long as there is a privacy feature to protect your identity, this is a very viable marketing tool.

Here's how to use them to greatest effect.

Visit the job banks—there's a good selection in the resource section—and search for appropriate job openings. Most of these job banks have a powerful device called an "e-mail alert." The alert allows you to identify the type of work you are seeking and receive an e-mail from the site every time a suitable job is advertised by one of their clients. You don't want these e-mails to come to you indiscriminately at work, so be sure to use your personal e-mail address.

The resume banks will work well for you too. From an employer's point of view, these resume banks are like big fish tanks. The fishing analogy works for you too; your resume in resume banks is like having a baited hook in the water while you go about your business. Resume banks often trash your resume after 90 days, so if you are looking longer than this you will need to go back and reload. Actually, it is not a bad idea to keep a resume posted on an ongoing basis; it will keep you aware of who is looking for what and how much they are paying. It's like keeping your finger on the pulse of the market. Use the free online course at careerbrain.com and the online resources section at the end of the book.

If you are writing as a result of an online job posting, you should mention both the Web site and the date you found it on:

> *"I read your job posting on your company's Web site on January 5th and felt I had to respond..."*

> *"Your online job posting regarding a _____ on CareerCity.com caught my eye, and your company name caught my attention."*

> *"This e-mail, and my attached resume, are in response to your job posting on _____."*

Help-wanted Advertisements

A first step for many is to go to the want ads and do a mass mailing. Bear in mind, there should be a method to your madness when you do this. Remember, if it is the first idea that comes to *your* mind, hitting the want ads will be at the front of everyone else's thoughts, too.

A single help-wanted advertisement can draw hundreds of responses. The following ideas might be helpful:

- Most newspapers have an employment edition every week (usually Sunday, although sometimes mid-week), when, in addition to their regular advertising, they have a major drive for help-wanted ads. Make sure you always read this edition of your local paper.

- So-called authorities on the topic will tell you not to rely on the want ads—that they don't work. Rockinghorse droppings! Want ads don't work only if you are too dumb to know how to use them. Look for back issues. Just because a company is no longer advertising does not necessarily mean that the slot has been filled. The employer may well have become disillusioned—and is now using a professional recruiter to work on the position. They may have filled the position; perhaps the person never started work or simply did not work out in the first few months. Maybe they hired someone who did work out and now they want another one. When you go back into the want ads you'll find untold opportunities awaiting you, and instead of competition from 150 other job hunters responding to this Sunday's want ad there may be just one or two people vying for the slot.

  I had a letter from a *Knock 'em Dead* reader recently who told me he had landed a $90,000 job from a seven-month-old want ad he came across in a pile of newspapers in his father-in-law's garage! (You see? There is a use for in-laws, after all.)

- In many instances jobs are available but just aren't being advertised. It's what the press refers to as the hidden job market. Likewise, in some high-demand occupations where want ads aren't famous for drawing the right caliber of professional, the employer may only run one or two major "institutional" ads a year for that type of position.

- Cross-check the categories. Don't rely solely on those ads seeking your specific job title. For example, let's say you are a graphic artist looking for a job in advertising. You should flag all advertising or public relations agencies with any kind of need. If they are actively hiring at the moment, logic will tell you that their employment needs are not restricted to that particular title.

If you are writing as the result of a newspaper advertisement, you should mention both the publication and the date. Do not abbreviate advertisement to "ad" unless space demands, and remember to underline or italicize the publication's title:

> "I read your advertisement in the Daily Gotham on October 6th and, after researching your company, felt I had to write . . ."

> "I am responding to your recent advertisement offering the opportunity to get involved with _____."

> "In re: Your advertisement in the Columbus Dispatch on Sunday the 8th of November. As you will notice, my entire background matches your requirements."

> "Your notice regarding a _____ in _____ caught my eye, and your company name caught my attention."

> "This letter and attached resume are in response to your advertisement in _____."

Networking

Networking is one of those dreadful words from the 1970s that unfortunately is so entrenched we might as well learn to live with it. Strip the hyperbole and it just means communicating with everyone you can get hold of—professional colleagues, academic peers, or personal contacts—whether you know them well or not.

I must admit my attitude toward networking among professional colleagues and personal friends has undergone a change. In earlier times I pooh-poohed the idea as a cop-out employed by the weak-willed. I said the only way to go was to bite the bullet, pick up the telephone, and make contact. This is still the fastest and most effective way. But I now recognize that for a job hunt to be most effective, direct mail has an important part to play. Even so, I still harbor fears that someone, once comfortable with networking among old friends, will unconsciously derail a job hunt by ignoring other and possibly more fruitful avenues of exploration for job opportunities. You would be wise to harbor the same fears; an effective job hunt is more than writing to and shooting the breeze with old cronies on the telephone.

What made me change my opinion? I consciously began to track my responses to requests for job hunting assistance.

To those requests from people I didn't know, I asked for a resume. If I received it in good time with a thoughtfully prepared accompanying letter, I would give that person help if I could.

To those requests from people with an introduction from someone I liked and respected, I gave time and consideration and, wherever possible, assistance.

To those requests from friends, people I had worked with at one time and *who had kept in touch* since we had worked together, I stopped everything and went through my Rolodex. I provided leads, made calls on their behalf, and insisted they keep in touch. I also initiated follow-up calls myself on behalf of these people.

To those requests from people who regarded themselves as friends but who had not maintained contact, or who had only reestablished contact when they wanted something, I looked through the Rolodex once but for some reason was unable to find anything. I wished them the best of luck. "Sorry I couldn't help you. If something comes to mind, I'll be sure to call."

Nothing works like a personal recommendation from a fellow professional—and you get that best by *being* a fellow professional. It is no accident that successful people in all fields know each other—they helped each other get that way.

If you are going to use business colleagues and personal friends in your job hunt, don't mess up and do it half-heartedly. We live in a very mobile society, so you shouldn't restrict yourself to family, friends, and colleagues just where you are looking. Everyone can help—even Aunt Matilda in Manila: Maybe she just happens to have had her cousin's wife's brother, who is a senior scientist at IBM, as her house guest for a month last summer and he is now forever in her debt for the vacation of a lifetime. Maybe not, but still, people know people, and they know people not just here but all over. Sit and think for a few minutes; you will be amazed at the people *you* know all over the country. Every one of them has a similar network.

Here are some tips for writing letters asking for assistance. If you feel awkward writing a letter to certain contacts, use these guidelines as a basis for the telephone conversation you'll have instead.

1. Establish connectivity. Recall the last memorable contact you had or someone in common that you have both spoken to recently.

2. Tell them why you are writing: "It's time for me to make a move; I just got laid off with a thousand others and I'm taking a couple of days to catch up with old friends."

3. Ask for advice and guidance: "Who do you think are the happening _____ companies today?" "Could you take a look at my resume for me? I really need an objective opinion and I've always respected your viewpoint." Don't ask specifically, "Can you hire me?" or "Can your company hire me?"

4. Don't rely on a contact with a particular company to get you into that company. Mount and execute your own plan of attack. No one has the same interest as you in putting bread on your table.

5. Let them know what you are open for. They will invariably want to help, but you have to give them a framework within which to target their efforts.

6. Say you hope you'll get to see each other again soon or "one of these days." Plan on doing something together. Invite them over for drinks, dinner, or a barbecue.

7. When you do get help, say thank you. And if you get it verbally, follow it up in writing. The impression is indelible, and just might get you another lead.

8. You never know who your friends are. You will be surprised at how someone you always regarded as a real pal won't give you the time of day and how someone you never thought of as a friend will go above and beyond the call of duty for you.

9. Whether they help you or not, let them know when you get situated, and maintain contact in one form or another at least once a year. A career is for a long time. It might be next week or a decade from now when a group of managers (including one of your personal network) are talking about filling a new position and the first thing they will do is say "Who do we know?" That could be you . . . if you establish "top of the mind awareness" now and maintain it.

If you are writing as the result of a referral, say so and quote the person's name if appropriate:

> *"Our mutual colleague, John Stanovich, felt my skills and abilities would be valuable to your company . . ."*

"The branch manager of your San Francisco branch, Pamela Bronson, has suggested I contact you regarding the opening for a _____."

"I received your name from Henry Charles last week. I spoke to Mr. Charles regarding career opportunities with _____, and he suggested I contact you. In case the resume he forwarded is caught up in the mail, I enclose another."

"Arthur Gold, your office manager and my neighbor, thought I should contact you about the upcoming opening in your accounting department."

Direct-Research Contacts

The internet is now the most comprehensive job hunting resource. There are many Web sites that provide company profiles, and often you can e-mail the companies you're interested in right from their Web site. In addition to researching contacts, you can look up information on the status of the company you're interested in, do salary surveys, get advice on finding a job, and post your resume on online resume banks. CareerCity.com is an excellent example of such a site. This site features a meta job search tool that allows you to search millions of jobs instantly, provides descriptions and links to 27,000 of the biggest U.S. companies, has comprehensive salary surveys in all fields, provides free resume posting, and has many other useful tools.

Most companies are also listed in one of the reference sources in your library. Take the time to do library research and you will discover job opportunities that 90 percent of your professional competitors never dreamed existed. The business reference section can give you access to numerous research books that can help:

- Standard and Poors
- The Directory of Directories
- State Directory of Manufacturers
- Contacts Influential
- The National Job Bank

Again, the reference librarian will be pleased to help you. Search each of the appropriate reference works for every company within the scope of your search that also falls within your geographic boundaries.

Your goal is to identify and build personalized dossiers on the companies in your chosen geographic area. Do not be judgmental about what and who they might appear to be: You are fishing for possible job openings, so cast your net wide and list them all. Only if you present yourself as a candidate for all available opportunities in your geographic area of search is there any realistic chance of landing the best possible opportunity.

Unfortunately, no single reference work is ever complete. Their very size and scope mean that most are at least a little out of date at publication time. Also, no single reference work lists every company. Because you don't know what company has the very best job for you, you need to research as many businesses in your area as possible, and therefore you will have to look through numerous reference books.

Copy all the relevant information for each company. You'll want to include the names of the company's president and chairman of the board, a description of the complete lines of company services and/or products, the size of the company, and the locations of its various branches. Of course, if you find other interesting information, copy it down, by all means. For instance, you might come across information on growth or shrinkage in a particular area of a company; or you might read about recent acquisitions the company has made. Write it all down.

All this information will help you target potential employers and stand out in different ways. Your knowledge will create a favorable impression when you first contact the company; that you made an effort is noticed and sets you apart from other applicants who don't bother. The combination says that you respect the company, the opportunity, and the interviewer; combined, these perceptions help say that you are a different quality of job candidate.

All your efforts have an obvious short-term value in helping you with job interviews and offers. Who would *you* interview and subsequently hire? The person who knows nothing about your company, or the person who knows everything and is enthusiastic about it?

Your efforts also have value in the long term, because you are building a personalized reference work of your industry/specialty/profession that will help you throughout your career whenever you wish to make a job change.

Purchasing Mailing Lists

Posting your resume online is now widely available, but purchasing mailing lists from professional mailing list companies can also be cheap and effective. Chances are there is a mailing list of exactly the kinds of movers and shakers you want to work for. These lists can be broken down for you by title, geography, zip code—all sorts of ways. They are affordable, too; usually about $100 for a thousand addresses. To contact a broker, just look in your yellow pages under "mailing list brokers/compilers."

If you want the most comprehensive source catalog, call the Direct Marketing Association at (212) 768-7277. Ask for the publications department; for $30 you can get the List Brokerage Directory. This is the single most comprehensive source of mailing lists available. With compilation specialists in every conceivable area, this directory can certainly lead you toward the right list.

As we have noted, even the most up-to-date lists and directories are out of date by the time they get to you, so it is a good investment of time to call and verify that Joe Schmoe, VP of Engineering, is still there. Apart from the obvious goal of sending mail to the right person, if Joe is no longer there you may be able to find out where he went. If so, you'll have uncovered another opportunity for yourself.

(Note: Mailing lists can be effective, but be sure to read the envelopes section in chapter 5 before you purchase preprinted mailing labels.)

Associations

You're a member of an appropriate professional association, aren't you? Of course you are—or, if not, you will want to invest in membership just as soon as humanly possible. You don't know of an appropriate association? Your local research librarian will gladly lead you to an enormous blue and yellow tome published by Bowker called *The Encyclopedia of Associations*. Your gang will be listed there.

When you join an association, you get a membership roster to use to network amongst your peers. This is the modern-day equivalent of the "old boy" and "old girl" network. Also, for a nominal sum you can often pick up a preprinted mailing list or the same on disk. (However, before you splurge on preprinted mailing labels, read about envelopes in chapter 5.)

Alumni/ae Associations

Many schools have an active alumni/ae association. The mailing list you can obtain from this source can vary from just names to names and occupations and (sometimes) names of employers. Being a fellow alumni/ae probably gives you claim to sixty seconds of attention. Nearly every working alumni/ae could be worthy of a networking letter (just check through the examples) and a follow-up call. Never ever underestimate the power of "the old school tie."

Employment Agents

There are essentially three categories: State employment agencies, private employment agencies, and executive recruiters.

State Employment Agencies

These are funded by the state labor department and typically carry names like State Employment Security, State Job Service, or Manpower Services. The names may vary, but the services remain the same; they will make efforts to line you up with appropriate jobs and mail resumes out on your behalf to interested employers who have jobs listed with them. It is not mandatory for employers to list jobs with state agencies, but more and more are taking advantage of these free services. Once the bastion of minimum-wage jobs, these public agencies now list positions with salaries reaching $100,000 a year.

If you are moving across the state or across the country, your local employment office can plug you into what is known as a national job bank, which theoretically can give you access to jobs all over the nation. However, insiders agree that it can take up to a month for a particular job from a local office to hit the national system. The most effective way to use this service is to visit your local office and ask for an introduction to the office in your destination area. Then send them a cover letter with your resume and follow up with a phone call.

Private Employment Agency Sources

The following are a few sources for employment service listings, from temporary help through local employment agency, contingency, and retained headhunters. Depending on who you are and what you are looking for, any or all of these categories could be of interest to you. Here is some contact data for the most comprehensive lists and directories available.

National Association of Personnel Consultants
3133 Mt. Vernon Avenue
Alexandria, VA 22305
(703) 684-0180

National Directory of Personnel Consultants, $30.00 (includes shipping and handling). Identifies companies by occupational specialization and geographical coverage. Includes employment agencies, contingency, and retained search companies in membership. The industry's premier organization, with thousands of reputable contacts.

Directory of Executive Recruiters
Kennedy & Kennedy Inc.
Kennedy Place, Rte. 12 South
Fitzwilliam, NH 03447
(603) 585-2200

Directory of Executive Recruiters, $47.95 (pb). Details on 2,000 retained and contingency firms throughout North America.

National Job Campaigning Resource Center
Box 9433
Panama City Beach, FL 32417
(904) 235-3733

Ken Cole is the president of this organization, which should be known as Legwork Central. The company provides many of the research services offered by the top outplacement firms, but it is supported by the individual consumer. Among its unique and exciting job-hunting products are:

101 industry-specific directories of top contingency and retained search firms throughout the U.S. These are updated quarterly and provide pinpoint accuracy for just $15.00 a directory. A great deal.

Executive Research Directory. $88.00. This is a tremendous resource for the senior-level executive. Perhaps you need firms engaged in the development of artificial intelligence. This directory provides you with the names of people who can track this information down for you and save you the legwork.

Senior Executive Research Package. $125.00. Includes the Executive Research Directory and a printout of the 400 research directors at many of the nation's leading search firms.

National Association of Temporary Services
119 South State Asaph Street
Alexandria, VA 22314-3119
(703) 253-2020

> A self-addressed stamped envelope with a polite request will get you a free listing of temporary help companies in the state of your choice. A full listing of 7,300 firms is available for $160.00. The information is also available on disk. Ask for prices.

Don't restrict yourself to any single category in this area. Executives, especially, should not turn their nose up at local employment agencies. Often a local agency has better rapport and contacts with the local business community than the big-name search firm. I have also known more than one "employment agency" that regularly placed job candidates earning in excess of $250,000 a year. Don't get hung up on agency versus search firm labels without researching the firms in question; you could miss some great opportunities.

Business Magazines

There are a number of uses here. The articles about interesting companies can alert you to growth opportunities, and the articles themselves can provide a neat little entry in your cover letter. Most professional trade magazines rely more or less on the contributions of industry professionals. So articles bylined by Nate Sklaroff, vice president of Openings at Sesame Furnaces, could go into a little dossier for strictly targeted mailings. It's also a neat idea to enclose the clipping with your letter. These mailings to sometime authors can be tremendously rewarding. Writing is hard, and writers have egos of mythical proportions (just ask my editor). A little flattery can go a long way.

By the same token, you can write to people who are quoted in articles. It's great to see your name in print; in fact there is only one thing better, and that is hearing that someone *else* saw your name in print and now thinks you're a genius. (Of course, you should bear in mind that most of these magazines also carry a help-wanted section.)

These ideas are just some of the many unusual and effective ways to introduce yourself to companies. Browse through all of the sample letters in chapter 7 to uncover other effective ideas.

Mass Mailings and You

Your first effort with a cover letter is to find an individual to whom you can address it. As noted earlier, "Sir/Madam," or "To whom it may concern" says you don't care enough about the company to find out a name—they will pay more attention to the candidates who do. A name shows you have focus and guarantees that a specific individual will open and read your letter. You also have someone to ask for by name when you do your follow-up—important when you are interview hunting.

Must you send out hundreds or even thousands of letters in the coming weeks? I spoke to a woman on a call-in TV show recently who had "done everything and still not gotten a job." She explained how she had sent out almost 300 letters and still wasn't employed. I asked her several questions that elicited some revealing facts: She had been job hunting for almost two years (that equals two or three letters a week), and there were, conservatively, 3,000 companies she could work for. (That equals a single approach with no follow-up to only one in ten potential employers.) Two employer contacts a week will not get you back to work—or even on the track. Only if you approach and establish communication with every possible employer and follow up properly will you create the maximum opportunity for yourself.

In the world of headhunters the statistical average is seven hundred contacts between offers and acceptances. These are averages of professionals representing only the most desirable jobs and job candidates to each other. When I hear the oft-quoted statements that it takes a white collar worker about eight months to get a job nowadays, I have a feeling those seven hundred or so contacts are being spread out needlessly. If you approach the job hunt in a professional manner, the way executive search professionals and employment agents approach their work, you can be happily installed on the next rung of your career ladder within a few weeks or months.

I am not recommending that you immediately make up a list of seven hundred companies and mail letters to them today. That isn't the answer. Your campaign needs strategy. While every job-hunting campaign is unique, you will want to maintain a balance between the *number* of letters you send out on a daily and weekly basis and the *kinds* of letters you send out.

The key is to send out a balanced mailing representing all the different types of leads, and to send them out regularly and in a volume that will allow you to make follow-up calls. There are many headhunters who manage their time so well that they average over fifty calls a day, year in and year out. While you may aim at building your call volume up to this number, I recommend that you start out with more modest goals.

To start the campaign:

Source	Number of Letters Per Day
Internet job postings	10
Newspaper ads	10
Networking	10 (5 to friends, 5 to professional colleagues)
Direct-research contacts (online searches, reference works, magazines, etc.)	10
Headhunters	10

Do You Need to Compose More Than One Letter?

Almost certainly. There is a case for all of us having letters and resumes in more than one format. The key is to do each variation once and do it right; and that, as we have seen, means keeping your work comprehensively backed up on disk. This way, even for future job hunts, the legwork will already be done, and you'll be ready regardless of when opportunity or necessity comes knocking.

In fact, you may find it valuable to send upward of half a dozen contact letters to any given company, to assure that they know you are available. To illustrate, let's say you are a young engineer desirous of gaining employment with Last Chance Electronics. It is well within the bounds of reason that you would mail cover or broadcast letters to any or all of the following people, with each letter addressed by name to minimize its chances of going straight into the trash:

- Company President
- Vice President of Engineering
- Chief Engineer
- Engineering Design Manager
- Vice President of Human Resources
- Technical Engineering Recruitment Manager
- Technical Recruiter

The Plan

A professionally organized and conducted campaign will proceed on one of two plans of attack. Both of these plans should have an e-mail and traditional snail mail dimension. So when I talk about "mail" and "mail campaign," understand it to embrace both communication mediums.

Approach #1

A carefully targeted rifle approach of a select group of companies. You will have first identified these "super-desirable" places to work as you researched your long list of potential employers. You will continue to add to this primary target list as you unearth fresh opportunities in your day-to-day research efforts.

In this instance you have two choices:

1. Mail to everyone at once, remembering that the letters have to be personalized and followed up appropriately.
2. Start your mailings off with one to a line manager and one to a contact in human resources. Follow up in a few days and repeat the process to other names on your hit list.

With the e-mail dimension of your campaign, you can bookmark any target companies. This way you can check in on their advertised openings on an ongoing basis.

Approach #2

A carpet-bombing strategy designed to reach every possible employer on the basis that you won't know what opportunities there are unless you go find out. (Here, too, you must personalize and follow up appropriately.)

Begin the process with a mailing to one or two contacts within the company and then repeat the mailings to other contacts when your initial follow-up calls result in referrals or dead ends. Remember, just because Harry in engineering says there are no openings in the company, that's not necessarily the case; always find out for yourself. Don't rely on hearsay. Even if he doesn't have a need himself, any one contact could well know the person who is just dying to meet you.

Once you have received some responses to your mailings and scheduled some interviews, your emphasis will change. Those contacts and interviews will require follow-up letters and conversation. You will be spending time preparing for interviews.

This is exactly the point where most job hunts stall. We get so excited about the interview activity we convince ourselves that "This will be the offer." The headhunters have a saying, "The offer that can't fail always will." What typically happens is that the offer doesn't materialize, and we are left sitting with absolutely no interview activity. We let the interview funnel empty itself.

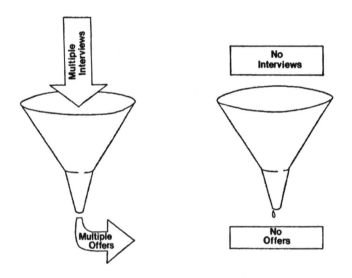

The more contacts you send out, the more follow-up calls you can make to schedule interviews. The more interviews you get, the better you feel and the better you get at interviewing. The better you get at interviewing, the more offers you get.

So no matter how good things look, you must continue the campaign— you have to maintain activity with those companies with whom you are in negotiation. But you must also maintain your marketing schedule. The daily plan now looks like this:

Source	Number of Letters Per Day
Internet Job Postings	5
Newspaper ads	5
Networking (associations, alumni/ae, colleagues)	5
Direct-research contacts (online searches, reference work, magazines, etc.)	5
Headhunters	5
Follow-up letters and calls	15–20

Small but consistent mailings have many benefits. The balance you maintain is important, because most job hunters are tempted simply to send the easy letters and make the easy calls (i.e., network with old friends). Doing this will knock your job hunt out of balance and kick you into a tailspin.

Even when an offer is pending, you must keep plugging, and by that I include all variations on "Harry, you've got the job and we're glad you can start Monday; the offer letter is in the mail." Yeah, just like the check in the proverb. Never accept the "yes" until you have it in writing, have started work, and the first paycheck has cleared at the bank! Until then, keep your momentum building. It is the professional and circumspect thing to do.

Following Up: A Cautionary Tale

In theory, your perfect letter will generate a 100 percent response. But there is no perfect letter, and this is a less-than-perfect world. Although you will get calls from your mailing, if you sit there like Buddha waiting for the world to beat a path to your door, you may wait a long time.

Not long ago a pal of mine put a two-line ad in the local paper for a programmer analyst. By Wednesday of the following week he had received over a hundred responses. Ten days later he was still plowing through them when he received a follow-up call (the only one he did receive) from one of the ad respondents. The job hunter was in the office within two hours, returned the following morning, and was hired by lunchtime.

The candidate's paperwork was simply languishing there in the pile waiting to be discovered. The follow-up phone call got it discovered. The call made the interviewer sort through the enormous pile of paper, pull out the letter and resume, and act on it. Follow-up calls work.

You'll notice that many letters in chapter 7 mention that they will follow up with a phone call. This allows the writer to explain to any inquisitive receptionist that Joe Shmoe is "expecting my call" or that it is "personal."

I find it surprising that so many professionals are nervous about calling a fellow professional on the phone and talking about what they do for a living. After all, isn't this exactly what you do at a party when you run into a fellow professional and stand around talking shop? To help reduce any nervousness, understand that there is an unwritten professional credo shared by the vast majority of successful professional people: You should always help another if it isn't going to hurt you in the process.

If you are not already successful in management, you need to know the principle outlined in my management books *Hiring the Best* and *Keeping the Best*: "The first tenet of management is getting work done through others." A manager's success is truly based on this single idea. Managers are always on the lookout for competent professionals in their field for today and tomorrow. In fact, the best managers maintain a private file of great professionals they can't use today but want to keep available. I know of someone who got a job as a result of a letter retained in these files. She got the interview (and the job) from the broadcast letter she'd sent eight years earlier.

No manager will ever take offense at a call from a competent fellow professional. To know exactly how to make the call and what to say, you will want to look at the chapter entitled "Painting the Perfect Picture on the Phone" in *Knock 'em Dead*.

To ensure that you keep track of the contacts you have sent and the results of the follow-up phone calls, create a Contact Tracker.

How to Use the Contact Tracker

I recommend that you make your own Contact Tracker on a spreadsheet program. Create columns for the company name, telephone number, e-mail address, and contact name. This will help you structure your job hunting days. A mailing today will allow you to have a follow-up plan set and ready to go at the appropriate time. As a rule of thumb, a mailing sent today is ripe for follow-up four to eight days from now. Any sooner and you can't be sure the mail has arrived; much later and it may already have gotten lost or been passed on. In addition to your Contact Tracker, it may be helpful to use your computer address book to keep track of the companies you contact.

You will know that your job hunt is on track when you are filling in more contacts every day as a result of a mailing, and creating a second Contact Tracker as a result of your follow-up calls.

If you follow the advice in this book, you will get interviews. If you follow the advice in *Resumes That Knock 'em Dead* and *Knock 'em Dead*, you will get multiple job offers. When you get your first job offer, you will want to read the section on multiple offers in *Knock 'em Dead*, which will show you how to turn many of these generated contacts into additional interviews and competitive offers.

Every month I hear from people who use these techniques effectively. Recently I spoke to a gentleman on a radio call-in show who had been out of work for some months. He had bought the books and followed my advice to the letter and had generated four job offers in only five weeks. I have lost count of the number of similar encounters I've had over the years. Follow my advice in letter and spirit and the same good fortune can be yours. After all, good fortune is really only the intersection of opportunity, preparation, and effort.

7 | Sample Letters

Here's the real meat and potatoes of the book— the sample letters you can use as models for your own.

Now we come to the letters. Apart from the sender's name and address (the personal stationery aspect), all letters adhere to Houghton Mifflin's *Best Writer's Guide* specifications. To those who might notice these things, it is important that we present an impeccable attention to detail.

E-mail Response to Online Job Posting (Technical Sales Representative)

Dear Ms. _____ :

Please accept this letter as application for the Technical Sales Representative position currently available with your company, as listed on Monster.com. My confidential resume is attached for your review and consideration, and I believe you will find me well qualified.

Detailed on my resume you will find a solid background in Sales and Marketing, with over two years in technical sales. In this capacity, I have developed an expertise in new and key account acquisition, new territory development and management, contract negotiation, and customer service. I am confident that my experience in these areas will prove to be an asset to ABC Corporation.

Additionally, I am familiar with blueprints, part number breakdowns, and the bidding process of our major accounts, which include _____, _____, _____ and _____ Corp. I have doubled my sales from $40,000/month to $80,000/month in just two years, and I am known for effectively identifying and resolving problems before they affect related areas, personnel, or customers.

I would welcome the opportunity to discuss with you how I might make similar contributions to the success of ABC Corporation. I look forward to hearing from you to schedule a personal interview at your convenience.

Sincere regards,

Jane Swift
(516) 555-1212
jswift@careerbrain.com

E-mail Response to Online Job Posting (Teacher)

Dear Ms. _____ :

I noted with interest your June 13, 2000 job posting on CareerCity.com for a Grade 2 Teacher for a leave replacement (9/00—-12/00). As a certified teacher with experience teaching this grade level and first-hand knowledge of P.S. 111 through extensive volunteer activities, I believe that I am an excellent candidate for this position.

I understand that you need someone who is self-directed and who possesses the necessary qualities for managing another teacher's class—flexibility, good humor, rapport with parents, familiarity with the school culture, and the ability to go beyond the lesson plans in accordance with meeting the current needs. At this point, I welcome the challenge of making a positive impact on the minds of elementary school aged children. I am committed to achieving this goal through ongoing professional development to learn the latest effective teaching methods.

I have attached my resume to provide more information on my strengths and career achievements. I am also open to other opportunities in the school. If after reviewing my material you believe that there is a match, please call me. Thank you for your consideration.

Sincere regards,

Jane Swift
(516) 555-1212
jswift@careerbrain.com

E-mail Response to Online Job Posting (Investment Banker)

Dear Mr. _____:

In response to your job posting that was posted for a _____ on your company's Web site, I have attached my resume for your consideration.

My experience as an administrative investment banker and assistant to a Vice Chairman is, I believe, readily adaptable to your needs. I have spent five years in a position best described as "doing whatever needs to be done" and have capitalized on my ability to undertake a large and widely varied array of projects, learn quickly, find effective solutions to problems, and maintain a sense of humor throughout.

My years as a line and administrative professional have also provided me with an unusual sensitivity to the needs of senior professionals. I have substantial computer experience and am fully computer literate. I have been told my verbal and written communication skills are exceptional.

I believe your firm would provide a working atmosphere to which I would be well suited, as well as one where my diverse experience would be valuable.

My salary requirements are reasonable and negotiable based on the responsibilities and opportunities presented.

Sincerely,

Jane Swift
(516) 555-1212
jswift@careerbrain.com

E-mail Response to Online Job Posting (Legal Administrator)

Dear Ms. _____:

I am responding to your job posting on Hotjobs.com for a legal administrator of a law firm. I wrote to you on (date) about law administrator positions in the metropolitan _____ area. I have attached another resume of my educational background and employment history. I am very interested in this position.

I have been a legal administrator for two 21-attorney law firms during the past six years. In addition, I have been a law firm consultant for over a year. Besides my law firm experience, I have been a medical administrator for over ten years. I believe that all of this experience will enable me to manage the law firm for this position very successfully. I possess the management, marketing, computer, accounting/budgeting, financial planning, personnel, and people-oriented skills that will have a very positive impact on this law firm.

I will be in the _____ area later in the month, so hopefully, we can meet at that time to discuss this position. I look forward to hearing from you, Ms. _____, concerning this position. Thank you for your time and consideration.

Very truly yours,

Jane Swift
(516) 555-1212
jswift@careerbrain.com

E-mail Response to Online Job Posting (Summer Job)

Dear Mr. _____:

I am excited about your advertisement on CareerCity.com for a summer intern. An internship with ABC Corporation is an ideal opportunity for me to enhance the skills I am developing as a third-year student, majoring in _____ at the University of _____.

The professional competency I have developed in other jobs (see attached resume) will enable me to assist you in meeting departmental goals. I would benefit from the experience of working with professionals and for a corporation with the strongest reputation in the industry.

I would like very much to be part of your team. I am available to meet with you at your convenience.

Sincerely,

James Sharpe
(516) 555-1212
jsharpe@careerbrain.com

E-mail Response to Online Job Posting (Customer Service Supervisor)

Dear _____ :

I've been a member of the _____ Educational Foundation for several years, and rely on you for exceptional programs. I've attached my resume and would like to be considered for the position listed on Jobs.com as Customer Service Supervisor.

I have ten years of business experience, including managerial and supervisory work, and have hired, trained, and supervised high-quality, responsive work groups. In addition to the work you see listed, I've been called upon to help design and facilitate "Face to the Customer" training programs for front-line workers. I also have access television experience, and am, as I said before, quite familiar with your programs.

On those occasions when I've spoken to members of your Customer Service staff, they have been very helpful. I'd like a chance to be part of that group and of the _____ Educational Foundation.

I look forward to hearing from you.

Sincerely,

Jane Swift
(516) 555-1212
jswift@careerbrain.com

E-mail Response to Online Job Posting (Production Supervisor)

Dear Ms. _____:

In response to the job posting on your company's Web site, please consider my resume in your search for a Production Supervisor.

With a hi-tech background in *Fortune* 500 companies, I feel well qualified for the position you described. I am presently responsible for the coordination of production in three assembly and test areas which employ 35 union personnel. Maintaining control of work of this magnitude and complexity requires my ability to function independently, and a willingness to make decisions quickly and effectively.

I am accustomed to a fast-paced environment where deadlines are a priority and handling multiple jobs simultaneously is the norm. I enjoy a challenge and work hard to attain my goals. Constant negotiations with all levels of management and union employees have strengthened my interpersonal skills. I would like very much to discuss with you how I could contribute to your organization.

I am seeking an opportunity to excel in a more dynamic company and am looking forward to relocating to the _____ area.

Please contact me at your earliest convenience so that I may share with you my background and enthusiasm for the job. Thank you for your time and consideration.

Sincerely,

James Sharpe
(516) 555-1212
jssharpe@careerbrain.com

E-mail Response to Online Job Posting (Jewelry Sales)

Dear Ms. _____ :

It is with great pleasure that I introduce myself, James Sharpe. I am asking you to consider me for the position you posted on CareerCity.com, for a _____ .

Please let's get together to discuss the part I could play in your operation. My family is currently in the import and export business in Egypt, exporting goods to London and other cities in Europe. They operate five offices in Egypt as well as maintaining offices in Hamburg, Germany, and London, England. While a student at Alexandria University, I worked for the family business. Additionally, I have many business connections throughout the Middle East.

I feel my experience could prove invaluable to your business and help develop the costume jewelry market in North Africa. I have faith that I can handle this territory in a highly professional manner. I have spent a lot of time and effort developing my marketing and sales skills, and I am sure that our relationship would prove to be mutually beneficial.

Please call me; it will only take a few minutes of your time and could prove to be the most profitable few minutes you ever spent. Together we can make this a *bright* year for everyone.

I look forward to hearing from you.

Sincerely yours,

James Sharpe
(516) 555-1212
jsharpe@careerbrain.com

E-mail Response to Online Job Posting (Production Manager)

Dear Mr. C. K. _____ :

I am interested in employment as a production manager with your firm. I know that my education and experience have prepared me for the position you have available.

For the past 10 years I have worked as a manager in manufacturing facilities. My company's annual evaluations of me have cited my ability to get the job done "on time and under budget," as well as the high employee morale in my department. I also have extensive hands-on experience as a machinist. Details of my education and experience are in the enclosed resume.

I know I can make a significant contribution to your company. May I come in, at your convenience, so we can discuss my qualifications more fully?

Sincerely,

James Sharpe
(516) 555-1212
jsharpe@careerbrain.com

Response to Newspaper Advertisement (Assessment Coordinator)

18 Central Park Street, Anytown, NY 14788
(516) 555-1212   jswift@careerbrain.com

JANE SWIFT

2 PAGES VIA FAX   (Date)
DEPT. HD 212-555-9999

Your advertisement in the New York Times, on June 9, 2000, for an **Assessment Coordinator** seems to perfectly match my background and experience. As the International Brand Coordinator for Kahlúa, I coordinated meetings, prepared presentations and materials, organized a major off-site conference, and supervised an assistant. I believe that I am an excellent candidate for this position as I have illustrated below:

YOUR REQUIREMENTS	MY QUALIFICATIONS
A highly motivated, diplomatic, flexible, quality-driven professional	Successfully managed project teams involving different business units. The defined end results were achieved on every project.
Exceptional organizational skills and attention to detail	Planned the development and launch of the Kahlúa Heritage Edition bottle series. My former manager enjoyed leaving the "details" and follow-through to me. Coverdale project management training.
College degree and minimum 3 years relevant business experience	B.A. from Vassar College (1994). 5+ years business experience in productive, professional environments.
Computer literacy	Extensive knowledge of Windows & Macintosh applications.

I'm interested in this position because it fits well with my new career focus in the human resources field. Currently, I am enrolled in NYU's adult career planning and development certificate program and working at Lee Hecht Harrison.

I have enclosed my resume to provide more information on my strengths and career achievements. If after reviewing my material you believe that there is a match, please call me. Thank you for your consideration.

Sincere regards,

Jane Swift

Jane Swift

JS
enclosure

Response to Newspaper Advertisement (Adjunct Faculty)

JANE SWIFT

18 Central Park Street, Anytown, NY 14788
(516) 555-1212   jswift@careerbrain.com

Phillip _____   (Date)
(Title)
ABC College
1 Industry Plaza
Anytown, NY 12096

Dear Mr. _____:

I was very excited to learn of your need for **Adjunct Faculty** in both *Reading* and *Elementary Education*. Having spent all of my professional life in Education, both as a teacher and my own continuing professional development, I realize the number of resumes you must receive on a daily basis. However, from my experience on selection committees, I know how valuable a few always turned out to be.

The purpose of this communication is to introduce myself and then to meet with you about an **adjunct teaching position** in your department. I'm well aware that in today's job market you will find people with more college teaching experience than I've had, though you *won't find anyone willing to work harder*. My record is one of solid accomplishments in both my teaching assignments and program development projects.

Review of my resume will further acquaint you with my qualifications:
- Well grounded and *knowledgeable in classroom dynamics*.
- *Proven* track record in developing and implementing *successful classroom interventions* to *maximize student achievement*.
- Possess *strong consultative skills* for teachers and parents alike.

My background, skills, and talents are in all aspects of Elementary Education and Staff Development: curriculum design; enrichment; language arts; literature; poetry; interdisciplinary programming; and helping students (special needs through gifted and talented) maximize their educational opportunities.

I am confident that my experience and skills would provide your students with the background to successfully "hit the ground running" when they enter their own classrooms in the future. I would appreciate the opportunity to meet with you, share ideas, and discuss ways in which my expertise would be an excellent addition to your college's teacher preparation program. I will call you over the next several days to schedule an appointment. In the interim, thank you for your consideration, attention, and forthcoming response.

Sincerely,

Jane Swift
Jane Swift

Response to Newspaper Advertisement (Teacher)

JANE SWIFT

18 Central Park Street, Anytown, NY 14788
(516) 555-1212   jswift@careerbrain.com

Phillip _____   (Date)
(Title)
ABC School
1 Industry Plaza
Anytown, NY 12096

Dear Mr. _____:

Please accept this letter and accompanying resume as application for the position of *Biology/Life Science Teacher* that was advertised in the *New York Times*. I am certified to teach Biology, General Science, and Earth Science in New York state. I am well aware that in today's job market you will find teachers with more years of experience than I have had, though you won't find anyone willing to work harder. My record is one of solid accomplishments in my teaching assignments.

As a science teacher, I have come to believe in two fundamental ideologies that allow me to focus on what is important in setting up a proper environment for learning. The first is that science must be a major part of education today so that students will be able to function in the world of tomorrow. The second belief is that within every child is a spark waiting to be ignited by the teacher into a flame of learning. These two beliefs coupled with my enthusiasm and love for learning make me a perfect match for your school district.

Review of the accompanying resume will show how well my qualifications match those of the position. Among my qualifications are:

- *Enthusiastic, high-energy educator* with proven track record in fostering academic learning and enhancing student creativity. Believe in making learning as much fun as possible.
- *Proven expertise* in taking academic subject matter and "*making it come alive*" for the student through well-planned, hands-on activities; fostering development of creative and critical thinking skills.
- *Acknowledged for raising the bar* in elevating students' standards and igniting their scientific curiosity.
- *Demonstrated ability to consistently individualize instruction*, based on students' interests and needs, at the most appropriate level.

I am confident that this background provides the skills that you require for this position and that an interview would demonstrate that my expertise would be an excellent addition to your school's educational program. I look forward to the opportunity to discuss in greater detail how my experience would benefit the Science Department. In the interim, thank you for your consideration, attention, and forthcoming response.

Yours truly,

Jane Swift

Jane Swift

Response to Newspaper Advertisement (Marketing Manager)

James Sharpe

18 Central Park Street, Anytown, NY 14788
(516) 555-1212   jsharpe@careerbrain.com

(Date)

Emily _____
(Title)
ABC Corporation
1 Industry Plaza
Anytown, NY 12096

Dear Ms. _____:

Your recent advertisement for a New Products Marketing Manager in the May 31 Sunday *New York Times* really captured my attention, as your requirements are a *custom-fit* to my experience and interests. For the past six years I have pursued an increasingly successful career in marketing management. My management and marketing *Skills* enabled me to achieve extremely high performance levels.

I am confident that my comprehensive management experience would serve as an asset to your organization. My record is one of increased responsibility, variety in job assignments, and solid accomplishments. The enclosed resume will provide you with a brief outline of my experience and accomplishments. Please allow me to highlight my skills as they relate to your stated requirements:

YOUR REQUIREMENTS	MY QUALIFICATIONS
• Drive and manage the marketing of new product development projects and product launch	• *Launched* 900 MHz communication product *driving sales growth from $1M to $28M. Increased volume* from 10k units (product predecessor) to over 500k units sold in the first year.
• Solicit and evaluate new project ideas	• Conducted face-to-face meetings with retail buyers, at the national level, to obtain market feedback. • *Spearheaded development* of multi-faceted product tailored to specific needs and produced customized marketing plan.
• Perform market/competitive analysis, conduct market research and concept testing	• *Demonstrated success in analyzing marketplace* to develop matrix that demonstrates superiority of product line.

James Sharp
page 2 of 2

- Ability to manage independent projects/work on new product development

- Proven ability to *identify trends* by category utilizing product profiles. Conduct focus groups to enhance ease of use, determine feature mix, and identify colors and optimal packaging to *achieve significant product improvement/new product*.

- MBA degree preferred

- Hold *MBA* in *Marketing Management* from St. John's University.

I am accustomed to a *fast-paced* environment where deadlines are a priority and handling multiple jobs simultaneously is the norm. Continual interaction with clients, in addition to all levels of management and operations, have strengthened my interpersonal and negotiation skills. I approach my work with a strong sense of urgency, working well under pressure and change. I look forward to meeting with you personally so that we may discuss in greater detail how my expertise would best meet the needs of your organization. In the interim, thank you for your consideration, attention, and forthcoming response.

Best regards,

James Sharpe

James Sharpe

JS
enclosure

Response to Newspaper Advertisement (Editor)

Jane Swift

18 Central Park Street, Anytown, NY 14788
(516) 555-1212   jswift@careerbrain.com

(Date)

Emily _____
(Title)
ABC Corporation
1 Industry Plaza
Anytown, NY 12096

Dear Ms. _____:

I'm writing in response to your ad in *The Sunday* _____ for an editor.

I have a bachelor's degree in communications from _____ University with an advertising major and art minor. My experience includes work at: _____ Advertising in Los Angeles, _____ in Portland, as well as freelance writing assignments for the _____ *Journal* and _____ Community College. I've enclosed a few writing samples for your review.

I have extensive editorial, proofreading, layout, and design experience, having served as the editor of my high school yearbook and previously as a section editor and staff member. The yearbook won first place in the _____ High School Press Conference for 20—. Most recently I completed a 32-page catalog paste-up and layout project for _____ Lab Sales in Hillsboro.

As a temporary secretary/word processor, I am responsible for creating a wide variety of documents and take great pleasure making sure each document looks good, reads well, and is error-free.

I'm organized and detail-oriented, work well under pressure and on deadline, enjoy working with a variety of people, and have a great attitude. I'm looking for a creative, challenging, growth-oriented position and would like the opportunity to learn more about your corporation and the position. What you need and what I can do sound like a match! I look forward to hearing from you.

Sincerely yours,

Jane Swift

Jane Swift

JS
enclosures
P.S. I will be out of town until Tuesday, June —th. However, a message may be left at my home number, 555-1212.

Response to Newspaper Advertisement (Accounting Manager)

James Sharpe

18 Central Park Street, Anytown, NY 14788
(516) 555-1212   jsharpe@careerbrain.com

(Date)

Phillip _____
(Title)
ABC Corporation
1 Industry Plaza
Anytown, NY 12096

Dear Mr. _____:

Re: File No. 213

I have nine years of accounting experience and am responding to your recent advertisement for an Accounting Manager. Please allow me to highlight my skills as they relate to your stated requirements.

Your Requirements	**My Experience**
A recognized accounting degree plus several years of practical accounting experience.	Obtained a C.A. degree in 1995 and have over four years' practical experience as an Accounting Manager.
Excellent people skills and demonstrated ability to motivate staff.	Effectively managed a staff of 24 including two supervisors.
Strong administrative and analytical skills.	Assisted in the development of a base reference library with Microsoft Excel for 400 clients.
Good oral and written communication skills.	Trained four new supervisors via daily coaching sessions, communication meetings, and technical skill sessions.

I believe this background provides the management skills you require for this position. I would welcome the opportunity for a personal interview to further discuss my qualifications.

Yours truly,

James Sharpe

James Sharpe

JS
enclosure

Response to Newspaper Advertisement (International Sales Manager)

JANE SWIFT

18 Central Park Street, Anytown, NY 14788
(516) 555-1212   jswift@careerbrain.com

(Date)

Phillip _____
(Title)
ABC Corporation
1 Industry Plaza
Anytown, NY 12096

Dear Mr. _____:

Re: International Sales Manager, *Globe & Mail*, September —, 20—

I was recently speaking with Mr. _____ from your firm and he strongly recommended that I send you a copy of my resume. Knowing the requirements for the position, he felt that I would be an ideal candidate. For more than eleven years, I have been involved in international sales management, with seven years directly in the aerospace industry. My qualifications for the position include:

- establishing sales offices in France, Great Britain and Germany;
- recruiting and managing a group of 24 international sales representatives;
- providing training programs for all of the European staff, which included full briefing on our own products as well as competitor lines;
- obtaining 42%, 33% and 31% of the French, German, and British markets, respectively, dealing with all local engine and airframe manufacturers; and
- generating more than $32 million in sales with excellent margins.

My Bachelor of Science degree in electrical engineering was obtained from the University of _____ and my languages include French and German.

I feel confident that an interview would demonstrate that my expertise in setting up rep organizations and training and managing an international sales department would be an excellent addition to your growing aerospace corporation.

I look forward to meeting with you, Mr. _____, and will give you a call to follow up on this letter the week of (date) _____.

Yours truly,

Jane Swift

Jane Swift
JS
enclosure

Response to Newspaper Advertisement (Executive Assistant)

JAMES SHARPE

18 Central Park Street ◆ Anytown, NY 14788
(516) 555-1212 jsharpe@careerbrain.com

(Date)

Box 9412
New York, NY 01234

Dear _____:

I was very pleased to learn of the need for an Executive Assistant in your company from your recent advertisement in _____. I believe the qualities you seek are well matched by my track record:

Your Needs	My Qualifications
Independent Self-Starter	• Served as company liaison between sales representatives, controlling commissions and products. • Controlled cash flow, budget planning and bank reconciliation for three companies. • Assisted in the promotion of a restaurant within a private placement sales effort, creating sales materials and communicating with investors.
Computer Experience	• Utilized Lotus in preparing financial spreadsheet used in private placement memoranda and Macintosh to design brochures and flyers. • Have vast experience with both computer programming and the current software packages.
Compatible Background	• Spent 5 years overseas and speak French. • Served as an executive assistant to four corporate heads.

A resume is enclosed that covers my experience and qualifications in greater detail. I would appreciate the opportunity to discuss my credentials in a personal interview.

Sincerely,

James Sharpe

James Sharpe

JS
enclosure

Power Phrases

Consider using adaptations of these key phrases in your responses to newspaper advertisements.

I believe that I am particularly well qualified for your position and would like to have the opportunity to meet with you to explore how I may be of value to your organization.

Your advertisement #5188 in the March 25th edition of The _____ has piqued my interest. This position has strong appeal to me.

I am confident that with my abilities I can make an immediate and valuable contribution to _____.

I would be pleased if you contacted me for an interview.

I was recently speaking with Mr. _____ from your firm and he strongly recommended that I send you a copy of my resume. Knowing the requirements for the position, he felt that I would be an ideal candidate.

I've had both large and small company experience and it is my preference to work in a smaller operation where goals are measurable, results are noticeable and contributions really make a difference!

I feel confident that an interview would demonstrate that my expertise in setting up rep organizations, and training and managing an international sales department, would be an excellent addition to your growing _____ company.

I look forward to meeting with you, Mr. _____, and will give you a call to follow up on this letter the week of September —th.

The opportunity to work with your client is appealing to me, and I would appreciate an opportunity to discuss the position further. I look forward to hearing from you soon.

I believe this background provides the management skills you require for this position. I would welcome the opportunity for a personal interview to further discuss my qualifications.

In response to your ad, please consider my resume in your search for a Sales Service Coordinator.

I look forward to hearing from you in the near future to schedule an interview at your convenience, during which I hope to learn more about your company's plans and goals and how I might contribute to the success of its service team.

I am accustomed to a fast-paced environment where deadlines are priority and handling multiple jobs simultaneously is the norm. I enjoy a challenge and work hard to attain my goals. Constant negotiations with all levels of management and union employees have strengthened my interpersonal skills. I would like very much to discuss with you how I could contribute to your organization.

I am seeking an opportunity to excel in a dynamic company and am looking forward to relocating to _____.

Please contact me at your earliest convenience so that I may share with you my background and enthusiasm for the job.

Your ad captured my attention.

My personal goal is simple: I wish to be a part of an organization that wants to excel in both _____ and _____. I believe that if I had the opportunity to interview with you it would be apparent that my skills are far-reaching.

Although I'm far more interested in a fine company and an intriguing challenge than merely in money, you should know that in recent years my compensation has been in the range of $45,000 to $60,000.

May we set up a time to talk?

What you need and what I can do sound like a match!

Please find enclosed a copy of my resume for your review. I believe the combination of my _____ education and my business experience offers me the unique opportunity to make a positive contribution to your firm.

As you will note in my resume I have not only "grown up" in and with the Operations and Warehousing area of a major (apparel) (consumer products) company, I have also established my expertise and my value to a discriminating and brilliant employer who depended upon me—on a daily basis—to represent and protect his interests and contribute significantly to his profitability.... I am seeking an opportunity to replicate this situation and again utilize my considerable abilities to dedicate myself to the profitability of my employer.

I am available to meet with you to discuss my qualifications at your convenience. I can be reached at _____. I would like to thank you in advance for your time and any consideration you may give me. I look forward to hearing from you.

Having been born and raised in the _____ area and wishing to return to this area to work as a _____, I have been researching _____ firms that offer the type of experience for which my previous education and work experience will be of mutual benefit. Highlights of my attached resume include: _____.

Please consider my qualifications for the position of _____ which you advertised.

As you will note on the enclosed resume, the breadth of my expertise covers a wide area of responsibilities, thereby providing me with insights into the total operation.

Recently, I saw an advertisement in the _____ for a position as a Technical Trainer. My candidacy for this position is advanced by my experience in three areas: training, support, and a technological background.

I thrive on challenge and feel that my skills and experience are easily transferable.

I would appreciate an opportunity to discuss my abilities in more depth, and am available for an interview at your earliest convenience.

Is the ideal candidate for the position of _____ highly motivated, professional, and knowledgeable in all functions concerning _____? Well, you may be interested to know that a person possessing these qualities, and much more, is responding to your ad in the _____ for this position.

I very much enjoy working in a team environment and the rewards associated with group contribution.

The skills you require seem to match my professional strengths.

I have a strong background in telemarketing small and medium-size businesses in the _____ District and outlying areas.

I look forward to hearing from you soon to set up an appointment at your convenience. Please feel free to give me a call at my office at _____ or leave a message at my home number, _____.

As a recent MBA graduate, my professional job experience is necessarily limited. However, I believe that you will find, and previous employers will verify, that I exhibit intelligence, common sense, initiative, maturity, and stability, and that I am eager to make a positive contribution to your organization.

I read, with a great deal of interest, your advertisement in the October 20 _____, issue of _____.

Please allow me to highlight some of my achievements which relate to your requirements: _____.

I would greatly appreciate the opportunity to discuss this position in a personal interview. I may be contacted at _____ to arrange a meeting.

I would appreciate an opportunity to meet with you. At present I am working as a temp but am available to meet with you at your convenience. I look forward to meeting you.

Thank you for taking the time recently to respond to my questions concerning a _____ position with _____.

I will be in your area Friday, December —th, and will call you early next week to see if we might schedule a meeting at that time.

This experience has provided me with a keen appreciation for the general practice of _____.

A salary of $30,000 would be acceptable; however, my main concern is to find employment where there is potential for growth.

"Cold" E-mail—To a Potential Employer (Summer Internship)

Dear Mr. _____:

Ms. Jane Smith suggested that I contact you to discuss the contribution that I could make to ABC Corporation in a Contract Design Internship this summer. I am currently a student at The Interior Design Institute and am anxious to begin my professional design career. Unlike many of my peers whose only experience is academic, I offer not only strong educational credentials but also practical, "hands-on" business experience.

My strength is being able to work with people to generate ideas that work. My career has been focused in the areas of advertising project coordination, customer relations management, and events planning. Former managers would describe me as capable, motivated, and detail-oriented.

The most rewarding work has always centered on creativity and design. As a child, I made barrettes, boxes, and dolls and sold them to local stores. In high school, I took every art and photography course that I could and even won a tri-state photography contest. Then I earned a degree in business administration and began working in marketing. Once I made the decision to make a career change, I began to create again. I made and sold pillows, blankets, painted furniture, pictures with beads, mosaics on tables and mirrors, water-colored lampshades, etc. Friends suggested that I should do it for a living. I agreed and quickly commenced my formal design training. I have excelled in my coursework and am looking forward to bringing my creativity and business acumen to this profession.

I have attached my resume to provide more information on my strengths and career achievements. I'm also prepared to show you a preliminary portfolio of my work. I look forward to speaking with you to further pursue this opportunity. Thank you for your consideration.

Sincerely,

Jane Swift
(516) 555-1212
jswift@careerbrain.com

"Cold" E-mail—To a Potential Employer (Business Manager)

Dear Ms. _____ :

Having grown up in Anytown, I was excited to learn of your need for an experienced Business Manager for the public school system. After several years in town management, with interviewing and hiring authority, I realize the number of resumes you receive regularly. However, I remember how valuable a few always turned out to be.

The purpose of this communication is to introduce myself and then to meet with you about the opportunity for me to relocate to my hometown and give something back. My confidential resume is enclosed for your review and consideration, and I am certain that you will find me very well qualified. Please allow me to highlight several aspects of my background:

- More than six years successful experience in municipal government with another two years in public accounting.
- Proven track record in managing significant budgets.
- Significant expertise in working with federal and state grants.
- Proven ability to maximize efficiency and expedite workflow.
- Demonstrated ability in managing capital improvement projects.

Although the accompanying resume illustrates my strengths well, I am certain of my abilities to make a significant contribution early on and that a personal interview would better demonstrate how I could meet the needs of Anytown Public Schools. I look forward to the opportunity of discussing in person how my expertise could best fit your needs and contribute to the school system's continued success. In the interim, thank you for your consideration, attention, and forthcoming response.

Sincere regards,

Jane Swift
(516) 555-1212
jswift@careerbrain.com

"Cold" E-mail—To a Potential Employer (Administration)

Dear Mr. _____:

Are you looking for a seasoned administrator with diversified experience in human resources management, financial services management, project leadership and operational audits? I have seventeen years of human resources experience with extensive knowledge in staffing, strategic planning, compensation and benefits administration, research and policy development, employee relations and employee relocation.

I am seeking a position in the human resources area; however, I am interested in other administrative management opportunities that require my abilities.

I have attached my resume and I look forward to hearing from you to discuss my qualifications further.

Sincerely,

Jane Swift
(516) 555-1212
jswift@careerbrain.com

"Cold" E-mail—To a Potential Employer (Banking)

Dear Mr. _____ :

Please include my name in your job search data base. As requested, I have attached a copy of my current resume.

Banking today is definitely a sales environment. While my marketing skills will always be useful, my interests lead me now to seek a more distinct financial management position such as Controller, Treasurer, or Vice President of Finance.

Since my CPA will be completed in January 20—, my search may be somewhat premature, but my transcript and results, combined with my practical experience, should offset my temporary lack of an accounting designation. I would therefore like you to begin considering me immediately. As an Account Manager, I saw many different industries, and so would not feel constrained to any one sector.

Including a mortgage loan benefit, I am currently earning $4,500 per month plus a car allowance. This should provide you with an indication of my present job level. Your suggestions or comments would be appreciated. I am available for interviews, and can be reached at (516) 555-1212. Thank you.

Yours truly,

James Sharpe
jsharpe@careerbrain.com

"Cold" E-mail—To a Potential Employer (Software Development)

Dear Mr. _____:

ABC Corporation caught my attention recently as I began a search for a new employer in the Phoenix area. ABC Corporation is well known in the software industry for quality products and excellent customer service; it also maintains a strong reputation as a great employer. Your organization has created an environment in which people can excel, which is why I write you today.

I am very interested in joining your software development team. I am confident that my background and experience will meet your future needs. My current position is Application Developer for Ascend Corp. I enjoy it very much as it has provided me with extensive hands-on training in Visual Basic and other languages. However, I am ready to get more into the actual software writing, as well as return to the Mesa area. I possess a bachelor's degree in Computer Science as well as training in a variety of programming languages. I am also a fast learner, as demonstrated by my learning Visual Basic quickly after joining Ascend. Additionally, I plan to pursue my Master's degree and have begun the application process.

I would appreciate the opportunity to meet with you to discuss your goals and how I can help you meet them. I will call you soon to arrange a meeting at your convenience. In the meantime, please feel free to call for further information on my background and experience.

Thank you for your consideration and reply. I look forward to meeting you in the near future.

Yours truly,

Jane Swift
(516) 555-1212
jswift@careerbrain.com

"Cold" E-mail—To a Potential Employer (Retail Administration)

Dear Mr. _____:

After fifteen years in the retail administration field, I am seeking a new position and have attached my resume for your consideration.

You will notice one common thread throughout my career—I am an administrator and a problem solver. These talents have been applied successfully in office management, field operations, purchasing, communications, telephone skills, and organizing and structuring of various departments. These assignments have required close coordination with Senior Management. This diversity of accomplishments enables me to relate to other areas of business.

I am self-motivated and can work independently to get the job done efficiently in the least possible time.

I will be calling you on Friday, August —th to be sure you received my resume and answer any questions you might have.

Very truly yours,

James Sharpe
(516) 555-1212
jsharpe@careerbrain.com

"Cold" E-mail—To a Potential Employer (Corporate Communications)

Dear Ms. _____:

Perhaps you are seeking an addition to your communications team. A new person can provide innovative approaches to the challenges and opportunities of integrated corporate communications. You will discover from the attached resume that I have a results-oriented background in several key areas.

Although my career has been centered on well-established public relations agencies, I prefer to continue professionally on the client side. In fact, in a couple of instances (in the United States and overseas), I worked on-site within the client organizations.

I want to concentrate my diverse talents in the service of one company's communications efforts. I currently would consider opportunities in the $65-$85K range.

Feel free to call me to discuss any details.

Regards,

Jane Swift
(516) 555-1212
jswift@careerbrain.com

"Cold" E-mail—To a Potential Employer (Process Engineer)

Dear Mr. _____:

Please accept this letter as application for the Process Engineer position currently available with your company. My confidential resume is attached for your review and consideration.

My experience has afforded me exposure to numerous facets of process engineering, including troubleshooting, problem solving, tooling set-up, performance improvement projects, and quality assurance. I am confident that my expertise in these areas will prove to be an asset to ABC Corporation's manufacturing operations.

My current salary requirement would range mid- to high-20Ks, with specifics flexible, negotiable, and dependent upon such factors as benefit structure, responsibility, and advancement opportunity.

I look forward to hearing from you in the near future to schedule an interview at your convenience, during which I hope to learn more about your corporation, its plans and goals, and how I might contribute to its continued success.

Sincerely,

James Sharpe
(516) 555-1212
jsharpe@careerbrain.com

"Cold" E-mail—To a Potential Employer (Internship)

Dear Ms. _____:

I am interested in being considered for an internship. I am currently a senior at the University of Denver majoring in International Studies with a concentration in Latin America and a minor in Political Science.

My internships have increased my knowledge of International Relations and have enabled me to make use of my education in a professional environment. I am very serious about my International Relations education and future career and am eager to learn as much as possible throughout my internship. I am interested in working for your organization to gain practical experience and additional knowledge pertaining to my field of study.

My professional and academic background, along with my sincere interest in helping others, has enhanced my sensitivity to a diverse range of cultures. As a highly motivated professional, I enjoy the challenge of complex demanding assignments. My well-developed writing and communication skills are assets to an office environment.

I welcome the opportunity to elaborate on how I could make a substantial contribution to your organization as an intern. I look forward to talking with you soon. Thank you.

Sincerely,

Jane Swift
(516) 555-1212
jswift@careerbrain.com

"Cold" Cover Letter—To a Potential Employer (Education)

JANE SWIFT

18 Central Park Street, Anytown, NY 14788
(516) 555-1212   jswift@careerbrain.com

(Date)

Phillip _____
(Title)
ABC Corporation
1 Industry Plaza
Anytown, NY 12096

Dear Mr. _____:

As Assistant Principal and School-to-Careers Coordinator, I have had the opportunity to develop a state of the art, ninth-to-twelfth-grade career building program at Twin Falls High School. The program includes assessment, research, job search training, and job shadowing components that culminate in an eight-week internship for all students during their senior year.

As an active member of both Business and School Divisions of the Twin Falls School-to-Careers Partnership, I have contributed ideas to the original grant and have shared my expertise at numerous workshops and training sessions in New York state. Over the last five years, my ideas have evolved into a systemic approach to career awareness and I have become a strong advocate of the need to promote a symbiotic relationship between schools and business.

I would like to be considered for the position of Director of Career Services. I believe my broad administrative experience together with my strong background in school-to-careers programs will enable me to provide innovative leadership at ABC Corporation and make a significant contribution to the schools it serves.

My resume is attached for your review. I would welcome the opportunity to discuss my qualifications further in a personal interview. I can be reached at (516) 555-1212 in the daytime, and (516) 555-5555 in the evening.

Yours truly,

Jane Swift

Jane Swift
JS
enclosure

"Cold" Cover Letter—To a Potential Employer (Teacher)

JAMES SHARPE

18 Central Park Street ◆ Anytown, NY 14788
(516) 555-1212   jsharpe@careerbrain.com

Phillip _____   (Date)
(Title)
ABC School
1 Industry Plaza
Anytown, NY 12096

Dear Mr. _____:

Please accept this letter and accompanying resume as application for projected teaching positions in English and/or Religion at the Secondary Level. I am well aware that in today's job market you will find teachers with more years of experience than I have had, though *you won't find anyone willing to work harder*. My record is one of solid accomplishments in my teaching assignments.

The enclosed resume will provide you with a brief outline of my experience and accomplishments. In summary, it includes these achievements:

- Enthusiastic educator with proven track record in fostering academic learning and enhancing student creativity. Believe in making learning as enjoyable as possible.
- Demonstrated expertise in taking academic subject matter and "making it come alive" for the student through well-planned projects that promote development of creative and critical thinking skills.
- Demonstrated ability to consistently individualize instruction, based on students' interests and needs, at the most appropriate level.

Not mentioned on the resume is my own secondary school experience. I attended Portrush School in Portsmouth, Rhode Island, where my faith and reason were encouraged to grow in the presence of a small Benedictine community. I treasure all that I have gained from this experience.

Now I want to give something back and would welcome the opportunity to contribute to the personal and intellectual development of your students, whatever their particular needs might be. I am confident that this background provides the skills that you require for such positions and that a personal interview would demonstrate that my expertise would be an excellent addition to your school's educational program. I look forward to the opportunity to discuss in greater detail how my experience would benefit the students in your school. In the interim, thank you for your consideration, attention, and forthcoming response.

Sincerely,

James Sharpe
James Sharpe

JS
enclosure

"Cold" Cover Letter—To a Potential Employer (Electrical Engineering)

JANE SWIFT

18 Central Park Street, Anytown, NY 14788
(516) 555-1212   jswift@careerbrain.com

Phillip _____   (Date)
(Title)
ABC Corporation
1 Industry Plaza
Anytown, NY 12096

Dear Mr. _____:

My electrical engineering background, specifically, my successes working on many defense, combat, and Navy projects, is the chief asset I would bring to a position in your firm.

I understand that the primary function is to provide guidance for Navy JUPITER-I systems in electromagnetic environmental effects, shock and vibration, antenna blockage, and radar cross-section. I am thoroughly familiar with Navy acquisition programs in general, and I have also dealt almost exclusively with Navy civilian and uniformed personnel throughout my career, so I am well-versed in Navy project specifications, requirements, and protocol.

In my current position as Senior Systems Engineer for Lexmark, Inc., a firm dealing primarily in Navy contracts, I supervise the software systems and testing associated with the EAGLE Weapon System. And as the Chief Consulting Engineer with Consultant Associates, I deal with not only Navy security classification issues, but also those involving the Department of Defense.

Previously, as the manager of Development & Special Projects Test Engineering for Cendant, I participated in the development of the Navy's X-72 Test and Evaluation Master Plan for the X-72 Acquisition Program. While working with the X-72 Combat System Integration and Test Team, we produced the first operating X-72 class Combat System within extremely short time constraints, an accomplishment which led to the successful completion of the DOTT milestone event.

My strengths are not only in development, but also in testing and analysis. Again, at Cendant, when faced with the loss of data during an initial shock trial of the EAGLE cruiser, I developed the following solution: we located video cameras at key equipment indicator panels and display consoles. The equipment recorded the data processes, which I then analyzed and suggested corrective action. A similar video recording technique was used to solve a problem on the JUPITER-I antenna.

I believe my Navy and electrical engineering background is a quality match for the requirements stated for a position in your organization. Kindly review my resume, then please contact me at your earliest convenience to schedule a professional interview.

Yours truly,

Jane Swift

Jane Swift

"Cold" Cover Letter—To a Potential Employer (Pharmaceutical Sales)

JAMES SHARPE

18 Central Park Street, Anytown, NY 14788
(516) 555-1212   jsharpe@careerbrain.com

Emily _____   (Date)
(Title)
ABC Corporation
1 Industry Plaza
Anytown, NY 12096

Dear Ms. _____:

I currently hold a sales management position for a very successful retail company. My talents to achieve high sales volume, work cooperatively with diverse personalities, and focus on providing exceptional customer service has allowed me to excel in customer relations and succeed in sales and marketing.

I have always enjoyed a challenge and have made the decision to extend my experience to the pharmaceutical sales field. Pharmaceutical sales has been an interest of mine for some time and I am confident that my background and skills in customer service, human relations, and product distribution would transition well into pursuing this change. What I may lack in specific experience in your business, I more than make up for with my dedication, energy, and determination.

I thoroughly understand the importance of developing customer relations, generating revenue from sales potential within a designated territory, and maintaining accurate customer information. I have the aptitude and willingness to learn the necessary technical medical materials to promote your products. I am fully capable of projecting a positive and professional image of an organization and its products and I strongly believe I possess the necessary skills and qualifications your organization seeks to be successful in this field of work.

Your time in reviewing my confidential resume is greatly appreciated. I will follow up next week to answer any questions you may have regarding my qualifications. At that time, I would like to discuss the possibility of setting up a personal interview at your convenience. Please contact me if you would like to speak sooner.

Very truly yours,

James Sharpe

James Sharpe

JS
enclosure

"Cold" Cover Letter—To a Potential Employer (Recruiter)

James Sharpe

18 Central Park Street, Anytown, NY 14788
(516) 555-1212   jsharpe@careerbrain.com

(Date)

Alice _____
(Title)
Krieger, Skvetney, Howell
Executive Search Consultants
2426 Foundation Road
Anytown, NY 14788

Dear Ms. _____:

Having spent several years as an executive recruiter, I realize the number of resumes you receive on a daily basis. However, I remember how valuable a few always turned out to be.

The purpose of this communication is to introduce myself and then to meet with you about joining your organization.

When asked which business situations have been the most challenging and rewarding, my answer is the time spent in the search profession.

My background, skills and talents are in all aspects of sales and sales management. My research indicates that your expertise is in this area.

I have enclosed a resume which will highlight and support my objectives. I would appreciate the opportunity to meet and exchange ideas. I will call you over the next several days to make an appointment. If you prefer, you may reach me in the evening or leave a message at (516) 555-1212.

Thank you and I look forward to our meeting.

Sincerely,

James Sharpe

James Sharpe

JS
enclosure

JAMES SHARPE

18 Central Park Street, Anytown, NY 14788
(516) 555-1212   jsharpe@careerbrain.com

(Date)
Emily _____
(Title)
ABC Corporation
1 Industry Plaza
Anytown, NY 12096

Dear Ms. _____:

With this letter and resume I would like to offer myself for a position in sales or project management that fully utilizes my professional skills and personal abilities.

Upon graduating from high school, I thought I wanted to be an electrician and successfully accomplished that goal. Over time, however, I have found that I enjoy, and am successful in, positions involving greater interaction with people.

I prefer an opportunity offering growth and advancement based upon individual merit and capability. My background reflects extensive successful experience within the electrical/construction industry, and I would like to utilize that experience in a position that will also allow me to use my communication, negotiation, and sales skills to secure new business and maintain existing customers.

I have the ability to establish and maintain effective communication and rapport with peers, clients, and management. I have proven business knowledge, as well as customer service, sales, and expediting abilities. In addition, I am efficient, organized, and detail oriented—and I believe in thorough follow-up.

My experience and education provide a solid base and broad understanding of business-related operations and practices. I am keenly aware of the importance of completing assignments on time, within budget, and to the client's total satisfaction.

I am interested in securing a position within your company where my abilities and qualifications can be fully applied for our mutual benefit. I welcome an opportunity to meet with you and elaborate on how I can make a substantial contribution to your company's profitability. I will call you in a few days to further discuss my qualifications in detail. Thank you.
Sincerely,

James Sharpe

James Sharpe

JS
enclosure

"Cold" Cover Letter—To a Potential Employer (Publishing)

JAMES SHARPE

18 Central Park Street ◆ Anytown, NY 14788
(516) 555-1212 jsharpe@careerbrain.com

(Date)

Phillip _____
(Title)
ABC Corporation
1 Industry Plaza
Anytown, NY 12096

Dear Mr. _____:

In the interest of exploring opportunities in the publishing industry, I have enclosed my resume for your review.

Over the last two years, I have gained valuable knowledge and experience in many aspects of personnel assistance, office procedures, and administrative operations. Recently I volunteered my time to edit a cookbook and have been responsible for editing the newsletter for my fraternity. I consider myself a good writer and an avid reader and have always wanted to get into publishing. With my considerable energy, drive, and ability to work long hours, I believe I could make a positive contribution to your organization, and I would appreciate the opportunity to discuss my qualifications at your earliest convenience.

Should any questions arise regarding the information on my resume, or if you need personal references, please do not hesitate to contact me through the address or telephone number listed above.

Thank you for your time and consideration. I look forward to meeting with you.

Respectfully,

James Sharpe

James Sharpe

JS
enclosure

"Cold" Cover Letter—To a Potential Employer (General)

JANE SWIFT

18 Central Park Street, Anytown, NY 14788
(516) 555-1212   jswift@careerbrain.com

(Date)

Emily _____
(Title)
ABC Corporation
1 Industry Plaza
Anytown, NY 12096

Dear Ms. _____:

I am very interested in obtaining a position with your organization. Enclosed please find my resume for your review.

You will find most of the necessary background information contained in my resume. However, I would like to mention that I am available for immediate employment. I am also exploring the job market to obtain a position with a firm that will appreciate my skills and willingness to work eagerly with other people. I can definitely offer you longevity.

As my resume indicates, I am a Filipina and only arrived in the United States in 19— after my marriage to an American. I hope that this will explain my limited work record in this country. Also, English is the second language in the Philippines. It is spoken from childhood and is taught from grade one in school, so I am fluent in the language. Frankly, all I need to prove my abilities is an employer in need of an employee who is used to hard work and who has a strong work ethic.

I would like very much to schedule a personal interview where we can discuss my enthusiasm and qualifications for a position with your organization. I can be reached at the address and telephone number listed above.

Thank you for your time; I look forward to a favorable response.

Sincerely yours,

Jane Swift

Jane Swift

JS
enclosure

"Cold" Cover Letter—To a Potential Employer (International Sales)

JANE SWIFT

18 Central Park Street, Anytown, NY 14788
(516) 555-1212   jswift@careerbrain.com

(Date)

Phillip _____
(Title)
ABC Corporation
1 Industry Plaza
Anytown, NY 12096

Dear Mr. _____:

I received your name from Mr. _____ last week. I spoke to him regarding career opportunities with _____ and he suggested contacting you. He assured me that he would pass my resume along to you; however, in the event that he did not, I am enclosing another.

As an avid cosmetics consumer, I understand and appreciate the high standards of quality that your firm honors. As you can see from my enclosed resume, I have had quite a bit of experience in the international arena. My past experience working overseas has brought me a greater understanding of international cultures and traditions, as well as a better understanding and appreciation of our own culture. These insights would certainly benefit a corporation with worldwide locations, such as your own. In addition, I have gained first-hand experience in the consumer marketplace through my various sales positions. I have noticed your recent expansion into the television media and am sure that an energetic individual would surely be an asset to ABC in this, as well as other, projects.

I would very much like to discuss career opportunities with ABC. I will be calling you within the next few days to set up an interview. In the meantime, if you have any questions I may be reached at the number above. Thank you for your consideration.

Sincerely,

Jane Swift

Jane Swift

JS
enclosure

Power Phrases

Consider using adaptations of these key phrases in your "cold" letters to potential employers.

My twenty-two-year operations management career with a multi-billion-dollar _____ company has been at increasing degrees of responsibility. While I have spent the last five years in top management, I am especially proud of my record — I started as a driver many years ago, and like cream, have risen to the top. I have consistently accomplished all goals assigned to me, particularly overall cost reductions, improved productivity, and customer service. Some of my achievements are:

Your recent acquisition of the _____ chain would indicate an intent to pursue southeastern market opportunities more vigorously than you have in the past several years. I believe that my retail management background would complement your long-range strategy for _____ very effectively.

With the scarcity of qualified technical personnel that exists today, it is my thought that you would be interested in my qualifications as set forth in the attached resume.

In approximately three months, I am moving to _____ with my family, and am bringing with me fifteen solid years of banking experience — the last eight in branch operations management. I would like particularly to utilize this experience with your firm.

I have noticed that you conduct laser exposure testing at your facility. If there is a need for laser technicians in this endeavor, I would like to be considered for a position.

As you can see from my resume, I am a psychology major and was president of our debating society in my senior year. I feel both would indicate a talent for sales. I did some selling in my summer job in 20— (ABC Books), and found not only that I was successful, but that I thoroughly enjoyed it.

The position you described sounds challenging and interesting. After receiving your comments about the job requirements, I am convinced that I can make an immediate contribution toward the growth of _____ and would certainly hope that we may explore things further at your convenience.

The opportunity to put to use my medical knowledge as well as my English degree would bring me great pleasure, and it would please me to know that I was bringing quality to your company.

I feel that the combination of _____'s educational environment and my desire to learn as much as possible about the data processing field could only bring about positive results.

If you think after talking to me and reading my resume that there might be an interest with your client company, I would be very interested. I have been put in many situations where I had to learn quickly, and have always enjoyed the challenge.

My accomplishments include:

As my resume indicates, I have demonstrated commitment to clients and to my employer's goals. That track record is consistent in my career endeavors as well as in my life as a whole. I dedicate myself to whatever task is at hand, marshal my resources and stay with the project until it is completed—to my satisfaction. Since my goals and demands are even more stringent than my employers' expectations, I consistently exceed quotas and objectives.

You will notice one common thread throughout my career — I am an administrator and a problem solver.

Currently I would like to consider opportunities in the $65-$85K range.

My confidential resume is enclosed for your review and consideration.

My current salary requirement would range mid-to-high $50Ks, with specifics flexible, negotiable, and dependent upon such factors as benefit structure, responsibility, and advancement opportunity.

Having spent several years as a _____, I realize the number of resumes you receive on a daily basis. However, I remember how valuable a few always turned out to be.

My research indicates that the company's expertise is in this area.

I would like the opportunity to discuss with you how we could mutually benefit one another. You may leave a message on my answering machine at my home and I will return the call. I look forward to hearing from you very soon.

I'm a clear communicator equally at ease with senior management, governmental officials and control agencies, vendors and contractors, construction/labor force. I'm a hard-driving manager who is project driven and is accustomed to inspiring the best job performance possible from associates and employees. I'm also creative enough to be in compliance with agency requirements without sacrificing profit or deadlines.

This job does seem to be the right challenge for me; I know that with my strong Java skills and manufacturing background experience I will be an asset to your company.

Hoping to meet you in person, I thank you for your time.

I will be calling you on Friday, August —, 20— to be sure you received my resume and to answer any questions you might have.

I have enclosed a resume which will highlight and support my objectives. I would appreciate the opportunity to meet and exchange ideas. I will call you over the next several days to make an appointment. If you prefer, you may reach me in the evening or leave a message at (516) 555-1212.

"Cold" E-mail—To Employment Industry Professional (IT Professional)

Dear Mr. _____:

As an IT specialist, with extensive experience managing a IBM mainframe environment, I am contacting organizations such as yours that seek to recruit top-level technical staff. Due to a restructuring at my current company, I am exploring opportunities where I can contribute significant expertise with IBM equipment and systems as well as networking.

In my current capacity of MIS Manager for a manufacturer I have been a key player in spear-heading the following efforts:

- integrating networking technologies into a mainframe system.
- incorporating EDI into manufacturing software.
- developing custom accounting software.

My diverse role requires me to "wear many hats," including interfacing extensively with all department managers, training staff on new systems and PC applications, along with ensuring security and top maintenance of the system. Throughout my tenure at XYZ Corp, I have kept the organization's system up-to-date with the most current technology, resulting in labor and telecommunications savings as well as improved reporting.

With my background in both manufacturing and corporate systems development, I offer an organization great flexibility. I welcome the opportunity to meet with you to explore areas of mutual benefit. Attached is my resume for your review.

In order to present my credentials more fully, I will follow up with you to answer any questions you may have. Thank you for your consideration.

Sincerely,

James Sharpe
(516) 555-1212
jsharpe@careerbrain.com

Dear Ms. _____ :

My background inspecting power supplies for NASA and federal government contracts, along with my professional training in electronics engineering technologies, are among the chief assets I would bring to the position of Technician.

For eight years I was the Lead Product Assurance Inspector for Lockheed Martin, where I worked on several notable projects including the Defense Meteorological Space Platform and the Mars Observer. My work involved not only component and complete assembly inspections, but also documentation, testing, and collaboration with NASA and government inspectors.

My resume shows that I have completed several NASA certifications, and I hold a degree in Electronics Engineering Technologies.

I am confident that my technical background well equips me for success in the technical position you have available. Kindly review my resume, then please contact me at your earliest convenience to schedule a professional interview.

Very truly yours,

James Sharpe
(516) 555-1212
jsharpe@careerbrain.com

"Cold" E-mail—To Employment Industry Professional (Computer Professional)

Dear Ms. _____ :

My broad background in all aspects of computers, from design and installation through user training and maintenance, coupled with my business operations expertise, are the assets I would bring to a position with one of your clients.

Currently I hold a management level position with MainLine Graphics, a firm that designs and builds flight simulators for U.S. and foreign governments. I provide the electronics expertise in completing approximately 12 major projects annually, which means I conceptualize the simulators' computerized mechanisms, direct the design and manufacturing processes, then install and test the systems at clients' sites around the globe.

In addition to providing technical expertise, the other major aspect of my job involves aggressively targeting new business. At a point when MainLine was facing an essentially saturated U.S. market, I designed and implemented an Internet Web site, then had it translated into several languages to target international clientele. The site generated 80% of our new business within one year.

Other assets I would bring to this position include skill in relocating entire company computer systems from existing facilities to new or expanded sites, as well as experience servicing all major brands of PCs. I am extremely familiar with nearly every computer-associated component, program, or operating system on today's market.

Thank you in advance for taking a few moments to review my resume. I am confident that the experience you'll find outlined therein will be valuable to your firm. Kindly contact me at your earliest convenience to schedule a professional interview.

Best regards,

James Sharpe
(516) 555-1212
jsharpe@careerbrain.com

"Cold" E-mail—To Employment Industry Professional (Programmer/Analyst)

Dear Ms. _____:

My certification in computer programming, along with my professional background in electro-mechanical engineering, are among the primary assets I would bring to a programmer/analyst position with one of your clients.

As part of my training at Computer Institute in South Fork, NJ, I was required to design, write, code, edit, and modify an e-commerce Web site. The project succeeded not only because of my skill in applying my technical knowledge, but also because of my strict attention to detail.

Currently I'm employed at Dynamic Pharmaceuticals in Price Point, NJ, executing experiments on electrical/mechanical equipment I was involved in manufacturing to ensure conformance to customers' specifications.

I am also committed to furthering my professional education, which is key for success in this field. I plan to augment my knowledge by attending and completing relevant courses.

I am confident this background well equips me for success with one of your clients. Kindly review my resume, then please contact me at your earliest convenience to schedule an interview.

Very truly yours,

James Sharpe
(516) 555-1212
jsharpe@careerbrain.com

л—To Employment Industry Professional (Technology Project Manager)

_____:

oficient and experienced project manager with a passion for technology, I am rou-
with challenges and the need to evaluate diversified programs and their ability to
mee.   ting requirements.

As you will note, my resume may not look like others you receive. My resume is beyond reciting
job titles and duties – it reveals results. Having a complete picture of my expertise and experience
is very important. For several years, I have spearheaded and developed various programs to meet
organizational needs.

I possess solid experience in systems integration, hardware and software analysis, and systems life
cycle management. In addition to my managerial and technical experience, I will offer your company decisive leadership, dedication, and commitment to excellence.

The attached resume is submitted in confidence. I prefer that my present employer not be contacted until a position is officially offered. Your time and consideration is appreciated. I will contact your office next week to follow up and answer any questions you may have. Please feel free
to contact me if you would like to speak sooner.

Sincerely,

James Sharpe
(516) 555-1212
jsharpe@careerbrain.com

"Cold" E-mail—To Employment Industry Professional (IT Management)

Dear Mr./Ms. _____ :

Leading information technology projects for high-growth companies is my area of expertise. Throughout my career I have been successful in identifying organizational needs and leading the development and implementation of industry-specific technologies to improve productivity, quality, operating performance, and profitability.

In my current position at XYZ company, I have initiated and managed the technological advances, administrative infrastructures, training programs, and customization initiatives that have enabled the company to generate over $3 million in additional profits in the past year. The scope of my responsibilities have included the entire project management cycle, from initial needs assessment and technology evaluations through vendor selection, internal systems development, beta testing, quality review, technical and user documentation, and full-scale, multi-site implementation.

My technological and management talents are complemented by my strong training, leadership, and customer service skills. I am accustomed to providing ongoing support and relate well with employers at all levels of an organization, including senior executives. Most notable are my strengths in facilitating cooperation among cross-functional project teams to ensure that all projects are delivered on time, within budget, and as per specifications.

Originally hired for a one year contract at XYZ company, I have been offered a permanent position within the company. However, I am interested in greater challenges and would welcome the opportunity to meet with you to determine the contributions I can make to your client. I will call you next week to set up an appointment.

Sincerely,

James Sharpe
(516) 555-1212
jsharpe@careerbrain.com

"Cold" E-mail—To Employment Industry Professional (Systems Integration)

Dear Company Representative:

My solid background in electrical engineering supported by extensive management and product development experience are key assets that I can contribute to your client's future success.

Throughout my career I have worked with cutting-edge technologies, including **embedded microprocessors, RF, telecommunications,** and **wireless,** in the development and manufacture of products for varied industries. In all of my positions, integrating software, firmware, and hardware to create unique applications has been a key strength. Some of these applications, that proved quite marketable include development of custom instrumentation and PC-based network for tracking vehicles in transit. In addition, I have also played an important role in both the sales and customer support process, helping A+ Corp. win its largest municipal contract with the city of New Orleans.

Currently, I am exploring opportunities in the telecommunications industry where I can contribute significant expertise in systems integration. I welcome the opportunity to meet with you to explore areas of mutual benefit. Attached is my resume for your review.

In order to present my credentials more fully, I will follow up with you to answer any questions you may have. Thank you for your consideration.

Sincerely,

Jane Swift
(516) 555-1212
jswift@careerbrain.com

"Cold" E-mail—To Employment Industry Professional (IT/IS Management)

Dear Mr. _____ :

In today's turbulent market, it can be difficult to find a highly skilled MIS professional with strong leadership, management, and interpersonal skills. If you seek such a candidate who is ready for change, we have good reason to meet. Please find my resume attached for your review and consideration for an IT/IS management position.

I possess extensive experience in both management and Information Technology/ Information Systems. I also possess numerous certifications from both Novell and Microsoft and have become an expert in network design, installation, and administration. I have been recognized and awarded for my technical abilities and top performance. In addition, my leadership skills stretch across management and team environments. For the past nine years, I have successfully managed technical professionals, including training, leading, motivating, and building high-performance teams. My management abilities have led to significant cost savings and new business for my employers. Also, I possess a Bachelor of Science degree in Information Systems Management and am currently pursuing my master's degree in MIS.

After meeting with me, I think you'll agree I possess the necessary qualifications to lead an IS department into the future. I would appreciate the opportunity to discuss with you how I can make a quick and valuable contribution to your organization. I will call you next week to set up a meeting at your convenience. In the meantime, please don't hesitate to contact me for more information.

I look forward to meeting you in the near future. Thank you for your time and consideration.

Sincerely,

James Sharpe
(516) 555-1212
jsharpe@careerbrain.com

"Cold" E-mail—To Employment Industry Professional (Systems Administrator)

Dear Ms. _____:

If you seek a new Systems Administrator who is more than just technically oriented, but also people oriented, then we have good reason to meet. As you'll find on my attached resume, I possess extensive technical skills and experience. What is more difficult to portray on a brief resume is my people skills.

Several colleagues, supervisors, subordinates, and end-users have commended me for my interpersonal skills. I am dedicated to helping others with their technical issues and sharing my knowledge to help them complete their work more efficiently. My job is to serve as a support person, there to keep the system operating smoothly for end-users, as well as to provide them training. I also understand that most technical projects are a team effort. Again, I have been recognized for my abilities as a team player as well as a team leader. I have a proven track record in taking projects and running with them, but the successes are a result of the combined efforts of the whole team. Whether it's a matter of motivating others, coordinating tasks, or just doing my part, I can do it.

My technical skills speak for themselves. My primary focus has been on Windows NT. In fact, I am currently pursuing my Microsoft Certified Systems Engineer designation. My plans are to attain this at about the time I leave the military. I will be able to bring this added expertise to an employer.

A meeting at your convenience would be greatly appreciated. Please feel free to contact me to schedule a time or to gain further information on my background. I am sure you will agree that I am right for the job after reviewing my resume and meeting with me in person.

Thank you for your time and prompt reply. I look forward to meeting you in the near future.

Best regards,

James Sharpe
(516) 555-1212
jsharpe@careerbrain.com

"Cold" Cover Letter—To Employment Industry Professional (Project Management)

18 Central Park Street, Anytown, NY 14788
(516) 555-1212   jswift@careerbrain.com

JANE SWIFT

(Date)

Phillip _____
(Title)
ABC Corporation
1 Industry Plaza
Anytown, NY 12096

Dear Mr. _____:

ABC Corporation is well known to professionals throughout the region as the leading customer service recruitment company; it also maintains a strong reputation as a great employer. Your organization has created an environment in which people can excel, which is why I write you today.

I present to you my skills, achievements, proven leadership, and demonstrated ability to achieve quality and bottom-line results. I possess extensive experience in project management, system implementation, operations manager, and client relations. I have restructured and turned around a struggling department, achieved top levels of customer and employee satisfaction, and drastically improved the company edge in the market. This has been rewarded with promotions and a reputation of getting the job done. Briefly, some of my accomplishments include:

- As Global Customer Support manager of XYZ Solution Center, I formed a global support office. I supported, staffed, directed, and streamlined the Solution Center, resulting in an increase of customer satisfaction from 20% to 80%.
- As a Project Coordinator, I structured and established standard operating procedures for system implementation, turning a very dissatisfied customer into a customer who implemented the company Warehouse Management System in more than 15 sites.
- As a Project Implementation Manager for the "Societe des Alcool de Quebec," I worked with a foreign government agency, communicating effectively in the customer's language and defusing many conflicts between all parties. I provided an exemplary Implementation Requirement Document, used by the company as a template in later projects.
- I designed, developed, tested, and implemented an Intelligent Computer Aided Instruction system using new learning concepts that was recognized by the Fairfax County School System and helped the company in getting the funds needed from NIST.
- As operations manager at Utility Management, I automated and improved productivity levels to a record high through motivation and re-engineering of the entire operations.

Jane Swift
Page 2 of 2

I am confident that I can provide similar benefits to one of your clients as a member of your management team. I would appreciate the opportunity to meet with you to determine how I can contribute to your company's future success.

Thank you for your consideration and reply. I look forward to meeting you and your team.

Sincerely,

Jane Swift
Jane Swift

JS
enclosure

"Cold" Cover Letter—To Employment Industry Professional (CPA)

JAMES SHARPE

18 Central Park Street, Anytown, NY 14788
(516) 555-1212   jsharpe@careerbrain.com

Emily _____   (Date)
(Title)
ABC Corporation
1 Industry Plaza
Anytown, NY 12096

Dear Ms. _____ :

As I am just completing the requirements for my MBA in Accounting at City Institute of Technology, I am exploring potential opportunities with a well-established firm that will lead to a career as a CPA. I hope to join an organization where I can learn and grow within the accounting profession and build a long-term relationship. With these goals in mind, I have enclosed for your consideration and review a resume that briefly outlines my credentials.

Some of the key experiences I can bring to an entry-level position with your firm include:

- **Administering Accounts Receivable and Payroll for an engineering firm that was also engaged in construction and some custom manufacturing.**
- **Preparing individual tax returns as part of a volunteer program in conjunction with CIT.**
- **Serving as Treasurer of a campus organization, Delta Beta Gamma, which encompassed maintaining financial records and providing financial reports to the auditing CPA and to the national organization.**
- **Proficiency with basic Windows and Microsoft Office applications, as well as a keen interest in technology and high-tech businesses.**

I am confident that my education and experience to date provide me with skills that would be beneficial to your firm and its clients. I would enjoy speaking with you in person to discuss the possibilities that exist and how I can best serve the needs of your firm and your clients. Please call me at **(516) 555-1212** to arrange a convenient date and time for us to meet. I look forward to opening a dialogue with you soon.

Very truly yours,

James Sharpe

James Sharpe
JS
enclosure

"Cold" Cover Letter—To Employment Industry Professional (Quality Assurance)

JANE SWIFT

18 Central Park Street, Anytown, NY 14788
(516) 555-1212   jswift@careerbrain.com

(Date)

Phillip _____
(Title)
ABC Corporation
1 Industry Plaza
Anytown, NY 12096

Dear Mr. _____:

Reliability. Problem Solving. Attention to Detail. Innovation. These are a few of the many qualities I have developed as a Quality Assurance Technician. If you are looking for a topnotch Electrical Engineer, look no further. I have over 15 years experience in quality assurance and quality control and have not only designed better consumer friendly products but have improved sales of existing products.

Because delivering solid productivity increases has been the norm throughout my career in the electronics field, I have achieved superior results at Continuum Biomedical, HMT Technologies, Wheco Electronics, 3M Healthcare, Irwin Magnetic, and Xircom Electronics. As a result, you get a Quality Assurance Technician who is productive from day one. My commitment to you would be the same: simplify processes, improve products, develop workforce competencies, and boost output while completing projects ahead of time and under budget.

Qualifications I can bring to your clients are outlined on the enclosed resume. Given my technical skills, familiarity with the product line, and understanding of your clients' needs, I could step into the position and be of immediate assistance.

Please contact me at my home telephone number to arrange a convenient time to meet. Thank you for your time; I look forward to speaking with you soon.

Yours truly,

Jane Swift

Jane Swift
JS
enclosure

"Cold" Cover Letter—To Employment Industry Professional (Internet Sales and Marketing)

JANE SWIFT

18 Central Park Street, Anytown, NY 14788
(516) 555-1212   jswift@careerbrain.com

(Date)

Phillip _____
(Title)
ABC Corporation
1 Industry Plaza
Anytown, NY 12096

Dear Mr. _____ :

A start-up company is only as good as the people behind it, and when you're in the Internet arena you need people who are experienced and knowledgeable in this quickly growing and ever-changing medium. I believe one of your searches is over if you seek an entrepreneurial-minded Sales & Marketing professional with expertise in formulating, managing, and marketing new Internet services.

As my enclosed resume briefly summarizes, I possess hands-on experience in starting an Internet-based venture. This background encompasses all aspects of starting a business—market research, business plan development, investor financing, marketing and sales, and more. I also have an excellent track record in sales, including lead generation, cold calling, presentation delivery, and closing. Additional strengths include:

- **Communication skills**—As a financial consultant, I marketed to top-level executives and business owners with net worths in the millions. This required the ability to communicate on their level and explain complex terms in their language. Also, seven years of teaching has honed my communication as well as leadership skills. In addition to my Physics degree, I also pursued minors in both English and History at the University of California, Berkeley.
- **Analytical skills**—Earning a Bachelor's degree in Physics required numerous courses that were intense in analyzing subject material and drawing educated conclusions. Progressing my way through the ranks in the financial industry also involved strong analytical ability, as I had to evaluate several investment vehicles to ensure I offered the most appropriate ones to my clients. Finally, during the start-up of my company, I performed extensive market and competition analysis, along with financial analysis.

Jane Swift
Page 2 of 2

- **Perseverance**—There are many areas in my background that give evidence to my perseverance. Graduating with a Physics degree from a well-known university is one. Becoming one of the top financial consultants on my special team with PaineWebber is another: I started at the bottom and worked my way up, learning as I went along. When I wasn't reaching my goals, I dedicated myself to learning new skills and honing existing ones in order to reach success. Also, being an entrepreneur requires commitment and perseverance to succeed.

I think you'll agree after reading the enclosed resume and meeting with me in person that I have the qualifications you seek for your Sales & Marketing Manager position. I would appreciate the opportunity to meet with you to discuss how I might benefit one of your clients. I will call you next week to schedule a time at your convenience. In the meantime, please feel free to contact me for further information.

I look forward to meeting you in the near future. Thank you for your time and consideration.

Sincerely,

Jane Swift
Jane Swift

JS
enclosure

"Cold" Cover Letter—To Employment Industry Professional (Executive Computer Specialist)

JAMES SHARPE

18 Central Park Street, Anytown, NY 14788
(516) 555-1212   jsharpe@careerbrain.com

(Date)

Emily _____
(Title)
ABC Corporation
1 Industry Plaza
Anytown, NY 12096

Dear Ms. _____:

My experience installing and maintaining computer networks, hardware, and software, along with my skills in training users and developing cost-saving applications, are the assets I would bring to the position of Executive Computer Specialist.

I am a Certified Novell Administrator. And my technical skills include expertise in Novell Netware, MS DOS and Windows, as well as experience with hardware including Cabletron, and software including the Microsoft Office Suite.

My computer expertise has saved my employers production time and costs. As a Senior Computer Specialist, I installed a Personal Computer LAN utilizing the Novell Netware Networking System. I saved $35,000 and used the savings to upgrade the equipment installation. Also in that position I designed and implemented a system to cut printing costs. The system is projected to save the government $4 million over four years.

I have also developed software packages, including "point of sale" software and mortgage software, which was for commercial sale.

I believe my skills and experience will make me succeed in the position of Executive Computer Specialist. Kindly review my resume, then contact me at your earliest convenience to schedule a professional interview.

Very truly yours,

James Sharpe

James Sharpe

JS
enclosure

"Cold" Cover Letter—To Employment Industry Professional (Executive Computer Specialist)

James Sharpe

18 Central Park Street, Anytown, NY 14788
(516) 555-1212   jsharpe@careerbrain.com

(Date)

Emily _____
(Title)
ABC Corporation
1 Industry Plaza
Anytown, NY 12096

Dear Ms. _____ :

Managing state-of-the-art technology and communications systems to support high growth initiatives, strengthen internal operating capabilities, improve employee productivity and reduce operating costs is my area of expertise. Combining over fifteen Novell, Microsoft and industry-leading certifications with a B.A. degree and more than ten years of experience in the technology and communications industry, I have delivered business solutions for Fortune 500 multi-site corporations, as well as small start-up companies.

The scope of my systems engineering and technical experience is diverse and includes:

- Novell, Microsoft, Citrix and Cisco network architecture design, installation/integration and support
- internet and intranet messaging and connectivity
- client/server implementation
- integration, management and support of PC, Macintosh and DEC Alpha hardware
- relational database systems management
- installation/integration of voice and data communications and telecommunications
- security systems, backup/data recovery systems and remote access systems
- end user application support
- software and hardware based voice mail
- telephone switch/system installation

James Sharp
Page 2 of 2

Equally important is my experience in technical and operations management, finance, budgeting and accounting, purchasing/leasing and contractual negotiations, staff development and training, new business development, and customer relations. Being an extremely innovative professional with strong leadership skills, I am able to create corporate and technological visions and deliver results and solutions. Additionally, my interpersonal and communication skills are excellent and I take exceptional personal pride in my work.

Although secure in my current position, I am confidentially seeking a more challenging position. If you are in need of a professional with my qualifications, I would welcome the opportunity to meet with you to discuss the contributions I can make to your organization. Please be advised that I am receptive to relocation.

Best regards,

James Sharpe

James Sharpe

JS
enclosure

"Cold" Cover Letter—To Employment Industry Professional (Vice President)

18 Central Park Street, Anytown, NY 14788
(516) 555-1212   jswift@careerbrain.com

JANE SWIFT

(Date)

Mr. _____
(Title)
Krieger, Skvetney, Howell
Executive Search Consultants
2426 Foundation Road
Anytown, NY 14788

Dear Mr. _____:

In the course of your search assignments, you may have a requirement for an organized and goal-directed Vice President. My present position provides me with the qualifications and experience necessary to successfully fulfill a Vice President position. Key strengths which I possess for the success of an administrative position include:

- Direct line operations responsibility improving gross margin to 8.0%.
- Planning and developing over $15 million in new construction projects.
- Reduction of departmental operating expenses to 1.1% below budget.
- Negotiating and developing contractual arrangements with vendors.

I have the ability to define problems, assess both large-scale and smaller implications of a project, and implement solutions.

The enclosed resume briefly outlines my administrative and business background. My geographic preferences are the midwest and southeast regions of the country. Relocating to a client's location does not present a problem. Also, I possess an MBA degree from _____ University, and a BS degree in Business Administration from _____University. Depending upon location and other factors, my salary requirements would be between $130,000 and $150,000.

If it appears that my qualifications meet the need of one of your clients, I will be happy to further discuss my background in a meeting with you or in an interview with the client. I will be contacting your office in the near future to determine the status of my application.

Sincerely,

Jane Swift

Jane Swift

JS
enclosure

"Cold" Cover Letter—To Employment Industry Professional (Senior Manager)

JAMES SHARPE

18 Central Park Street ◆ Anytown, NY 14788
(516) 555-1212 jsharpe@careerbrain.com

(Date)

Mr. _____
ABC Company
1 Industry Plaza
Anytown, NY 12096

Dear Mr _____:

Mentored by Bob _____, founder of _____, I successfully progressed within his privately held organization for twelve years serving on the **Board of Directors of 13 separate companies** and holding positions including **Treasurer, Vice President of Finance** and ultimately **President.** During my tenure the company grew from 7 employees to more than 1,000 while **revenues increased from $3 million to $108 million.** My enclosed resume gives further detail.

My reason for contacting you is simple. I am interested in exploring any senior management opportunities which may be available through your organization and would also be interested in interim or consulting roles. Geographically speaking, I have no limitations and am available for relocation throughout the U.S. and abroad. Due to the level and quality of my performance I feel it pertinent to state that I am only willing to consider positions consistent with my current income level. I have the experience, the talent and the energy to turn around, create or grow a dynamic organization.

I have built my career on my commitment and ability to create open lines of communication between the Board of Directors and senior management to **protect the investments of my organization** and to **assure the attainment of the target return.**

I look forward to hearing from you in the near future to discuss any mutually beneficial opportunities. If you do not at present have a need for a professional with my experience but know of someone who may, please be so kind as to pass my letter and resume on to that individual, or simply call me.

Sincerely,

James Sharpe

James Sharpe

JS
enclosure

"Cold" Cover Letter—To Employment Industry Professional (International Operations)

James Sharpe

18 Central Park Street, Anytown, NY 14788
(516) 555-1212   jsharpe@careerbrain.com

(Date)

Ms. _____
(Title)
ABC Corporation
1 Industry Plaza
Anytown, NY 12096

Dear Ms. _____:

Over the years, I have built a successful career in **international operations and project management** on my ability to quickly and accurately assess situations, identify problems and focus on strategies which obtain results. I am currently seeking a challenging opportunity with an internationally focused, growth-oriented organization. I am willing to explore interim assignments and consulting projects as well as senior management opportunities. My enclosed resume details some of my accomplishments and credentials.

I have extensive experience in **diplomacy and international public affairs** dealing with foreign government officials, Heads of State, and Ambassadors as well as Fortune 100 senior executives. Building effective teams and inspiring others to peak performance are among my strengths. I am particularly adept at living and working effectively in foreign countries and with individuals of various cultural backgrounds. As such I am interested in opportunities both in the U.S. and abroad.

Feasibility studies, crisis resolution and **international risk assessment** are areas where I excel. Unit construction and operations, mining/drilling and industrial equipment procurement, sales and distribution are areas where I may be of particular assistance, but my skills are transferable to virtually any industry.

I look forward to hearing from you to discuss any mutually beneficial opportunities that you may be aware of. Please feel free to pass along my resume to others who may have a need for a professional of my caliber.

Sincerely,

James Sharpe

James Sharpe

JS
enclosure

Power Phrases

Consider using adaptations of these key phrases in your "cold" letters to employment service professionals.

I am an optimist, thrive on challenges, lead by example, and readily adapt to situations. If your client — international or domestic — would benefit from these kinds of qualities we should get to know each other. If you will call or write at your convenience, I look forward to telling more about my background.

As a dedicated listener, I am usually designated for client/customer relations and produce notable results in client/customer retention—even under the least favorable conditions.

An industry association referred to _____ as an active and selective executive search firm, and mentioned your name because of your work in logistics. I liked that referral and think our meeting would be mutually beneficial.

I would like to talk with you personally to further discuss our meeting. I suggest next week, the week of October —, when you have a free minute. I have asked my staff to forward your message immediately in case I am unavailable when you call. I look forward to hearing from you.

Please include my name in your job search data base.

Including a mortgage loan benefit, I am currently earning $4,500 per month plus a car allowance. This should provide you with an indication of my present job level. Your suggestions or comments would be appreciated.

For 25 years, my family operated one of the most prestigious landmark inn/restaurants on Long Island. From the age of 6, I was a part of the family workforce—I couldn't wait to "help." That attitude pervades my work ethic and I'm grateful for the training that helped me to develop an attitude of service, teamwork and pride in performance and product.

One of your clients is looking for me, if not today then sometime in the near future. I know good people are hard to find because I've had to find them myself.

I have the depth of experience it takes to make a positive contribution.

Income is in the mid-five figures, but the right opportunity is the motivating factor. References and resume are available. With my well-rounded professional background I look forward to a new and interesting career opportunity through your firm.

I'm a natural "enroller" because my enthusiasm is contagious and I personally project credibility—people are inclined to (1) cooperate and participate wholeheartedly on projects with which I'm involved, (2) favorably consider products I recommend, and (3) be open to my efforts on their behalf when they experience problems or dissatisfaction.

The following are some highlights of my track record for your consideration:

I understand your clients frequently ask you to locate senior operating executives with much higher than average ability to accomplish difficult jobs quickly and profitably.

It is my goal to play an integral part in the development, operation and success of a small to mid-sized company where the diversity of my experience and the level of my commitment can be used to their fullest advantage and I can have the satisfaction of seeing the results of my efforts…really impacting profitability!

Please call at your convenience this week so we can explore potential opportunities more fully. Use the home number, please; our company's uncertain financial status is stirring up the office rumor mill. Thank you for your time and attention.

I am a motivated and dedicated leader. Many of my staff have worked for me from 10 to 30 years. My enthusiasm for meeting goals and accomplishing objectives has been contagious and I know how to reward outstanding performance without disturbing a profit and loss balance. My employees and I thrive on a "family" environment with no loss of respect or production.

As a former business owner, I am well aware of the needs, concerns and challenges facing management. By the same token, I am accustomed to operating with the best interests of the total business in mind and at heart, as well. I operate expeditiously, constantly seeking the best use of time, effort, resources and money…for my staff and myself.

My experience as an entrepreneur as well as an employee of a powerful, demanding employer gives me the unique ability to empathize the needs of management as well as the aggressiveness necessary to represent management effectively.

I'm seeking an opportunity to join an employer that can benefit from my expertise and experience while offering me the opportunity for challenge, continued professional growth as well as commensurate compensation.

I'm a dedicated listener and an accomplished problem solver, always seeking to assist clients in accomplishing their mission. My clients experience and express a sense of trust and confidence in me and my recommendations because my sincerity and my efforts invested on their behalf are evident and consistent. They never have a doubt that I really care and will operate in their best interests.

Broadcast E-mail (Senior Buyer/Purchasing Agent/ Purchasing Manager)

Mr. / Ms. _____:

SENIOR BUYER * PURCHASING AGENT * PURCHASING MANAGER

Do you cringe at the high costs your company incurs for goods and services?

Do you need someone who will maximize vendor resources, working hard to secure lower-cost, longer-term contract?

Do you need someone on board who will immediately slash supply costs and streamline purchasing operations?

With more than 20 years in purchasing, retail sales management, store expansions, and new product research and market launch, I believe I may offer just what you're missing.

In my esteemed career with Major Company, a premier auto parts and accessories distributor, I have:

- Directed procurement of over $200M of goods and services, accounting for 60% of MC's total purchasing budget.
- Launched 3 private label programs, garnering $500K in additional profits during the first year of distribution.
- Recouped $300K in stolen merchandise and prosecuted the employee responsible.
- Generated $3M in savings by cultivating partnerships and negotiating long-term contracts with key suppliers.

With the right opportunity, I'd be perfectly willing to relocate. With regard to salary, I understand that flexibility is essential and would consider a compensation package appropriate for a person with my outstanding qualifications and dynamic track record of accomplishments.

If you're tired of seeing your company's profits slip through your fingers, call me today to schedule a business meeting. I can't wait to discuss how I can benefit your purchasing operation right away. I can be reached at (516) 555-1212 to arrange our interview.

Very truly yours,

James Sharpe
(516) 555-1212
jsharpe@careerbrain.com

Broadcast E-mail (Industrial Safety and Health Officer)

Dear Mr. _____ :

As an industrial safety and health officer with experience in a unionized heavy manufacturing environment, I feel my background may be of interest to you. My qualifications include:

- A degree in Industrial Relations and Personnel.
- Five years of experience in planning, developing, implementing and maintaining programs designed to prevent occupational injury, illness and property damage—as well as complementary safety contests, individual recognition programs, and safety promotions.
- Experience in the use of industrial hygiene-monitoring equipment such as noise dosimeters, air-sampling pumps, detector tubes, toxic and explosive gas monitors, etc., and in field investigation of serious incidents and work refusals.
- Administration of employer correspondence concerning claims for compensation benefits or company appeals, including communications with injured workers, their representatives, benefits staff, and the company lawyer.

In addition to the above, I have been actively involved with the formulation of accident prevention policies and safety rules and procedures. I have also handled grievances and arbitrations concerning safety issues and abuse of the workers compensation system.

In the event that you feel I might be able to assist your organization's occupational health and safety program, I would welcome the opportunity for a personal interview.

Yours truly,

James Sharpe
(516) 555-1212
jsharpe@careerbrain.com

Broadcast E-mail (New Product Marketing)

Dear Mr. _____ :

If you are looking for a successful executive to take charge of new product marketing, you will be interested in talking to me.

Ten years of experience in every aspect of marketing and sales in different industries gives me the confidence to be open to opportunities in almost any field. My search is focused on companies that innovate, because I am particularly effective at new product marketing. I have successfully managed new product-marketing research, launch planning, advertising, product training, and sales support, as well as direct sales. In my current position with XYZ Company, I created several products and marketing approaches on which other operating divisions in the company based their programs.

My business education includes a Marketing MBA from _____ University's School of Management, and provides me with a variety of useful analytical tools in managing problems and maximizing opportunities. My superior sales track record guarantees that I bring the reality of the marketplace to each business situation; I know what sells and why.

Currently, my total compensation package is in the low seventies; I am looking for a company that rewards performance consistently.

Since I am currently weighing several interesting opportunities, please contact me immediately if you are conducting any searches that might be a good fit. Relocation is no problem.

Thank you in advance for your consideration.

Sincerely,

James Sharpe
(516) 555-1212
jsharpe@careerbrain.com

Broadcast E-mail (Senior Marketing Executive)

Dear Mr. _____:

I recently learned of your firm's excellent record of matching senior marketing executives with top corporations. I also have learned that you have an officer-level marketing assignment in process now—I am a serious candidate for your client's vacancy. Please consider some successes:

- After joining _____ as Marketing Director, I revitalized a declining processed-meats product category in less than a year, introducing better-tasting formulas and actually reducing product costs by over $100,000. Dramatic new packaging enhanced appetite appeal, and fresh promotion strategies doubled previous sales records.
- I have carefully crafted and fine-tuned many new product introductions and line extensions, such as _____ turkey, _____ processed meats, and _____'s deodorant maxi-pads.
- My sales/marketing experience dates from 1990, when I formed a direct sales company to pay for my _____ MBA (now the top-rated program in the U.S.A., I'm proud to say). Much of my subsequent success springs from strong working relationships with sales management and joint sales calls with field reps and marketing brokers. I have designed events like the _____ program, and _____'s sponsorship of the Indy 500 Williams racing team.
- I have a strong personal and professional interest in consumer electronics. I consult professionally and have successfully adapted marketing techniques for home and commercial satellite systems, "high-tech" audio/video, and radio communications equipment.

Please inform your client I am fluent in French and I quickly absorb other languages. If your client challenges executives with the greatest of responsibilities and rewards them for remarkable performance, please contact me as soon as possible. I'll quickly repeat my past successes.

Sincerely,
Jane Swift

JS

Broadcast E-mail (Logistics)

Dear Mr. _____:

An industry association referred to your organization as an active and selective executive search firm, and mentioned your name because of your work in logistics. I liked that referral and think our meeting would be mutually beneficial.

I have a successful career of using logistics to cut costs and improve profits, usually in concert with other parts of the business. For example:

- I supervised the start-up of several remote offices to assist our plants in improving their distribution operations. By offering customized service, and through sharp negotiations, we saved over $500 million in various operations and warehouse costs.
- I directed the efforts of sizeable computer resources in the design and installation of a major application that saved $2.5 million in carrier costs. The application became the standard throughout the company's forty-six locations.
- Working with International Sales, I have established various Quality Control programs that have improved the timeliness and accuracy of product and paperwork delivery. Customer complaints plummeted to virtually zero, and remain there today.

A recent reorganization has reduced the number of senior management positions available within my company. I have concluded that another firm may offer a position and career advancement more in line with my personal expectations.

I would like to talk with you further. I suggest next week, the week of October 29, when you have a free minute. I have asked my staff to forward your message immediately in case I am unavailable when you call. I look forward to hearing from you.

Sincerely,

James Sharpe
(516) 555-1212
jsharpe@careerbrain.com

Broadcast E-mail (Vice President Asset Liquidation)

Dear Mr. _____ :

In recent years, as the Vice President of Lease Asset Liquidation with XYZ U.S.A., I successfully engineered the recovery of $23 million in assets, almost 3 times the original buyout offer of $8 million. Throughout my career I have been instrumental in developing and implementing work-out and liquidation strategies and as such I have earned a strong reputation as a professional who gets the job done.

My reason for contacting you is simple. I am interested in project opportunities that will serve both to challenge and to utilize my abilities in asset liquidation management. My current project will be completed within the next four to six weeks. I am currently considering offers and intend to make a decision by February 1st.

The attached summary details some of my accomplishments. I look forward to hearing from you to discuss any mutually beneficial opportunities. Please feel free to pass along my resume to others who may have a need for my professional assistance.

Sincerely,

James Sharpe
(516) 555-1212
jsharpe@careerbrain.com

Broadcast E-mail (Health Care Manager)

Dear Ms. _____:

Recently I was hand-picked to prospect new business in an expansion territory. By creating a new "communication loop" I was able to stimulate product awareness. This resulted in a 500% increase in business participation and generated more than $2.4 million in annual revenues. As a result of my performance I have received four promotions in just 36 months. My attached resume will itemize my credentials.

As you are probably aware, however, XYZ Healthcare is soon to merge with Anycorp; and although I know I will have a solid place with the company subsequent to the merger, I feel the time has come for me to look at other opportunities. Due to the level and quality of my performance (I more than doubled my income last year and will do the same this year) I feel it pertinent to state that I am only willing to consider positions that will allow me to be compensated appropriately.

I trust that you will treat this correspondence, as well as my resume, with utmost confidentiality. I look forward to hearing from you in the near future to discuss any mutually beneficial opportunities—which need not necessarily be in the health care area.

Sincerely,

James Sharpe
(516) 555-1212
jsharpe@careerbrain.com

Broadcast Letter (Database Engineer)

(Date)
Phillip _____
(Title)
ABC Corporation
1 Industry Plaza
Anytown, NY 12096

Jane Swift

18 Central Park Street, Anytown, NY 14788
(516) 555-1212   jswift@careerbrain.com

Dear Mr. _____ :

Empowering your employees with the information and tools necessary to make better strategic business decisions is very likely to improve your company's competitive advantage and profitability. I can do this through insightful strategic planning and the delivery of superior data warehouse and decision support systems.

My extensive career experience in data warehousing, database administration, and business systems development, coupled with my commitment to exceed customer expectations and my focus on achieving sustainable strategic competitive advantage, are the primary assets I would bring to your Director of Database Engineering position. I have successfully delivered numerous data warehouse projects that were effectively aligned with company strategic objectives. I am also highly skilled at directing teams on complex initiatives and improving processes, communication, teamwork, and quality.

As a senior-level employee of R & M Information Technology, Inc., I have established an excellent track record for successfully managing large complex projects. Notably, I managed a $10 million development project for Management Source One, building and implementing their first enterprise data warehouse and certain downstream divisional data marts. So successful was this project that within three months after implementation it established itself as the recognized supreme source of accurate company data for all of Management's North American business units. Additionally, it met tight service level commitments over 97% of the time and experienced no downtime due to programming error.

As a Project Leader/Manager for Churchman's Business Systems, Inc., I also managed the development of a large data warehouse. I led the design and development efforts for this data warehouse of sales information for their Specialty Products division. This was the first data warehouse developed at Churchman's that successfully met user expectations.

An additional asset I would bring to your organization is competency in correlating data warehousing functions with overall company goals. I am skilled in providing counsel to senior managers and executives and adept at monitoring data warehouse systems to continually ensure their value and usefulness to an organization as a whole.

I am confident that this experience well equips me for success as your Director of Database Engineering. Kindly review my resume, then please contact me at your earliest convenience to schedule a professional interview.

Sincerely,

Jane Swift
Jane Swift

Broadcast Letter (Senior Technical Sales)

JAMES SHARPE

18 Central Park Street, Anytown, NY 14788
(516) 555-1212   jsharpe@careerbrain.com

Emily _____   (Date)
(Title)
ABC Corporation
1 Industry Plaza
Anytown, NY 12096

Dear Ms. _____:

As a seasoned Technical Sales and Marketing Consultant, I've generated considerable new business for my previous employers, and now I'd like to do the same for you. For the past 15 years I have pursued an increasingly successful career in telecommunications sales and marketing. Among my accomplishments are:

SALES
Qualified to spearhead the entire sales cycle management process, from initial client consultation and needs assessment through product demonstration, price and service negotiations, and final sales closings.

MARKETING
Success in orchestrating all aspects of developing a gainful marketing strategy, from competitive market intelligence and trend analysis, product development, launch, and positioning to distribution management and customer care.

TELECOMMUNICATIONS & NETWORK SOLUTIONS
Recognized for pioneering technology solutions that meet the needs of complex customer service, logistics, and distribution operations. Able to test operations to ensure optimum systems functionality and availability, guide systems implementation across multiple platforms, and deliver user training and support programs that outpace the competition.

I hope you will contact me in the very near future. You'll find my address and telephone number listed above. I would welcome the opportunity to contribute my skills to the success of your marketing team and look forward to learning about any available opportunities in your corporation.

Very truly yours,

James Sharpe

James Sharpe
JS
enclosure

Broadcast Letter (Telecommunications)

Jane Swift

18 Central Park Street, Anytown, NY 14788
(516) 555-1212   jswift@careerbrain.com

(Date)
Emily _____
(Title)
ABC Corporation
1 Industry Plaza
Anytown, NY 12096

Dear Ms. _____ :

If you need someone with proven international success *who will really listen* to your clients' needs and has leaped over cultural barriers to forge some of the most profitable technical opportunities in the telecommunications field, I am your #1 choice for any opportunity in international or domestic sales or marketing.

Since 1994, my work in strategic partnering, developing alliances, creating new opportunities, and exceeding multinational clients' expectations has helped my employers more than double their sales. However, follow-up, tenacious attention to detail, and my ability to listen have critically solidified long-standing relationships with major players worldwide.

With a global leader in telecommunications, I received 3 promotions in 4 years due to my success in managing contacts, motivating staffs, and implementing marketing campaigns that delivered ROI threefold.

Since 1998 I have ...
- Marketed a full range of data and voice communication services to multinational corporations and Internet service providers in Japan, Southeast Asia, Canada, and Western Europe.
- Brought in 28 new global accounts representing up to a 250 percent increase in business—currently handle brand management efforts for DWDM on pace to exceed annual goal; managed 20 accounts requiring broadband connectivity to international locations.
- Created the first transcontinental ATM circuit and earned one of the most prestigious awards in the company.
- Trained technical associates in ATM and employed knowledge of DWDM, SONET, SDMS, and TCP/IP technology to create some of the most cost-effective networks on the planet.

If these proven successes sound like a go-getter you need on staff ...
- Consider that, in just 2 years with a system software developer, I added $1.5M in new business, trained an all-Japanese staff in direct marketing principles, and launched direct sales campaigns that increased client awareness of our services.

Jane Swift
Page 2 of 2

Additionally, my efforts with an international contractor …

- Partnered the parent company with Japan-based joint venture interests that enabled the first US-built airport in Japan.
- Kept Japanese executives and high-ranking government officials apprised of progress—and landed 2 additional opportunities for a total of $10M in business in just a year.

Technically speaking …

- I have worked with ATM, Frame Relay, Private Line, SONET, DWDM, SNA/SDLE, SDMS and IP, and managed networks and a diverse array of hardware and software packages—in addition to holding numerous Novell and Windows specialized certifications.

I love calling on clients who have been abused by other reps, because I know my negotiating skills, ability to cross cultural barriers and generate win-win opportunities will get the decision-maker to sign every time.

Reviewing my attached resume, you will note doctoral, master's, and bachelor's degrees—and a host of quantifiable results and technical training that serve only to enhance my drive and enthusiasm. I will gladly set aside time to meet with you and discuss how my knowledge of technology, client relations, and strategic partnering can become your biggest asset.

I will take the liberty of contact you on Monday at 10 a.m. If you need to reach me, please feel free to contact me at 516-555-1212. Thanking you in advance for the opportunity to meet with you, I am

Sincerely yours,

Jane Swift

Jane Swift

JS
enclosure

Broadcast Letter (Senior R&D Engineer)

JAMES SHARPE

18 Central Park Street ◆ Anytown, NY 14788
(516) 555-1212   jsharpe@careerbrain.com

**SENIOR R&D ENGINEER … patent holder … launched x# new products…
recognized worldwide … created win-win alliances … cornered global markets…**

(Date)

Phillip _____
(Title)
ABC Corporation
1 Industry Plaza
Anytown, NY 12096

Dear Mr. _____:
If your R&D-to-market time needs a sense of urgency, creativity, and a seasoned coordinator of people and priorities, I am one individual you need to discuss the ABD POSITION. Here's why:

- STRATEGIC PLANNING: Etched long- and short-term technological plans that kept a $2B manufacturer ahead of its competition since 1999
- COORDINATED RESOURCES: 20+ years in planning, reviewing, and benchmarking technical performance, meeting budgetary goals, and coordinating interlaboratory and interdepartmental efforts
- IGNITED STAFFS' CREATIVITY: Led efforts and piqued an in-house multidisciplinary R&D staff's synergy; got x# new products to market
- ENRICHED KNOWLEDGE: Trained sales, marketing, and technical staffs since 1995; well-known for abilities to communicate new ideas, selected for numerous assignments in product training worldwide
- MOVED THE MARKET TO OUR PRODUCT: Recognized expert—created the need for cutting-edge technology in the cutting tool market by featuring results in technical articles for leading publications
- INTEGRATED OPERATIONS: 1 of 2 individuals to integrate a newly acquired company's R&D with parent company's
- IGNORED STIGMAS: First person to involve marketing with R&D—created pathway between R&D and marketing, bringing projects to market in record time; landed $10 million+ in new accounts—only non-salesperson to get a one-of-a-kind annual sales award
- IMPECCABLE RECORD: Achieved 70 to 80 percent first-time success rate in field testing for all products developed; hold x# US patents; consulted worldwide by engineers and scientists; published; presenter at technical conferences since post-doctoral fellowship

- MORE -

James Sharpe
2 of 2

Reviewing my credentials and past results, you will note they occurred in the XYZ field. However, I am confident the core *technical, interpersonal, and organizational expertise I bring to your staff and customers would easily retrofit* at ABC CORPORATION.

If you need *a driven problem solver who can get your people moving to the work,* I am readily available to discuss how I can channel my more than 2 decades of success as your ABD POSITION at ABC CORPORATION. I will be in the area next month, and would prefer to meet with you then.

I am in a position to move to the Bay area, and *am ready to demonstrate how I can reignite your R&D efforts and create a flurry of opportunity.* Should you need added information, please do not hesitate to contact me at 516-555-1212 or jsharpe@career-brain.com.

Sincerely,

James Sharpe
James Sharpe

JS
enclosure

Broadcast Letter (Multilingual Sales Manager)

James Sharpe

18 Central Park Street, Anytown, NY 14788
(516) 555-1212   jsharpe@careerbrain.com

**Fluent in Spanish ... time management skills ... 8 years front line experience ...
service-oriented positions ... trainer ... presentation expertise ...**

(Date)

Emily _____
(Title)
ABC Corporation
1 Industry Plaza
Anytown, NY 12096

Dear Ms. _____:

If you know *your customers and operations deserve attention to detail,* as well as a high-energy individual who is *fluent in Spanish and makes people a #1 priority,* I am one individual you need to interview for an ZYX position at ABC Corporation.

Reviewing my credentials, you will note I have taught high school since 1996. This exposure to *daily planning, keeping people motivated and moving to the work* can be an immediate asset at ABC, and here are some areas up-front that align with your needs ...

— SUCCESS IN DIRECT COMMUNICATION: Whether with students, decision-makers or the general public, my presentation skills kept people interested, involved and properly served ...

— MULTILINGUAL ABILITIES: Fluent in Spanish, Japanese and Russian — despite having a Spanish-only background, mastered the dialects of Russian and Japanese and was teaching classes upon hire at a school district ...

— ALWAYS LOOKING FOR IMPROVEMENTS: Successfully integrated technology with additional conversational strategies ... working for a distributor as an undergraduate, took initiative to revamp routing — increased productivity and service ... increased a student's competency from 31 percent to 100 percent while an undergrad ...

James Sharpe
Page 2 of 2

— FOCUS ON SERVICE: Made individual needs a priority since 1996 as a teacher — adept in varying approach per individual personalities and priorities…

— MOTIVATED: Worked up to 30 hours weekly while pursuing degree … proven abilities to juggle diverse assignments opened door for additional assignments and leadership roles…

I seek to channel my communication, presentation, customer service, training and organizational skills, and the ZYX opportunity at ABC Corporation matches my goal for a transferable opportunity. *You would benefit from someone with a proven track record in front line positions, and your customers and operations will have a team player who knows how to set goals, meet goals, and keep customers' needs at the forefront.*

I will take the liberty of contacting you on _____ at _____ to confirm your receipt of my information and briefly discuss how my energy and talents could be your asset. I would also like to arrange our meeting at that time. Should you need to reach me prior, I can be contacted at 516-555-1212 or jsharpe@careerbrain.com

Best regards,

James Sharpe

James Sharpe

JS
enclosure

Broadcast Letter (Management)

JANE SWIFT

18 Central Park Street, Anytown, NY 14788

(516) 555-1212   jswift@careerbrain.com

(Date)

Phillip _____
(Title)
ABC Corporation
1 Industry Plaza
Anytown, NY 12096

Dear Mr. _____:

People will only give you what you're willing to accept. That's why my staffs employed "The Golden Rule" every day, treating customers the way they themselves would like to be treated.

If you need someone with a technical background who has hired and kept top talent challenged and on their toes to deliver exemplary service, then consider that in 20+ years…
— I translated my knowledge of physics and business into profits and operational success—for my staffs, my employers, and myself.
— I took on the lead engineering position in my second year with an industry giant, skipping over the traditional 12-year career path—I simply outworked everyone and never said I couldn't do something or get it done on time or within budget.
— I earned full latitude in decision making after proving my team's understanding of a new target market's needs—I introduced more products than my successors, improved processes, and cut manufacturing and warranty costs by roughly $1M the first year.
— Operations I had an impact on experienced extremely low employee turnover—and employees met or exceeded customer expectations 100 percent of the time.

I've made sure my staffs are so service-oriented that the customer doesn't have to ask for warranty repairs or "the next step"—they have the answers or already have performed the warranty work.

And when my name is on a project, it always is on schedule within budget—and is a winner…
— When a relationship with a specialty manufacturer ended, I spearheaded development of an intake manifold line, analyzed and negotiated manufacturing costs, and selected vendors—and launched an 18-unit product line in 18 months that led the industry.
— The first race manifold we developed took the first 5 Chevrolet finishes in the 1985 Daytona 500 without prior testing by participating teams.

Jane Swift
Page 2 of 2

If you seek someone with the work ethic of a business partner, then I am your top choice for the
_____ opportunity with the ABC Corporation. I fully understand the nuts-and-bolts of customer service, and certainly can combine my financial know-how with proven success in the field
at ABC.

Right now I'm ready to step down from entrepreneurial management, simplify my role, and do
"one or three things" well for an organization that values integrity, hard work, and creativity.

If I sound like the person you need at ABC , then contact me right away to discuss the _____
opportunity. I can be reached at 516.555.1212 after 6 p.m. Monday through Friday, or at my
place of business at 516.555.5555 during regular business hours. I will take the liberty of contacting you on Monday at 10 a.m. to briefly screen my qualifications and arrange our interview.

Yours truly,

Jane Swift

Jane Swift
JS
enclosure

Broadcast Letter (HR Generalist)

18 Central Park Street, Anytown, NY 14788
(516) 555-1212   jswift@careerbrain.com

JANE SWIFT

HR GENERALIST
9 years advising senior decision-makers on employee matters...
5 years in benefits administration for $1B company and 5 affiliates...
15 years delivering HR presentations...
Open enrollment / benefits processing for professional employees...
13 years grievance / disciplinary meeting involvement...
10+ years training / development, entry through professional levels...
Worked through mergers and reorganizations...
Created award-winning concept for enrollment booklet...
Earned highest ratings throughout career...

(Date)

Phillip _____
(Title)
ABC Corporation
1 Industry Plaza
Anytown, NY 12096

Dear Mr. _____:

If your organization seeks someone to advance your human resource programs, consider my proven track record. I am ready for a challenge with ABC Corporation, as your recent growth needs someone acclimated to working with new subsidiaries and maintaining the bottom line. I absolutely am ready to step in as your Human Resource Director at ABC Corporation, as my commitment extends to all areas you seek to address.

I bring you and your employees objectivity, knowledge of policy/procedure implementation and interpretation, and hands-on work in an ever-emerging climate. Here are some highlighted abilities that can be put to work immediately at ABC Corporation...

— MET THE CHALLENGE: With little notification, stepped in and was an asset in a HR Directorship capacity; administered $20M in health and welfare benefits; initiated multi-tier health care plan to better suit regional product needs

— BENEFITS: 5 years working with open enrollment for all levels of employees—restructured benefits during 3 internal reorganizations

— REMAINED FLEXIBLE: Adapted to the needs of entrepreneurial organizations while continuing a career with conservative major utility company

— LEADERSHIP: Entrusted to step in for superiors due to track record in HR; #1 person consulted by senior managers of a $1B parent company and its 5 affiliates regarding HR or benefits; met with bargaining unit leadership, discussed and resolved grievances and complaints

— COMMUNITY INVOLVEMENT: Accepted leadership role in United Way Campaign, keynote speaker for regional fundraising appearances

— TRAINING / DEVELOPMENT: Delivered HR and benefits presentations since 1995, safety training, 2 years

— OVER/ABOVE: Traveled over 3-year period to help a newly formed company whose explosive growth took them to 2,000 employees in 3 years (coordinated staffing and benefit enrollment while maintaining existing workload); singled out for HR support for special finance division structure, took on policy making / interpretation and HR

If you need someone seasoned in policy making who can interface with decision-makers and keep you 100 percent compliant with federal regulations, I am one individual awaiting your call for an interview.

I prefer to take the lead in contacting you, so I will call on Monday at 10 a.m. to brief you on how my background can be an immediate asset and arrange our meeting. I can forward a resume for your review immediately. Should you need to reach me prior, I am at 516-555-1212.

Sincerely,

Jane Swift

Jane Swift

JS
enclosure

~ Benefits Enrollment ~ Multi-Tier Coverage ~ Labor Relations ~ Grievances ~ Arbitration ~
Job Bidding ~HCFA, HIPAA, COBRA Regulations ~ EEOC/PHR Compliance ~
Unemployment Compensation ~ Sexual Harassment ~ Safety Training ~
~ Background Investigations ~

Broadcast Letter (Interventional Radiology Fellow)

JAMES SHARPE

18 Central Park Street ◆ Anytown, NY 14788
(516) 555-1212   jsharpe@careerbrain.com

(Date)

Phillip _____
(Title)
ABC Hospital
1 Industry Plaza
Anytown, NY 12096

Dear Mr. _____:

If your next Interventional Radiology Fellow must be compatible with your team and ready to dig in to deliver consistent, accurate care, my background and qualifications warrant an immediate review for the opportunity. I am truly enthusiastic about the field and willing to roll up my sleeves for the year 2001 at ABC HOSPITAL/FACILITY and give you my personal best.

My nearly three years as a Radiology Resident with the X#-ranked hospital/research facility in the country offers first-hand exposure to procedures most residents and medical students only learn about in textbooks. In addition, my surgical background, enthusiasm and personal commitment to advancing the field can provide your patients and surgical staff a well-rounded perspective.

When I was exposed to the medical cures and solutions performed daily without the complications of traditional surgery, Interventional Radiology immediately earned my respect. Since then, I have pursued the field passionately.

I bring this same energy to ABC, and am available at your earliest convenience at 516-555-1212 (voice) or jsharpe@careerbrain.com to demonstrate how my talents will be an asset to your medical staff. I have enclosed my personal statement for your review.

Sincerely,

James Sharpe
James Sharpe

JS
enclosure

James Sharpe, M.D.
PERSONAL STATEMENT

As recently as five years ago, I would never have imagined I was going to be an Interventional Radiologist. I completed a BS in Electrical Engineering, invested just two months in that field, and found myself pursuing a challenge in medicine. After nearly two years in General Surgery, I witnessed procedures that changed *my* life as much as it would change my patients.'

I discovered Interventional Radiology as a General Surgery Resident, monitoring my critically ill patients while they were in the angiography suites. I was amazed at the medical magic radiologists were performing—curing medical problems through small holes in the skin, often the same day and with little anesthesia. Patients who were bleeding from arteries inaccessible to surgeons and may have previously died were now being saved and stabilized within hours.

As a Surgical Resident, I also evaluated CT scans and plain films on my pre- and post-surgical patients without the slightest consideration or regard for the power this technology wields. Interventional Radiology resembled surgery in that a procedure was performed, the patient was cured and went home…and it avoided the hassles. I was drawn to the angiography suite because I saw Interventional Radiology as Surgical Radiology or Percutaneous Surgery, and knew I had uncovered my true passion.

Since then, I have channeled my enthusiasm, dexterity and attention to detail, along with my desire to help others, in this direction. I now find myself more fulfilled than at any stage in my emerging career as a medical professional.

Everything I have done in the past has been built on the steps before, from Electrical Engineering to General Surgery to Radiology and to Interventional Radiology. The decision to subspecialize in Interventional Radiology is purely based on my love of the field, as I have never been happier than I am right now as a Radiology Resident at the Big City Medical Center.

One of my goals is to become an Interventionalist who invents catheters, pioneers new techniques, and discovers new procedures. I plan to practice in a setting that allows me to research and focus on this direction. I feel Interventional Radiology is the best-kept secret in medicine and know I finally found my calling.

Broadcast Letter (Information Systems Executive)

JAMES SHARPE

18 Central Park Street, Anytown, NY 14788
(516) 555-1212   jsharpe@careerbrain.com

(Date)

Alice _____ - (Title)
Krieger, Skvetney, Howell Executive Search Consultants
2426 Foundation Road, Anytown, NY 14788

Dear Ms. _____:

I am an experienced information systems executive who can make a major contribution for one of your clients. During my career with blue-chip companies including _____, _____, and _____, I have improved the efficiency of their information processing. These improvements include:

- Implementing cost reductions totalling more than $1,000,000
- Recommending and/or implementing organizational changes to streamline the organization yet improve customer service
- Taking a leadership position in the introduction of new methods or technologies
- Automating operations (reduced head count)
- Upgrading hardware and software from mainframes to PCs (improved quality, cost effectiveness and service levels), and integrating multiple vendors (IBM, DEC, Honeywell)

With the leading integrated professional services firm in the U.S., I developed a methodology to assess clients' information-processing effectiveness, resulting in prioritized recommendations for improvement and increased linkage to achieving business objectives. This has led to billings in excess of $3 million.

My formal education includes an M.B.A. and a B.S. in Engineering. I am seeking a change of employment that will return me to industry in an information systems executive position. While the majority of my experience has been in manufacturing environments, I have consulted in several others. Potential positions of interest would include Information Systems Director.

Although negotiable depending upon location and other factors, you should know that in recent years, my compensation has been in the range of $85,000 to $100,000.

I would be happy to discuss my background in a meeting with you. If you have any questions, do not hesitate to contact me at my home, or office at _____.

Sincerely yours,

James Sharpe

James Sharpe

JS

Broadcast Letter (Vice President of Sales and Marketing)

JANE SWIFT

18 Central Park Street, Anytown, NY 14788
(516) 555-1212   jswift@careerbrain.com

(Date)

Alice _____
(Title)
Krieger, Skvetney, Howell
Executive Search Consultants
2426 Foundation Road
Anytown, NY 14788

Dear Ms. _____:

I understand your client wants you to locate a Vice President of Marketing/Sales to create a new and aggressive business development function. I have successfully created and developed three marketing and sales functions. My association with leading companies and my track record of consistent accomplishments and increasing responsibility make me a viable candidate. My expertise will quickly achieve competitive advantage for your client.

While Vice President of Marketing and Strategic Planning at _____ Utility Services (a subsidiary of _____ Energy specializing in financial services, data and software), I . . .

- created a high-energy, highly skilled team of inside technical and sales personnel. This team and our external telemarketing and direct marketing companies increased customers 39% in a low growth industry.
- grew our basic service 128% and increased revenue another 31%.
- achieved a remarkable 16% direct response rate from senior financial executives and won a direct marketing award from an industry magazine. Two of our direct mail packages made the national finals for the prestigious direct marketing Echo awards presented by the Direct Marketing Association (DMA).

While Manager of the International Consulting Division at _____ I assisted in creating and developing this new division. From $0 we developed over $2.3 million in new business in only one year. I developed business worldwide by interacting with foreign nationals (public and private sector).

My demonstrated skills at quickly increasing new business would be most valued by a leading service firm desiring rapid growth and competitive advantage. Relocation would not be an issue. I look forward to hearing from you. I'll be available in the office this next week.

Sincerely,

Jane Swift

Jane Swift

JS

Broadcast Letter (Senior Executive)

James Sharpe

18 Central Park Street, Anytown, NY 14788
(516) 555-1212   jsharpe@careerbrain.com

(Date)

Alice _____ - (Title)
Krieger, Skvetney, Howell Executive Search Consultants
2426 Foundation Road, Anytown, NY 14788

Dear Ms. _____:

I have heard that you conduct searches for clients seeking senior executives with proven abilities, strong track records, and international experience. I have recently returned to the USA from Argentina, and it's unlikely you will find me through your normal sources, so I've decided to write directly and introduce myself.

American businesses starting up in Europe or Latin America will struggle against entrenched foreign competition and huge cultural differences. I've faced these and handled them more successfully than most Americans.

After becoming General Manager of a high-quality bakery company in Buenos Aires, Argentina, I reorganized sales, distribution, and warehousing. I rebuilt the demoralized sales force with leadership, communication, and enthusiasm. I set up an American-style distribution network to supply supermarkets, distributors, and smaller stores in the interior. After only a year, improvements I introduced expanded business one hundredfold to two bakeries on twenty-four-hour shifts, with one hundred fifty employees and sixteen trucks selling nationally.

With _____ (international public accountants and consultants), I consulted with principals of closely held Argentinian companies, particularly in general management, distribution, administration, and merchandising of industrial and consumer products. We quite successfully increased market share, built output, and added new outlets.

Before moving to Argentina, I built and directed a family-owned grocery chain (to eleven supermarkets, 850 employees and $60 million in sales from two stores and only $4.5 million) in a highly competitive Florida market. The company established a reputation for quality perishables and outstanding customer service; we introduced the first twenty-four-hour supermarket in Florida.

My wife and I returned to the U.S. because of Argentina's high inflation and an unstable political climate. I am an optimist, thrive on challenges, lead by example and readily adapt to situations. If your client—international or domestic—would benefit from these kinds of qualities we should get to know each other. If you will call or write at your convenience, I look forward to telling more about my background.

Sincerely,

James Sharpe

James Sharpe

JS

Broadcast Letter (Consultant)

James Sharpe

18 Central Park Street, Anytown, NY 14788
(516) 555-1212   jsharpe@careerbrain.com

(Date)

Ms. _____
(Title)
ABC Corporation
1 Industry Plaza
Anytown, NY 12096

Dear Ms. _____ :

Over the years, I have built a successful consulting business on my ability to quickly and accurately assess situations, identify problems and key in on strategies which obtain results. I have **increased the bottom line** for my clients by effectively reshaping organizations and improving productivity. Building effective teams and inspiring others to peak performance are among my strengths.

Feasibility studies, start-up management, turnaround situations, and **crisis resolution** are areas where I am able to be of particular assistance. Timber and natural resources are areas where I excel, but my skills are transferable to any industry.

Although I never lack work and consistently earn a six-figure income, I am always on the lookout for challenging interim assignments and consulting projects. **What motivates me most is making money for my clients.**

The enclosed summary details some of my accomplishments. I look forward to hearing from you to discuss any mutually beneficial opportunities. Please feel free to pass along my resume to others who may have a need for my professional assistance.

Sincerely,

James Sharpe

James Sharpe

JS
Enclosure.

Power Phrases

Consider using adaptations of these key phrases in your broadcast letters.

I hope this summary describes my experience and provides you with a better understanding of my capabilities. Thank you for your help.

If you feel that any of the strengths outlined in my resume could make a valuable contribution to your organization, please contact me to let me know of your interest.

Recently I read about the expansion of your company in the _____ Sun. As the _____ industry is of great interest to me, I was excited to learn of the new developments within ABC Corporation.

I feel confident that a short conversation about my experience and your growth plans would be mutually beneficial. I will be calling you early next week to follow up on this letter.

Currently, my total compensation package is in the low $70s; and I am looking for a company that rewards performance consistently.

I'm a responsive and responsible listener, maintaining a gracious and empathetic attitude, creatively troubleshooting, thoroughly researching options and making well-thought-out recommendations designed to establish and enhance customer/client relationships.

I am available for relocation and travel and am targeting compensation in the $50K range.

I fervently request more than your cursory consideration; I request your time to verify my claims. YOUR TIME WILL NOT BE WASTED.

Superior recommendations from industry leaders as well as verifiable salary history is available.

I hope you will not think me presumptuous in writing directly to you; however, in view of your position, I am led to believe that you are more aware of your organization's telecommunications personnel requirements than anyone else.

I am confident that with my experience I can make a significant contribution to your organization.

Throughout my career, I've been fortunate to represent quality merchandise and services and have learned just how to present them in their most favorable aspects. I know how to evaluate competition, to assess consumer/market needs, exploit a market niche, maximize profit margins, create and maintain a reputation for dependability and excellent service.

I am a self-starter looking to join a reputable firm, one that could benefit from an individual who is ready to give 110 percent. With over three years of sales experience, I have developed excellent interpersonal, organizational, and communication skills. I am a hard-working individual who is motivated by the knowledge that my earnings are directly related to the time, energy, and effort that I commit to my position.

I am personable, present a highly professional image, and deal effectively with both peers and clientele. I am confident you will agree that I should be representing your firm and not your competition. My salary requirements are negotiable. I will call you this week to set up a mutually convenient time for an interview.

Since beginning with ABC Company, my average commission has progressed from $400 to $650 weekly. My current salary or commission requirement would range upward of the mid-$20Ks, with specifics flexible and negotiable.

I look forward to hearing from you in the near future to schedule an interview at your convenience, during which I hope to learn more about the position, your company's plans and goals, and how I can contribute to the success of your team.

I am grateful for that environment and the faith that was demonstrated in my capabilities. I automatically moved into the role of Executive Assistant, constantly seeking ways to limit expenses, cut costs and generate additional profit for the company. I was exceptionally successful in that endeavor—while managing 5 operations, 3 warehouses, 6 Warehouse Managers and a staff of 60.

I am appreciative of the time you've spent reviewing this letter (and the accompanying material). I hope to hear from you in the very near future to arrange to meet in person and discuss just how my qualifications may be of value to your organization.

Networking E-mail (Employee Benefits Administration)

Dear _____:

It was a pleasure to speak with you on the telephone recently and, even more so, to be remembered after all these years.

As mentioned during our conversation, I have just recently reentered the job market and have ten years of experience with a 3,000-employee retail organization in the area of employee benefit administration. My experience includes pension plans, and dental, life, and disability insurance. I have been responsible for all facets of management of the company plan, including accounting, maintenance, and liaison with both staff and coverage providers.

My goal is to become a Benefits Manager in a larger organization with the possibility of advancement in other Human Resources areas. My preference is to remain in the Metropolitan _____ area.

For your information, attached is my resume. If any situations come to mind where you think my skills and background would fit or if you have any suggestions as to others with whom it might be beneficial for me to speak, I would appreciate hearing from you. I can be reached at the telephone number listed below.

Again, I very much enjoyed our conversation.

Yours truly,

James Sharpe
(516) 555-1212
jsharpe@careerbrain.com

Networking E-mail (Publishing)

Dear _____ :

It was a pleasure to meet with you for lunch today. I am grateful for the time you took out of your busy schedule to assist me in my job search.

It was fascinating to learn about the new technology which is beginning to play a major role in the publishing field today. I have already been to the book store to purchase the book by _____ which you highly recommended. I look forward to reading about his "space age" ideas.

I will be contacting _____ within the next few days to set up an appointment. I will let you know how things are progressing once I have met her.

Thanks again for your help. You will be hearing from me soon.

Yours sincerely,

James Sharpe
(516) 555-1212
jsharpe@careerbrain.com

Networking E-mail (Administrative Assistant)

Dear _____ :

_____ suggested that I contact you regarding employment opportunities.

After many years in the legal community, I have decided that a career change is due in order to use my interpersonal skills to their fullest. As you may know, a secretary/paralegal position offers little advancement unless you become a lawyer or move into the administrative areas. It is with this growth potential in mind that I desire to work with upper-level management in a corporate environment as an administrative assistant or executive secretary.

I am sending as attachments for your review a copy of my resume and letters of recommendation. I look forward to the opportunity of meeting with you at your convenience. I have recently resigned from _____ and may be contacted at my home phone number of (516) 555-1212. Thank you.

Very truly yours,

Jane Swift
(516) 555-1212
jswift@careerbrain.com

Networking Letter (Chief Information Officer)

18 Central Park Street, Anytown, NY 14788
(516) 555-1212   jswift@careerbrain.com

JANE SWIFT

Phillip _____   (Date)
(Title)
ABC Corporation
1 Industry Plaza
Anytown, NY 12096

Dear Executive Resources Team Members:

Never before have we experienced such a phenomenon as the information technology revolution. As a senior manager for information technology at the XYZ Office, I am routinely faced with IT challenges and the requirement to build solutions based on critical analysis, investigation, and planning of information management initiatives.

During the past 25+ years, I have spearheaded the analysis of emerging technology management across federal entities. Presently, I am overseeing a government-wide project to analyze private-sector best practices for managing telecommunications/network services in government agencies. The goal is stronger internal operating capabilities, reduced costs, and improved service levels. In addition, I have led analyses of the Life Cycle Management process, especially notable during an analysis of a department-wide XYZ Personnel system that resulted in improved planning of the multimillion-dollar project, increased systems security, and the potential to reduce operating costs for the department's civilian personnel organization by $100 million per year.

With a blend of IT and general management experience, I build alliances within and beyond my work team applying well-developed communication skills to communicate technical information in clearly understood ways. I am successful in achieving buy-in to necessary changes/improvements, with cost-containment results equaling hundreds of millions of dollars. Remaining current on technical issues, practices, and procedures, I can identify and recommend the most contemporary, cutting-edge business operating models.

In addition, the IT team members under my leadership have been promoted over the years, in part due to the ongoing mentorship and motivational environment available to them. I have influenced their appointment to leadership roles and receipt of numerous awards. Despite a rigorous schedule, challenging commitments, high-level goals, and multiple roadblocks to the end result, our team remains positive and upbeat, taking pride in their performance.

My goal is the Deputy Chief Information Officer position with the ABC Corporation/Office of the Chief Information Officer. I appreciate your consideration and look forward to speaking with you soon.

Sincerely,

Jane Swift

Jane Swift

JS
enclosure

Networking Letter (Hospitality Management)

James Sharpe

18 Central Park Street, Anytown, NY 14788
(516) 555-1212   jsharpe@careerbrain.com

(Date)

Bob _____
(Title)
Krieger, Skvetney, Howell
Executive Search Consultants
2426 Foundation Road
Anytown, NY 14788

Dear Bob:

We are members of the same professional association, the National Guild of Hospitality Marketing Professionals, and I need to call on your assistance. I have sixteen years of business management experience in marketing and sales with premier package goods and service firms. My accomplishments include the revitalization of established brands, new-product introduction, extensive advertising exposure, and marketing success in the fast-food restaurant field.

Perhaps you know of a company that could use this scope of experience. In this regard, I enclose a copy of my resume outlining a few of my more significant accomplishments.

My objective is to find a director-level position at a marketing-driven company where my skills can contribute to the firm's growth and profitability. My preference would be to stay in an industry associated with consumer goods or services.

I am not limited by location and would consider the opportunity whenever it presents itself. My minimum salary requirement is in the upper $60K range and will depend on location and potential. You may use this figure for your own analysis. My preference is that you do not discuss salary with a potential employer.

Please advise me of any opportunities that I might investigate. Your assistance will be appreciated.

Sincerely yours,

James Sharpe

James Sharpe

JS
enclosure

Networking Letter (Project Coordinator/Administrator)

JANE SWIFT

18 Central Park Street, Anytown, NY 14788
(516) 555-1212   jswift@careerbrain.com

(Date)

Phillip _____
(Title)
ABC Corporation
1 Industry Plaza
Anytown, NY 12096

Dear Phil:

I met you a couple months ago at the _____ convention. Since that time I have been serving in the capacity of Project Coordinator/Administrator of a program at Children's Hospital. However, this program is federally funded for a limited time, and my position will soon be coming to an end.

I am looking for a position in management and would appreciate any assistance you could provide. Enclosed are both a resume and letter of recommendation for your review. As you will note from my resume, I have broad management experience in a number of areas. I particularly enjoy the development and implementation of new programs.

My skills and experience include:

- Extensive background in all areas of staff management, budget development, strategic planning, public relations, and marketing.
- Excellent communication skills.
- Demonstrated ability to approach management from a broad base of management experience in a number of areas. I particularly enjoy the development and implementation of new programs.
- Career experience complemented by a Master's Degree in Health Administration and a Bachelor's Degree in Social Work.

Thank you in advance for your assistance. I look forward to meeting with you again.

Sincerely,

Jane Swift

Jane Swift

JS
enclosure

Networking Letter (General)

JAMES SHARPE

18 Central Park Street, Anytown, NY 14788
(516) 555-1212   jsharpe@careerbrain.com

(Date)

Phillip _____
(Title)
ABC Corporation
1 Industry Plaza
Anytown, NY 12096

Dear Phil:

I was over at _____'s house a few weeks ago to pick up some information to aid me in my job search. You guessed it, Phil, I'm in transition. I was one of the many who was caught in _____'s downsizing a few weeks ago. As part of the information _____ gave me, _____'s newsletter was included.

I am not calling you or sending this letter to ask you for a job, but I could use your help in my job search. If you know of a position in your company or can give me any leads, I would appreciate it greatly. I'm sure you know how difficult it can be to develop a solid resume, job leads, interviews, etc., and with the local economic situation such that it is, the job of finding a job is compounded. I've included a copy of my resume for your reference and file.

I can be contacted at either my home phone number (555-1212) or at the _____ Outplacement Center at 555-1414. I will call you in a few days to follow up.

Sincerely,

James Sharpe

James Sharpe

JS
enclosure

Networking Letter (Accounting)

JANE SWIFT

18 Central Park Street, Anytown, NY 14788
(516) 555-1212   jswift@careerbrain.com

(Date)

Alice _____
(Title)
Krieger, Skvetney, Howell
Executive Search Consultants
2426 Foundation Road
Anytown, NY 14788

Dear Alice:

Please find the enclosed copy of my most recent resume. As we discussed, I am beginning to put some "feelers" out in advance of the completion of my degree in December. I have worked very hard, and sacrificed a lot, in order to better my educational credentials. My GPA is currently a 3.8. I am certain that it will be a 3.9 when I graduate. I intend to further the process by passing the CPA (Certified Public Accountant) Exam in June. I have already applied to take the exam. In addition, I will begin work on my MBA in the fall.

I do not intend to target any specific type of job. I am open to most anything that my qualifications will fit. My only criteria are the following:

1. An employer who will reimburse me for at least a fair portion of my MBA program tuition and books.
2. A reasonable increase over my present salary.
3. A decent medical and dental plan.
4. An employer that allows its employees to grow within the organization; in other words, develops them for increased responsibility and upward mobility.

It sounds as if I'm asking for the world, but I know that situations like this exist. I also know that I have a lot to offer. I can guarantee that any employer who hires me will be more than pleased with my abilities and accomplishments.

I would appreciate any advice and/or referrals you might be able to give me.

Sincerely,

Jane Swift

Jane Swift

JS
enclosure

Power Phrases

Consider using adaptations of these key phrases in your networking letters.

It was good talking with you again. As promised, I am enclosing a copy of my resume for your information. If any appropriate opportunities come to your attention, I would appreciate it if you would keep me in mind.

After you have had a chance to look over the resume, please give me a call.

I am beginning to put some "feelers" out in advance of the completion of my degree in December.

I do not intend to target any specific type of job. I am open to most anything that my qualifications will fit. My only criteria are the following:

I would appreciate any advice and/or referrals you might be able to give me.

I am looking for a position in management and would appreciate any assistance you could provide.

As always, it was good to talk with you. Your positive outlook is catching. I've been called the eternal optimist, but I always feel more upbeat after a conversation with you.

Many thanks for the words of encouragement and taking the time from your busy schedule to help me. It truly is appreciated. I have never faced an unemployment situation like this before.

It was a pleasure to speak with you on the telephone recently and, even more so, to be remembered after all these years.

For your information, enclosed is my resume. If any situations come to mind where you think my skills and background would fit, or if you have any suggestions as to others with whom it might be beneficial for me to speak, I would appreciate hearing from you. I can be reached at the telephone numbers listed above.

He assured me that he would pass my resume along to you; however, in the event that it has not reached you yet, I am enclosing another.

Perhaps you know of a company that could use this scope of experience. In this regard, I enclose a copy of my resume outlining a few of my more significant accomplishments.

My objective is to find a _____ level position at a marketing driven company where my skills can contribute to the firm's growth and profitability.

I am not limited by location and would consider the opportunity wherever it presents itself.

First of all, let me sincerely thank you for taking the time and trouble to return my call last Monday. I found our conversation informative, entertaining, and (alas) a little scary. Needless to say, I genuinely appreciate your prompt response and generous, helpful advice.

Again, a thousand thanks for your time and consideration. If I might ask you one last favor, could you please give me your opinion of the revision? A copy is, as usual, enclosed.

I am writing to you in response to our recent conversation over the telephone. I thank you for your time and your advice. It was most generous of you and sincerely appreciated. Please accept my apologies for invading your privacy. I anticipated an address for written correspondence from an answering service.

*I look forward to hearing from you on your next visit to
_____.*

*I hope you'll keep me in mind if you hear of anything that's up
my alley!*

*I recently learned that your firm is well-connected with
manufacturers in the _____ area and does quality work.
We should talk soon, since it's very likely we can help each
other. I'll be in the office all next week and look forward to
hearing from you. I have alerted my secretary; she'll put your call
right through.*

*_____ suggested that I contact you regarding employment
opportunities.*

*After many years in the _____ community, I have decided
that a career change is due in order to use my interpersonal skills
to their fullest.*

Follow-up E-mail (after telephone contact) (General)

Dear Ms. _____ :

I appreciate the time you took yesterday to discuss the position at _____. I recognize that timing and awareness of interest are very important in searches of this type. Your comment regarding an attempt to contact me earlier this summer is a case in point.

Attached, as you requested, you will find an outline resume. I also believe that my experiences as a director of physical plant services are readily transferable to a new environment. I believe that I can contribute a great deal to the satisfaction of your client's needs.

Realizing that letters and resumes are not entirely satisfactory means of judging a person's ability or personality, I suggest a personal interview to discuss further your client's needs and my quali-fications. I can be reached directly or via message at (516) 555-1212, so that we may arrange a mutually convenient time to meet. I look forward to hearing from you. Thank you for your time and consideration.

Sincerely,

Jane Swift
(516) 555-1212
jswift@careerbrain.com

Follow-up E-mail (after telephone contact) (Arts Management)

Dear Ms. _____:

Per yesterday's conversation, I am forwarding a copy of my resume and am looking forward to our meeting in the very near future.

As we discussed, the positions which interest me are as follows:

Event/Arts Management
Promotions/Advertising/Public Relations
Corporate Training

I am a fanatic about image, excellence, and attention to quality and detail. As my academic and career background reveal, I have the tenacity of a rat terrier when it comes to task accomplishment.

I have never held an "eight-to-five" job and would most likely be bored to death if I had one. Therefore, I am looking for something fast-paced and challenging to my gray matter that will allow growth and advancement and an opportunity to learn. I am in my element when I am in a position to organize . . . the more details the better!

I'll give you a buzz on Tuesday, March —th to try to set an appointment for further discussion.

Sincerely,

Jane Swift
(516) 555-1212
jswift@careerbrain.com

Follow-up E-mail (after telephone contact) (Telemarketing)

Dear Ms. _____:

This letter is in response to our phone conversation this afternoon and your online job posting on CareerCity.com regarding the _____ position available.

My background includes experience (sales and technical) with a wide range of computer systems, as well as with industrial distributed process-control systems and measurement instrumentation. Considering the complexity of the equipment I've worked on and sold, most of the products being marketed will present no difficulty to me. The customer base would take a little time, but this would be nothing excessive.

I am a bright, articulate, and well-groomed professional with excellent telemarketing skills, sales instincts, and closing abilities. I would like to meet with you to discuss how I could contribute to the effectiveness and profitability of your operations.

Sincerely,

James Sharpe
(516) 555-1212
jsharpe@careerbrain.com

Follow-up E-mail (after telephone contact) (General)

Ms. _____ :

As per my telephone conversation with Stephanie of your office today, this letter will confirm our meeting on Friday, June 9, 20— at 2:00 P.M.

Again, thank you for your flexibility and for working out this time for us to meet at my convenience.

I look forward to continuing the discussion we had over the telephone in greater detail.

Very sincerely yours,

Jane Swift
(516) 555-1212
jswift@careerbrain.com

Follow-up Letter (after telephone contact) (Adjunct Faculty)

Jane Swift

18 Central Park Street, Anytown, NY 14788
(516) 555-1212   jswift@careerbrain.com

EDUCATOR / ADVOCATE / MENTOR
"Every leader a teacher, every teacher a leader, every student a success."

Emily _____   (Date)
(Title)
ABC Community College
1 Industry Plaza
Anytown, NY 12096

Dear Ms. _____:

I enclose my resume in follow-up to our conversation last week regarding the adjunct adult education position currently available at Anytown Community College. I appreciate very much your offer to forward my credentials to the appropriate individual.

With a Master's degree in Education Administration, Principal of Administration and Supervision certification through the state of New York, plus four years of cumulative experience in the classroom, I believe I possess the expertise and qualifications that are critical to leading your organization's adult students to successfully achieve their educational goals.

What do I offer your students?

- Effective listening and communication skills—a demonstrated ability to provide individualized instruction based on students' interests and needs.
- Encouragement and motivation—a creative, inviting atmosphere of interaction and participation.
- Sincere desire to reach them on a level they can understand, no matter what age, skill level, or cultural background.

I am excited at the opportunity to work with adult students, because I recognize that they are in that classroom because they want to be there. The adult population brings a unique flavor of enthusiasm and motivation that energizes and inspires me as an instructor and makes me eager to go above and beyond expectations to help them reach their goals.

In terms of salary, I realize that flexibility is essential and am therefore open to discussing your organization's compensation package for an individual with my distinctive talents. If you believe that I could play an important role on your educational team, please call me at (516) 555-1212 to arrange for an interview.

Sincere regards,

Jane Swift

Jane Swift
JS
enclosure

Follow-up Letter (after telephone contact) (Legal Assistant)

JANE SWIFT

18 Central Park Street, Anytown, NY 14788
(516) 555-1212   jswift@careerbrain.com

(Date)

Phillip _____
(Title)
ABC Corporation
1 Industry Plaza
Anytown, NY 12096

Dear Mr. _____:

Thank you for returning my telephone call yesterday. It was a pleasure speaking with you, and as promised, a copy of my resume is enclosed. As I mentioned, I have been working in law firms since the end of February, as well as working on weekends and in the evenings for over one year. At present, I am looking for a second or third shift to continue developing my word-processing and legal skills.

Although the majority of my positions have been more managerial and less secretarial, I have developed strong office skills over the years. While I was attending both undergraduate and graduate school, I worked as Administrative Assistants to Deans and Department Heads, in addition to working in other professional capacities.

_____ speaks very highly of me, and if you need to confirm a reference with him, please feel free to contact him at _____. In addition, I would be happy to furnish you with names of people I have worked for within law firms over the past year.

Within the next day, I will be contacting you to arrange a convenient meeting time to discuss the position you now have available. However, if you would like to speak with me, feel free to contact me at 555-1212.

Thank you again for calling yesterday. I look forward to speaking with you on the telephone, and meeting you in person.

Sincerely,

Jane Swift

Jane Swift

JS
enclosure

Follow-up Letter (after telephone contact) (Advertising Sales)

Jane Swift

18 Central Park Street, Anytown, NY 14788
(516) 555-1212   jswift@careerbrain.com

(Date)

Phillip _____
(Title)
ABC Corporation
1 Industry Plaza
Anytown, NY 12096

Dear Mr. _____:

Thank you for taking the time recently to respond to my questions concerning a _____ position with _____, as advertised in _____ (October —, 20—). As you suggested, I have enclosed my resume for your review and consideration.

As you will find detailed on my resume, I offer nearly two years of sales experience, with over one year of successful advertising sales for a $1 million regional business publication.

Within one year, I have developed a formerly neglected territory from approximately $50,000 to its current $180,000 in annual sales.

I have an excellent track record in customer retention, account penetration, low receivables, and consistent goal achievement. I have had experience working with client advertising agencies and directly with smaller clients. I am confident that I can make similar contributions to your sales efforts, and would consider an interview with _____ to be a tremendous career opportunity.

As I have mentioned, I am relocating to your area in January and I would welcome the opportunity to discuss my background and accomplishments with you in further detail. I will be in your area Friday, December —th, and will call you early next week to see if we might schedule a meeting at that time.

Best regards,

Jane Swift

Jane Swift

JS
enclosure

Follow-up Letter (after telephone contact) (Purchasing)

James Sharpe

18 Central Park Street, Anytown, NY 14788
(516) 555-1212 jsharpe@careerbrain.com

(Date)

Bob _____ - (Title)
Krieger, Skvetney, Howell
Executive Search Consultants
2426 Foundation Road
Anytown, NY 14788

Dear Mr. _____ :

In reference to our telephone conversation, enclosed is my _____ resume. I believe the one you have is written toward a purchasing position.

Since we last spoke I have been working as a business consultant for the _____ group of companies on projects in a number of different areas outlined below.

- Elected to serve as the Vice Chairman of the _____ Chapter 11 bankruptcy creditors committee including the two primary subcommittees reviewing offers to purchase the _____ operations.
- Spearheaded and supervised upgrading of the _____ companies' communications systems, including printing and copy machines, telecommunications systems, computer hardware and software systems, computer scanning system, computer filing system, and fax and modem transmission systems.
- Set up and implemented an auto and entry floor mat marketing program for _____ including pricing and product displays for retail sales outlets.
- Researched, purchased and installed a bar code labeling program for the companies' products, including label set up and printing systems to allow them to sell their products to _____ .
- Participated in the design and layout of a new logo for _____ division including specifications for all letterheads, forms, and printed communications materials.
- Provided major input for a factory-paid _____ point-of-sale system to display custom automotive floor mats.

Most of my projects should be wrapped up by the end of November, and so I will be looking for another company who could utilize my broad range of experience. Please let me know if you think you might have something for me.

Sincerely,

James Sharpe

James Sharpe

JS
enclosure

Follow-up Letter (after telephone contact) (Merchandising)

JAMES SHARPE

18 Central Park Street ◆ Anytown, NY 14788
(516) 555-1212 jsharpe@careerbrain.com

(Date)

Bob _____
(Title)
Krieger, Skvetney, Howell
Executive Search Consultants
2426 Foundation Road
Anytown, NY 14788

Dear Mr. _____:

As you will recall, we spoke about my qualifications for the opportunity with your New York client (account #5188), and you mentioned that you would be forwarding my resume for consideration.

I wanted you to have my updated resume, and I am enclosing several copies. I hope you'll send one to your client and keep another for your own files. I'm aware that you have many business leads and that my qualifications might pertain to other opportunities; please remember me if something arises that would tie in with my background.

My experience in grocery and merchandising areas is considerable, and I have an extensive network of business contacts in the Pacific Northwest. My many long-term professional relationships would benefit any employer in this area.

I'd like to meet with you to tell you more about my background and to show you some of the training and marketing materials I've developed. This would give you a better picture of my capabilities.

I'll be in touch with you in the near future to find out when we might get together. Thank you again for your consideration.

Sincerely yours,

James Sharpe

James Sharpe

JS
enclosures

Follow-up Letter (after telephone contact) (Manager)

James Sharpe

18 Central Park Street, Anytown, NY 14788
(516) 555-1212 jsharpe@careerbrain.com

(Date)

Bob _____
(Title)
Krieger, Skvetney, Howell
Executive Search Consultants
2426 Foundation Road
Anytown, NY 14788

Dear Mr. _____ :

THANK YOU for allowing me to tell you a little about myself. I have just completed my MBA (December, 20—) and would appreciate the opportunity to talk with your client companies who are in need of an experienced and seasoned manager. Whether the need is for general (operational) management, products, marketing, or sales, my substantial background in management, marketing, and technical products should be very valuable to your clients.

I have enclosed two resumes (marketing-oriented and operational-oriented) with some other information which you may find useful. With eyes firmly welded to the bottom line, I offer: the ABILITY to manage, build, and quickly understand their business; EXPERIENCE in domestic and international corporate cultures; INTELLIGENCE and the capacity to grasp essential elements; and the WILLINGNESS to work hard, travel, and relocate.

Realizing that most of your clients aren't looking for VPs, I'm not necessarily looking for fancy titles (but I am promotable). What I am looking for is that special position which will offer not only a challenge but a career opportunity with long-range potential. I know my successes will bring them (and me) rewards.

Resumes and letters are brief by their very nature and cannot tell the whole story. I will be happy to discuss with your client and you how my commitment to them will help solve their needs or problems and will definitely make good things happen! After all, isn't that the bottom line?

May we work together?

Very truly yours,

James Sharpe

James Sharpe

JS
enclosures

Power Phrases

Consider using adaptations of these key phrases in your follow-up letters after phone calls.

As you requested in our telephone conversation this morning, I am enclosing a copy of my resume for your review.

As you can see from my resume, I have some excellent secretarial experience.

I'll give you a buzz on Tuesday, March —th, to set an appointment for further discussion.

In reference to our telephone conversation, enclosed is my sales and marketing resume; I believe the one you have is written toward a purchasing position.

I am a bright, articulate, and well-groomed professional with excellent telemarketing skills, sales instincts, and closing abilities. I am seeking a dynamic position with a reputable firm. I would like to meet with you in person to discuss how I could contribute to the effectiveness of your clients' operations.

Again, thank you for your flexibility and for working out this time for us to meet at my convenience.

Please remember me if something arises that would tie in with my background.

My many long-term professional relationships would benefit any employer in this area.

I'd like to meet with you to tell you more about my background and to show you some of the training and marketing materials I've developed. This would give you a better picture of my capabilities.

As you suggested when we spoke last week, I have enclosed my resume for your review and consideration. I contacted you on the recommendation of _____ of _____, who thought that you may have an interest in my qualifications for a position in the near future.

I have long admired _____ for its innovations in the industry, and I would consider it a tremendous career opportunity to be associated with your organization.

Follow-up E-mail (after face-to-face meeting) (General)

Dear Mr. _____:

I appreciate the time you took today interviewing me for the position. I hope our 2-hour meeting did not throw off the rest of the day's calendar. I trust you will agree that it was time well spent, as I sensed we connected on every major point discussed.

Your insight on e-commerce was intriguing. My history in hi-tech, manufacturing, and biomedical industries and background in technology solutions seems to be a good match with the opportunities available in your company. As I mentioned, at Continuum Biomedical I initiated the marketing stratagems that opened our markets to Latin America. What I failed to mention is that I also have contacts with some e-commerce investors developing online portals targeted to Latin Americans.

I am very interested in the position and would like to touch base with you on Tuesday to see where we stand.

Sincerely,

James Sharpe
(516) 555-1212
jsharpe@careerbrain.com

Follow-up E-mail (after face-to-face meeting) (Sales Manager)

Dear Ms. Christianson:

Thank you for meeting with me yesterday to discuss the Sales Manager position for the Midwestern region.

I am excited at the prospect of teaming with you to revitalize this territory. The anticipated launch of the New Widget product line is particularly intriguing, and I am confident that my past experience with similar product introductions will be of great benefit to ABC Corporation in this effort.

To supplement what we discussed, I'd like to point out my 5 years of experience in capital medical equipment sales where I played a key role in spearheading the successful launch of several technologically advanced monitoring devices. In addition, I led a 15-member sales/marketing and product support team that earned the 1999 New Product of the Year award from Medical Devices International.

If I can answer additional questions about my qualifications and expertise, please call me at (516) 555-1212.

Yours truly,
Jane Swift
jswift@careerbrain.com

Follow-up E-mail (after face-to-face meeting) (Customer Service)

Dear Ms. Nese:

I would like to take this opportunity to thank you for meeting with me on Friday, January, 6. I found the time we spent together and with Ken to be both informative and enjoyable. After meeting with both of you, I feel even more confident that my demonstrated strengths and experience in customer service, coupled with my enthusiasm, will prove to be an asset for ABC Corporation.

In addition, my solid computer skills will prove to be most valuable in increasing productivity within the Customer Service department. Undoubtedly, the department transfer from Ohio to New York will provide many challenges, and I believe that my demonstrated organizational, analytical, and communication skills will serve to enhance and simplify this move.

In closing, I would like to again thank you for sharing your valuable time with me. If you have any other questions, or need to schedule another meeting, please feel free to contact me at the number or e-mail address listed below.

I look forward to hearing from you soon and in joining the team!

Sincere regards,

Jane Swift
(516) 555-1212
jswift@careerbrain.com

Follow-up E-mail (after face-to-face meeting) (Management)

Dear Mr. _____ :

The position we discussed Friday is a tremendously challenging one. After reviewing your comments about the job requirements, I am convinced that I can make an immediate contribution toward the growth and profitability of ABC Corporation.

Since you are going to reach a decision quickly, I would like to mention the following points, which I feel qualify me for the job we discussed:

1. Proven ability to generate fresh ideas and creative solutions to difficult problems
2. Experience in the area of program planning and development
3. Ability to successfully manage many projects at the same time
4. A facility for working effectively with people at all levels of management
5. Experience in administration, general management, and presentations
6. An intense desire to do an outstanding job in anything which I undertake

Thank you for the time and courtesy extended me. I will look forward to hearing from you.

Sincerely,

James Sharpe
(516) 555-1212
jsharpe@careerbrain.com

Follow-up E-mail (after face-to-face meeting) (Corporate Graphic Design)

Dear Mr. _____:

It was a pleasure speaking with you regarding my search for a position in corporate graphic design. Thank you for your initial interest.

The position I am looking for is usually found in a corporate marketing or public relations department. The titles vary; Graphic Design Manager, Advertising Manager, and Publications Director are a few. In almost every case the job description includes management and coordination of the corporation's printed marketing materials, whether they are produced by in-house designers or by an outside advertising agency or design firm.

I would like to stay in the _____ area; at least, I would like to search this area first. My salary requirement is $_____ a year.

My professional experience, education, activities, and skills uniquely qualify me for a position in Corporate Graphic Design. My portfolio documents over eight years of experience in the business, and includes design, project consultation, and supervision of quality printed material for a wide range of clients.

I hope you will keep me in your files for future reference. I will telephone your office next week to discuss my situation further.

Sincerely,

James Sharpe
(516) 555-1212
jsharpe@careerbrain.com

Follow-up E-mail (after face-to-face meeting) (General)

Dear Ms. _____:

It was a pleasure meeting with you last week in your office. I appreciate the time you spent with me, as well as the valuable information you offered. As we discussed, I have adjusted my resume in regard to my position with _____. I have attached the new resume with this e-mail so that your files can be updated.

_____, please allow me to thank you again for the compliment on my ability to present a strong interview. Please keep this in mind when considering me for placement with one of your clients.

Sincerely,

Jane Swift
(516) 555-1212
jswift@careerbrain.com

Follow-up E-mail (after face-to-face meeting) (Entry-Level)

Dear Mr. _____:

I would like to take this opportunity to thank you for the interview Wednesday morning at _____, and to confirm my strong interest in an entry-level position with your company.

As we discussed, I feel that my education and background have provided me with an understanding of business operations which will prove to be an asset to your company. Additionally, I have always been considered a hard worker and a dependable, loyal employee. I am confident that I can make a valuable contribution to your Group Pension Fund area.

I look forward to meeting with you again in the near future to further discuss your needs.

Sincere regards,

James Sharpe
(516) 555-1212
jswift@careerbrain.com

Follow-up E-mail (after face-to-face meeting) (Auditing)

Mr. _____:

Thank you for allowing me the opportunity to meet with you to discuss the EDP Audit position currently available at ABC Corporation. The position sounds very challenging and rewarding, with ample room for growth. I feel my background and qualifications prepare me well for the EDP audit position we discussed.

I have a great willingness and eagerness to learn more about EDP auditing, and feel that I am the type of individual who would blend in well with the EDP audit staff at ABC Corporation. I look forward to hearing from you.

Sincerely,

Jane Swift
(516) 555-1212
jswift@careerbrain.com

Follow-up Letter (after face-to-face meeting) (General Letter)

18 Central Park Street, Anytown, NY 14788
(516) 555-1212   jswift@careerbrain.com

(Date)

Phillip _____
(Title)
ABC Corporation
1 Industry Plaza
Anytown, NY 12096

Dear Mr. _____:

Thank you very much for taking the time to meet with me today. I enjoyed our discussion, and I'm now even more excited about the possibility of working for ABC and with your team.

It was great to learn that you are embracing technology as it relates to your business—both in terms of day-to-day operations and the future delivery of ABC's programs (e.g. on-the-spot training). I am very interested in, and have an affinity for, computer technology and would love to be a part of your efforts in this area.

I am confident that I could make a strong contribution to the continued growth of ABC. As we discussed, I have related experience in all of the required areas for the position. In addition, I look forward to taking a project management approach to establishing the new system for the delivery of the assessment workshops to your key client. This process would allow me to ensure that I am meeting your objectives and getting a system "up and running" within an established time frame. Having done this, I would continually review for improvement and focus on managing the enhancement of customer service.

I remain very interested in the position, and I look forward to hearing from you soon. If you require additional information in the meantime, I may be reached at (516) 555-1212.

Sincerely,

Jane Swift
Jane Swift

JS
enclosure

Follow-up Letter (after face-to-face meeting) (Store Manager)

JAMES SHARPE

18 Central Park Street, Anytown, NY 14788
(516) 555-1212   jsharpe@careerbrain.com

Emily _____   (Date)
(Title)
ABC Corporation
1 Industry Plaza
Anytown, NY 12096

Dear Ms. _____:

It was a genuine pleasure meeting with you last Tuesday. I appreciate the candid approach that prevailed during our discussion and feel you gave me a comprehensive understanding of the store manager position. I can see in it an opportunity to apply the sales/staff building techniques I have acquired over the years with Banana Republic.

In our discussion, you made clear the objectives, duties, and responsibilities of the position, involving a rapid and significant increase in volume, addressing customer service needs, and training/motivating sales staff—all with a cost-conscious approach. I have given considerable thought to the problems and challenges you described and am confident that I can begin to produce the results you want. My interpersonal skills, leadership abilities, and sales/marketing experience will prove advantageous in this respect.

Additionally, I'd like to draw your attention to my store management experience both at Jacobsen's and Banana Republic, which totals more than 7 years. At this level, I interacted directly with customers and was accountable for my own sales objectives as well as overall store operations. My ability to train sales associates is undertaken with a "train by example" approach and it is through my own experience that I am able to develop staff to peak levels.

As you can see, I am very interested in and feel well qualified for the position with ABC Corporation. I am convinced that it is just the kind of challenging opportunity I have been seeking and trust that we can meet again soon for further discussion. If you need additional information, the names of references, or would like to arrange another meeting, please do not hesitate to contact me at the above listed phone number or e-mail address.

Thank you once again for your interest and cordiality.

Very truly yours,

James Sharpe

James Sharpe

JS

Follow-up Letter (after face-to-face meeting) (Construction Manager)

James Sharpe

18 Central Park Street, Anytown, NY 14788
(516) 555-1212   jsharpe@careerbrain.com

Emily _____   (Date)
(Title)
ABC Corporation
1 Industry Plaza
Anytown, NY 12096

Dear Ms. _____:

We had the opportunity to speak briefly at last week's Chamber of Commerce meeting concerning the Construction Management position you are seeking to fill in Vancouver. I appreciate you filling me in on the details of the project and have enclosed my resume as you suggested.

As we discussed, I am well acquainted with ABC Corporation's brand and store concept, and I am excited to learn of the company's expansion plans over the coming decade. With my background in construction, maintenance, and project management as well as operations and strategic leadership, I believe I am primed to play a key role in this growth.

As Chief Executive Officer of Superior Landscape Design, I have been instrumental in leading the company to phenomenal success within a very short time, building the organization from start-up into a solid revenue generator reputed throughout the Pacific Northwest as an aggressive competitor in markets crowded by multimillion-dollar, nationally recognized companies.

I am currently in the process of selling the company and have been exploring opportunities with dynamic, growth-oriented organizations like yours that could benefit from my broad-based expertise in operations, organizational management, finance, and business development. Complementing my diverse leadership background is expertise in all the fundamentals of construction management, including the ability to see projects through to completion while exceeding quality standards.

Perhaps one of my strongest assets is my ability to cultivate long-lasting relationships with clients through attentive, direct communication. I have been highly successfully at defining complex project plans, establishing budgets, outlining scope of work, and directly soliciting qualified contractors utilizing the bid process. I also offer extensive experience navigating through the paperwork and bureaucracy, forging productive alliances with key regulatory agencies to streamline permitting and licensing and facilitate expedited project starts.

I would enjoy the opportunity to speak with you again in greater detail. Could we meet for lunch on Friday? I'll call your assistant in a few days to confirm the appointment.

Best regards,

James Sharpe

James Sharpe

JS

Follow-up Letter (after face-to-face meeting)
(Executive Assistant)

JAMES SHARPE

18 Central Park Street ◆ Anytown, NY 14788
(516) 555-1212 jsharpe@careerbrain.com

(Date)

Phillip _____
(Title)
ABC Corporation
1 Industry Plaza
Anytown, NY 12096

Dear Phillip _____:

The time I spent interviewing with you and Sandra gave me a clear picture of your company's operation as well as your corporate environment. I want to thank you, in particular, Phillip, for the thorough picture you painted of your CEO's needs and work style.

I left our meeting feeling very enthusiastic about the scope of the position as well as its close match to my abilities and work style. After reviewing your comments, Phillip, I think the key strengths that I can offer your CEO in achieving his agenda are:

- Experience in effectively dealing with senior level staff in a manner that facilitates decision-making.
- Proven ability to anticipate an executive's needs and present viable options to consider.
- Excellent communication skills — particularly, the ability to gain feedback from staff and summarize succinctly.

Whether the needs at hand involve meeting planning, office administration, scheduling or just serving as a sounding board, I bring a combination of highly effective "people skills" and diversified business experience to deal with changing situations.

With my energetic work style, I believe that I am an excellent match for this unique position. I welcome an additional meeting to elaborate on my background and how I can assist your CEO.

Sincerely,

James Sharpe

James Sharpe

JS

Follow-up Letter (after face-to-face meeting)
(Management Information Systems)

James Sharpe

18 Central Park Street, Anytown, NY 14788
(516) 555-1212   jsharpe@careerbrain.com

(Date)

Bob _____
(Title)
Krieger, Skvetney, Howell
Executive Search Consultants
2426 Foundation Road
Anytown, NY 14788

Dear Mr. _____:

Thank you for meeting with me this morning. Our associate _____ assured me that a meeting with you would be productive, and it was. I sincerely appreciate your counsel, insight, and advice.

I have attached my resume for your review. I would appreciate any feedback you may have regarding effectiveness and strength. I understand you may not have any searches under way that would be suitable for me at this time, but I would appreciate any future considerations.

As we reviewed this morning, I seek and am qualified for senior MIS positions in a medium to large high-tech manufacturing or services business. I seek compensation in the $150,000-and-above range and look to report directly to the business CEO. These requirements are somewhat flexible depending on a number of factors, especially potential of a new position. My family and I are willing to relocate to any area except New York City.

Please consider any associates, customers, or friends who may have contacts that would be useful for me to meet with. I have learned how important networking is, and will really appreciate some assistance from a professional like you.

Thanks again, Mr. _____, and please let me know if I can be of service to you. I wish you and your colleagues continued success and look forward to a business relationship in the future.

Best regards,

James Sharpe

James Sharpe

JS
enclosure

Follow-up Letter (after face-to-face meeting) (Assistant)

18 Central Park Street, Anytown, NY 14788
(516) 555-1212 jswift@careerbrain.com

JANE SWIFT

(Date)

Emily _____
(Title)
ABC Corporation
1 Industry Plaza
Anytown, NY 12096

Dear Ms. _____:

Thank you for the opportunity to discuss the position of assistant.

ABC Corporation is involved in one of the most pressing concerns of today: environmentally safe methods of disposing of solid waste materials. The challenge of creating proper disposal systems is paramount. I look forward to being a part of an organization that is focusing on furthering the technology needed to enhance our environment.

At ABC Corporation I would be able to:

- Be a productive assistant to management
- Be a part of a technologically developing industry
- Be in a position to learn and grow with the opportunities presented by your company
- Be involved in the excitement of a new expanding company

The skills that I have to offer ABC Corporation are:

- Professionalism, organization, and maturity
- Excellent office skills
- Ability to work independently
- A creative work attitude
- Research and writing skills
- Varied business background
- Willingness to learn

Again, thank you for considering my qualifications to become a part of your organization.

Sincerely,

Jane Swift

Jane Swift

JS

Follow-up Letter (after face-to-face meeting) (Sales)

Jane Swift

18 Central Park Street, Anytown, NY 14788
(516) 555-1212   jswift@careerbrain.com

(Date)

Phillip _____
(Title)
ABC Corporation
1 Industry Plaza
Anytown, NY 12096

Dear Mr. _____:

It was a pleasure to speak with you and Mr. _____ on Monday. Thank you for giving me the opportunity to express my enthusiasm regarding a sales position at ABC Corporation.

My extensive sales experience, along with my persistence and strong closing ability, make me confident that I can perform successfully in your company. I am able to effectively establish rapport without face-to-face contact and close a minimum of 40 percent of my sales by telephone. I am accustomed to working with professionals and feel confident that I can communicate the benefits of additional exposure and close a significant number of new and expanded advertisements for this segment.

I am an extremely capable professional with a high tolerance for stressful situations and the ability to recognize clients' needs and evaluate alternatives to ensure their satisfaction. Joining the sales team at ABC Corporation will enable me to continue to grow and be challenged while serving my customers.

It is important for me to be able to give and receive in my career, and the possibility of contributing to an organization like ABC Corporation that offers stability and opportunity is very appealing to me.

I have corrected the omission in my resume and enclosed an updated version for your reference. If I can provide any additional information, please let me know.

I sincerely appreciate every consideration you can give me for a position on your sales team. I feel strongly that I will be an asset to your staff and a valuable addition to your organization. I look forward to meeting you in person and continuing the interview process next week.

Sincerely,

Jane Swift

Jane Swift

JS
enclosure

Power Phrases

Consider using adaptations of these key phrases in your follow-up letters after face-to-face meetings.

Thank you for meeting with me this morning. Our associate _____ assured me that a meeting with you would be productive, and it was. I sincerely appreciate your counsel, insight, and advice.

I have attached my resume for your review. I would appreciate any feedback you may have regarding effectiveness and strength. I understand you may not have any searches under way that would be suitable for me at this time, but I would appreciate any future considerations.

Please consider any associates, customers, or friends who may have contacts who would be useful for me to meet with. I have learned how important "networking" is and will really appreciate some assistance from a professional like you.

Thanks again, _____, and please let me know if I can be of service to you. I wish you and your colleagues continued success and look forward to a business relationship in the future.

In addition to experiencing a very enjoyable and informative interview, I came away very enthusiastic about the position you are seeking to fill.

I hope _____'s consideration of candidates will result in our being together again soon.

During my drive home I savored the possibility of working for _____ in the _____ area, and I must say it was an extremely pleasing thought.

I look forward to meeting with you again and hope our discussion will precede a long-term working relationship.

I am looking forward to meeting _____ on August— at 10:00 A.M., at which time I will convince her of my abilities and prove I am the most qualified person for the position.

It was a pleasure meeting with you last week in your office. I appreciate the time you spent with me, as well as the valuable information you offered.

I hope you will take a few moments to review my resume and place it in your files for future reference. I will telephone your office next week to discuss my situation further.

Gone but not forgotten …

Thank you for our time together this afternoon. What I lack in specific experience in your business I more than make up for with my people power and my proven record of achievement, energy, and just pure tenacity.

Given the opportunity, I can succeed in your office. That makes you and me both successes. Is that worth the investment in training me?

I would like to take this opportunity to thank you for the interview this morning, and to express my strong interest in the position with _____.

I would welcome the opportunity to apply and to further develop my talents within your company.

Through my conversations with you and Mr. _____, I felt that the company provides exactly the type of career opportunity that I am seeking, and I am confident that I will prove to be an asset to your organization.

I trust our meeting this morning helped you further define the position. First and foremost, however, I hope that you came away from our meeting with a vision that includes my filling one of the many offices in _____. I certainly did.

I would like to take this opportunity to thank you for the interview on Thursday morning. I was very impressed with the operation, and I am enthusiastic about the prospects of joining your team.

Since we spent so much time discussing the subject, I have enclosed …

I look forward to hearing from you again to further discuss the position. Through my conversations with you and _____, I felt …

After reviewing your comments about the job requirements, I am convinced that I can make an immediate contribution toward the growth and profitability of _____.

Since you are going to reach a decision quickly, I would like to mention the following points, which I feel qualify me for the job we discussed:

The position in the _____ area is very attractive to me.

The interview confirmed that I want this career opportunity. Specifically, I want to work in the _____ department for you and _____. That is the simplest way to say it. I will call you this week to see what the next step is in the process.

Again, thank you for your time and interest.

It was indeed a pleasure to meet with you after working with you by telephone several years ago.

Thank you for taking time out of your busy schedule to meet with me on Tuesday, December —, 20—. I left the interview with an extremely favorable impression of your company.

I would like to take this opportunity to thank you for the interview on Friday morning, and to confirm my strong interest in the _____ position.

A career opportunity with _____ Corporation is particularly appealing because of its solid reputation and track record in research and development. I am confident that the training program and continued sales support will provide me with the background that I need to succeed in a _____ career.

I look forward to discussing my background and the position with you in greater detail.

I want to take this opportunity to thank you for the interview on Tuesday afternoon, and to confirm my strong interest in the position of _____ with XYZ Health Care Agency.

From our conversation, I feel confident in my ability to reach and exceed your expectations.

I am looking forward to spending a day in the field with a _____ representative. I will telephone you later this week to set up an appointment for my second interview.

Thank you for the time during my visit to _____ yesterday. I enjoyed our conversation at lunch and learned more about personal trust and investment services.

Thank you for your time and interest today. As I indicated, I am very new to this game of searching for employment and it is nice to start this effort on a positive note.

I am eager to hear from you concerning your decision; I know that you have several other candidates to meet with, so I will wait patiently. Good luck to you in your interview process; I know they must be difficult. Again, thank you so much for your time and consideration. I would welcome the opportunity to work for your company.

_____, the visit with you left me feeling positive about the possibility of working for _____. I would appreciate an opportunity to join your staff, and look forward to hearing from you.

"Resurrection" E-mail (Account Executive)

Mr. _____ :

I wanted to thank you for the interview we had on March —th, 20—. The position that was being offered sounds like something I would be interested in. However, I do understand your reasons for not choosing me for the position, and I thank you very much for your honesty.

Perhaps when you are looking for an account executive with five years of experience instead of ten, you will bear me in mind. I am determined to be your choice. I hope the fact that I came in a close second to someone with twice my chronological experience will help you keep me in mind.

I look forward to hearing from you, and thank you again for your time. With your permission I will stay in touch.

Sincerely,

Jane Swift
(516) 555-1212
jswift@careerbrain.com

"Resurrection" E-mail (Programmer)

Dear Ms. _____:

I must have been one of the first people you spoke with about the job posting, because at the time you seemed very interested in me. However, when I called you back, you had received so many calls for the position, you didn't know one from the other. That's understandable, so I hope I can stir your memory and, more importantly, your interest.

When I spoke with you I got the feeling we could both benefit from working together. I am a computer enthusiast, always looking for new applications and ideas to implement on the computer. I have a solid programming and project development background in both the Windows and Macintosh worlds. What's even better is my hobby: my work. I spend countless hours in one way or another doing things which concern computing.

You had asked if I had children and I do: a four-and-a-half-year-old daughter and a four-and-a-half-month-old daughter. You had some ideas for children's software and thought having kids would help when working on such software. My oldest uses _____ on my Macintosh at home and double-clicks away without any assistance from my wife or myself. She has learned a great deal from "playing" with it and is already more computer literate than I ever expected. We need more software like _____ to help stir the minds of our kids.

I have attached a resume for your perusal. But in case you don't want to read all the details, here it is in short:

- I have 6 years programming and development experience in Windows.
- I have 3 years programming and development experience on the Macintosh.
- I am currently the Senior Developer for Macintosh programming here at _____ Corp.

I look forward to speaking with you again, so please don't hesitate to call me, either at home (516-555-1212) or at work (516-555-1213) anytime.

Regards,

James Sharpe
(516) 555-1212
jsharpe@careerbrain.com

"Resurrection" E-mail (Product Manager)

Dear Ms. _____ :

Four months ago you and I discussed an opportunity at Active Products, and you were kind enough to set up meetings with _____ and _____ . Shortly thereafter, as you know, I accepted a position with _____ , where I am now.

For reasons I will go into when we meet, I would like to reopen our discussions. If you think such a conversation would be mutually beneficial. I hope we can get together. I'll call next week to see when you have a half hour or so of free time.

Sincerely,

James Sharpe
(516) 555-1212
jsharpe@careerbrain.com

"Resurrection" Letter (Wholesale Market Manager)

JANE SWIFT

---

18 Central Park Street, Anytown, NY 14788
(516) 555-1212   jswift@careerbrain.com

(Date)

Phillip _____
(Title)
ABC Corporation
1 Industry Plaza
Anytown, NY 12096

Dear Mr. _____:

I understand from _____ of _____ that the search is continuing for the Wholesale Market Manager position at _____ Bank & Trust. As you continue your search, I would like to ask that you keep in mind the following accomplishments and experiences that I would bring to the job:

1. Maximized relationships and increased balances through the sale of trust and cash management products.
2. Captured largest share of public funds market in _____ within three years and captured a disproportionate market share of insurance companies in _____.
3. Developed cash management and trust products tailored to the needs of my target market.
4. Marketed services through mass mailings and brochures, through planning and conducting industry-specific seminars, and through active participation in target market's industry professional organization.
5. Direct experience in all phases of wholesale commercial banking, including: market segmentation, prospecting, building and maintaining customer relationships, lending, and the sale of non-credit products and services.

Sincerely,

Jane Swift

Jane Swift

JS

P.S. I will call you next week, after you have seen the other candidates, to continue our discussion. In the meantime, please be assured of both my competency and commitment.

"Resurrection" Letter (Construction Manager)

JAMES SHARPE

18 Central Park Street, Anytown, NY 14788
(516) 555-1212   jsharpe@careerbrain.com

(Date)

Alice _____
(Title)
Krieger, Skvetney, Howell
Executive Search Consultants
2426 Foundation Road
Anytown, NY 14788

Dear Ms. _____ :

I am writing to you to follow up on the initial inquiry I wrote to you on July —th, 20—. At that time I forwarded you a cover letter and resume. I am in the construction management and business management fields. Since I have not had a response I can only assume that you do not have any currently active searches that meet my qualifications in process or that my file has been deactivated.

I am still in the market for an executive position that matches my qualifications and abilities. I am open to relocating throughout the United States and overseas. If any positions become available, I would be interested in hearing from you. If you need an updated resume, please write or call me and I would be most happy to forward you any information required.

Sincerely,

James Sharpe

James Sharpe

JS

P.S. I'll call in a couple of days to follow up on this letter.

"Resurrection" Letter (Entry-Level)

JANE SWIFT

18 Central Park Street, Anytown, NY 14788
(516) 555-1212   jswift@careerbrain.com

(Date)

Bob _____
(Title)
Krieger, Skvetney, Howell
Executive Search Consultants
2426 Foundation Road
Anytown, NY 14788

Dear Mr. _____:

I feel I should more thoroughly explain why I am willing to take even an entry-level position considering all my past experience. And that's just it—past experience.

For the past three years I ran my own small business, which, of course, kept me out of the job market. Meanwhile, computers took over the world! Fortunately, since moving here and doing temp jobs, I have gotten hands-on experience in data entry. I have also taken and finished a private course in Microsoft Word. So I guess that makes me computer literate, if not entirely experienced.

Nevertheless, I'm in no position to be proud or disdainful of clerical jobs, as I realize I must start somewhere. Fortunately, I enjoy all facets of office work (even filing), so that would not be a problem. I have enough faith in myself and my ability to learn quickly to know that some form of upper movement would be possible for me ... eventually.

Incidentally, even though I am on a temp job this week and possibly next, I do have an answering machine I check every couple of hours during the day. So please leave a message and I'll return your call soon after.

Thank you, and I look forward to hearing from you. I have enclosed another copy of my resume for you.

Sincerely,

Jane Swift

Jane Swift

JS
enclosure

Power Phrases

Consider using adaptations of these key phrases in your resurrection letters.

I turned down your job, but for reasons I will go into when we meet, I would like to reopen our discussions. If you think such a conversation would be mutually beneficial I hope we can get together. I'll call next week to see when you have a half hour or so of free time.

As you continue your search, I would like to ask that you keep in mind the following accomplishments and experiences that I would bring to the job.

I am still in the market for an executive position that matches my qualifications and abilities. I am open to relocating throughout the United States and overseas. If any positions become available, I would be interested in hearing from you.

I look forward to hearing from you, and thank you again for your time. With your permission I will stay in touch.

I hope I can stir your memory and, more importantly, your interest.

I look forward to speaking with you again, so please don't hesitate to call me either at home or at work anytime.

Nevertheless, I'm in no position to be proud or disdainful of clerical jobs as I realize I must start somewhere. Fortunately, I enjoy all facets of office work (even filing), so that would not be a problem. I have enough faith in myself and my ability to learn quickly to know that some form of upper movement would be possible for me ... eventually.

Incidentally, even though I am on a temp job this week and possibly next, I do have an answering machine I check every couple of hours during the day. So please leave a message and I'll return your call soon after.

Rejection of Offer E-mail (Department Manager)

Dear Ms. _____:

I would like to take this opportunity to thank you for the interview on Thursday morning, and to express my strong interest in future employment with your organization.

While I appreciate very much your offer for the position of Department Manager, I feel that at this stage of my career I am seeking greater challenges and advancement than the Department level is able to provide. Having worked in _____ management for over four years, I am confident that my skills will be best applied in a position with more responsibility and accountability.

As we discussed, I look forward to talking with you again in January about how I might contribute to ABC Corporation in the capacity of Unit Manager.

Sincere regards,

James Sharpe
(516) 555-1212
jsharpe@careerbrain.com

Rejection of Offer Letter (General)

18 Central Park Street, Anytown, NY 14788
(516) 555-1212   jswift@careerbrain.com

JANE SWIFT

(Date)

Phillip _____
(Title)
ABC Corporation
1 Industry Plaza
Anytown, NY 12096

Dear Mr. _____:

It was indeed a pleasure meeting with you and your staff to discuss your needs for a _____.
Our time together was most enjoyable and informative.

As we have discussed during our meetings, I believe a purpose of preliminary interviews is to
explore areas of mutual interest and to assess the fit between the individual and the position.
After careful consideration, I have decided to withdraw from consideration for the position.

My decision is based upon the fact that I have accepted a position elsewhere that is very suited to
my qualifications and experiences.

I want to thank you for interviewing me and giving me the opportunity to learn more about your
facility. You have a fine team, and I would have enjoyed working with you.

Best wishes to you and your staff.

Sincerely,

Jane Swift

Jane Swift

JS

Power Phrases

Consider using adaptations of these key phrases in your rejection of offer letters.

It was indeed a pleasure meeting with you and your staff to discuss your needs for a _____.

Our time together was most enjoyable and informative.

After careful consideration, I decided to withdraw from consideration for the position.

As we discussed, I look forward to talking with you again in _____ about how I might contribute to _____ in the capacity of _____.

Acceptance E-mail (General)

Dear Mr. _____:

I would like to express my appreciation for your letter offering me the position of _____ in your _____ Department at a starting salary of $53,000 per year.

I was very impressed with the personnel and facilities at your company in Dallas and am writing to confirm my acceptance of your offer. If it is acceptable with you I will report to work on November 20, 20—.

Let me once again express my appreciation for your offer and my excitement about joining your engineering staff. I look forward to my association with ABC Corporation and feel my contributions will be in line with your goals of growth and continued success for the company.

Sincerely,

James Sharpe
(516) 555-1212
jsharpe@careerbrain.com

Acceptance Letter (Executive Assistant)

18 Central Park Street, Anytown, NY 14788
(516) 555-1212   jswift@careerbrain.com

JANE SWIFT

(Date)

Phillip _____
(Title)
ABC Corporation
1 Industry Plaza
Anytown, NY 12096

Dear Mr. _____:

I am delighted to confirm my acceptance of the Executive Assistant position for Ichabod Crane, Senior Vice President of Marketing, at ABC Corporation. In reviewing our agreement, I will attend a 2-day orientation program at the Human Resources Complex, then begin my employment at the corporate headquarters on Monday, June 5.

In speaking with your assistant, I understand that ABC Corporation has an extensive health and insurance benefits program as well as a 401(k) company match plan. As we agreed, my compensation will be $112,000 annually, complemented by $5,000 in dedicated training funds, and will provide for 3 weeks of vacation leave each year.

I have spoken with Mr. Jameson on several occasions since our initial meeting, and I am more excited than ever to join the ABC Corporation team.

I look forward to seeing you again next week to finalize the paperwork.

Sincerely,

Jane Swift
Jane Swift

JS
enclosure

Acceptance Letter (Vice President)

JAMES SHARPE

18 Central Park Street, Anytown, NY 14788
(516) 555-1212   jsharpe@careerbrain.com

(Date)

Emily _____
(Title)
ABC Corporation
1 Industry Plaza
Anytown, NY 12096

Dear Ms. _____:

This letter will serve as my formal acceptance of your offer to join your firm as Vice President of _____. I understand and accept the conditions of employment which you explained in your recent letter.

I will contact your personnel department this week to request any paperwork I might complete for their records prior to my starting date. Also, I will schedule a physical examination for insurance purposes. I would appreciate your forwarding any reading material you feel might hasten my initiation into the affairs of _____.

Yesterday I tendered my resignation at _____ and worked out a mutually acceptable notice time of four weeks, which should allow me ample time to finalize my business and personal affairs here, relocate my family, and be ready for work at _____ on schedule.

You, your board, and your staff have been most professional and helpful throughout this hiring process. I anxiously anticipate joining the ABC team and look forward to many new challenges. Thank you for your confidence and support.

Yours truly,

James Sharpe

James Sharpe

JS

Power Phrases

Consider using adaptations of these key phrases in your acceptance letters.

I am delighted to accept _____'s generous offer to become their _____. All of the terms in your letter of October 13th are amenable to me.

My resignation was submitted to the appropriate managers at _____ this morning, but we are still working out the terms of my departure.

I am eagerly anticipating starting my new position, particularly at a firm with _____'s reputation. During the interim, I will stay in direct contact with _____ to assure a smooth initiation at _____. Thank you again for this opportunity.

We are still working out the terms of my departure from _____, but it is safe to say that I will report to _____ no later than November —th. It should be possible to confirm a starting date early tomorrow morning. I will telephone you directly when my erstwhile managers and I have a departure schedule completed.

_____ has scheduled my pre-employment physical for _____, and I do not expect any problems to arise. I have found several possible housing alternatives that I will be investigating and I do not expect any problems here, either.

I appreciate the confidence you demonstrated by selecting me to be _____.

I am confident that you made an excellent choice.

I feel that I can achieve excellent results for your firm, and I am looking forward to working with you. I am also anxious to get to know you and your corporation better.

This letter will serve as my formal acceptance of your offer to join _____. I understand and accept the conditions of employment that you explained in your recent letter.

I will contact your personnel department this week to request any paperwork I might complete for their records prior to my starting date. Also, I will schedule a physical examination for insurance purposes. I would appreciate your forwarding any reading material you feel might hasten my initiation into the affairs of _____.

Yesterday I tendered my resignation at _____ and worked out a mutually acceptable notice time of four weeks, which should allow me ample time to finalize my business and personal affairs here, relocate my family, and be ready for work at _____ on schedule.

You, your board, and your staff have been most professional and helpful throughout this hiring process. I anxiously anticipate joining the _____ team and look forward to many new challenges. Thank you for your confidence and support.

I look forward to making a contribution as part of your team.

I look forward to the challenges and responsibility of working in this position.

Resignation E-mail (General)

Dear Mr. _____:

This letter is to notify you that I am resigning my position with ABC Corporation effective Saturday, March 26, 2000.

I have enjoyed my work here very much and want to thank you and the rest of the MIS Department for all the encouragement and support you have always given me. In order to achieve the career goals that I've set for myself, I am accepting a higher level Systems Operator position with another company. This position will give me an opportunity to become more involved in the technical aspects of setting up networking systems.

Please know that I am available to help with any staff training or offer assistance in any way that will make my departure as easy as possible for the department. I want to wish everyone the best of luck for the future.

Sincerely,

James Sharpe
(516) 555-1212
jsharpe@careerbrain.com

Resignation Letter (Sales Representative)

JAMES SHARPE

18 Central Park Street ◆ Anytown, NY 14788
(516) 555-1212 jsharpe@careerbrain.com

(Date)

Phillip _____
(Title)
ABC Corporation
1 Industry Plaza
Anytown, NY 12096

Dear Mr. _____:

Please accept my resignation of my position as Sales Representative in the _____ area, effective January —, 20—. I am offering two weeks' notice so that my territory can be effectively serviced during the transition, with the least amount of inconvenience to our clients.

While I have enjoyed very much working under your direction, I find now that I have an opportunity to further develop my career in areas that are more in line with my long-term goals. I thank you for the sales training that I have received under your supervision. It is largely due to the excellent experience I gained working for ABC Corporation that I am now able to pursue this growth opportunity.

During the next two weeks, I am willing to help you in any way to make the transition as smooth as possible. This includes assisting in recruiting and training my replacement in the _____ territory. Please let me know if there is anything specific that you would like me to do.

Again, it has been a pleasure working as a part of your group.

Best regards,

James Sharpe

James Sharpe

JS

Resignation Letter (Vice President)

18 Central Park Street, Anytown, NY 14788
(516) 555-1212   jswift@careerbrain.com

JANE SWIFT

(Date)

Emily _____
(Title)
ABC Corporation
1 Industry Plaza
Anytown, NY 12096

Dear Ms. _____:

As of this date, I am formally extending my resignation as _____. I have accepted a position as Vice President of _____ at a university medical center in _____.

My decision to leave ABC Corporation was made after long and careful consideration of all factors affecting the institution, my family, and my career. Although I regret leaving many friends here, I feel that the change will be beneficial to all parties. My subordinate staff is readily able to handle the institution's operations until you find a suitable replacement. I intend to finalize my business and personal affairs here over the next several weeks and will discuss a mutually acceptable termination date with you in person.

Finally, I can only express my sincere appreciation to you and the entire board for all your support, cooperation, and encouragement over the past several years. I will always remember my stay at ABC Corporation for the personal growth it afforded and for the numerous friendships engendered.

Yours truly,

Jane Swift

Jane Swift

JS

Power Phrases

Consider using adaptations of these key phrases in your resignation letters.

I am offering two weeks' notice so that my territory can be effectively serviced during the transition, with the least amount of inconvenience to our clients.

While I have enjoyed very much working under your direction, I find now that I have an opportunity to further develop my career in areas that are more in line with my long-term goals. I thank you for the sales training that I have received under your supervision. It is largely due to the excellent experience I gained working for ABC Corporation that I am now able to pursue this growth opportunity.

During the next two weeks, I am willing to help you in any way to make the transition as smooth as possible. This includes assisting in recruiting and training my replacement in the _____ territory. Please let me know if there is anything specific that you would like me to do.

Again, it has been a pleasure working as a part of your sales force.

I have thoroughly enjoyed the work environment and professional atmosphere at _____. Your guidance and counseling have been the source of great personal and career satisfaction, and I am grateful.

These _____ years have made a considerable contribution to my career and professional development and I hope that I have likewise contributed during this time to the growth and development of ABC Corporation. I am grateful for the kind of associates I have had the opportunity to work with and the substantial support I have consistently received from management.

Thank-you E-mail (after hire) (Software Manager)

Dear Ms. _____:

I am happy to inform you that I received and accepted an offer of employment just after Thanksgiving. I am now employed by the _____ Corporation.

I would also like to thank you for all your help the past several months not only in my search for employment but also by your understanding and friendly words of encouragement.

My duties include responsibility of all Dun & Bradstreet software (General Ledger, Accounts Payable, Accounts Receivable, and Fixed Assets) for _____ worldwide plus the first-year training of several entry-level employees.

I am enjoying my new responsibility and being fully employed again, although at times I feel overwhelmed with all I have to learn.

If there is ever anything I can do for you please call me. I hope you and your family have a wonderful holiday season and much luck and happiness in the new year.

Sincerely,

James Sharpe
(516) 555-1212
jsharpe@careerbrain.com

Thank-you Letter (after hire) (General)

JAMES SHARPE

18 Central Park Street ◆ Anytown, NY 14788
(516) 555-1212 jsharpe@careerbrain.com

(Date)

Phillip _____
(Title)
ABC Corporation
1 Industry Plaza
Anytown, NY 12096

Dear Mr. _____:

I want you to be among the first to know that my job search has come to a very successful conclusion. I have accepted the position of _____ Director at _____, Inc. located in _____.

I appreciate all the help and support you have provided over the last several months. It has made the job search process much easier for me. I look forward to staying in contact with you. Please let me know if I can be of any assistance to you in the future. Thank you.

Sincerely,

James Sharpe

James Sharpe

JS

Power Phrases

Consider using adaptations of these key phrases in your thank-you letters.

I am writing not only to share this good news with you but most importantly to thank you for your efforts on my behalf. If there is ever anything that I can do for you, please do not hesitate to call on me.

Thank you for all your help. I have accepted a position as a _____ for _____.

I want you to be among the first to know that my job search has come to a very successful conclusion.

I appreciate all the help and support you have provided over the last several months. It has made the job search process much easier for me. I look forward to staying in contact with you. Please let me know if I can be of any assistance to you in the future.

I would like to extend my sincere thanks to you for your kind help and encouragement during my job search. If I can be of any assistance to you in the future, please do not hesitate to contact me. I was often reminded during the past few months that we too easily lose contact with old friends. Let's try to stay in touch.

If you ever get a chance to visit _____, on business or pleasure, please be sure to let me know.

If there is ever anything I can do for you please call me. I hope you and your family have a wonderful holiday season and much luck and happiness in the new year.

Just a quick note to bring you up-to-date with what I am doing.

Appendices

How to Jump-Start a Stalled Job Search

A short course on getting your job search back on track.

Jerry has been out of work now for a year. His severance package was really lousy—a week for every year of service, which amounted to seven weeks for him. The house, two cars, and three kids should have provided enough pressure to get Jerry's butt in gear, but they didn't.

Jerry told me that no one was calling him. No one would return his calls. It was a bad time of year, he would say, or his contacts were all stale. Often, he would just express amazement and bewilderment as to how he could be in such a predicament.

There was no mystery here. He wasn't getting calls because he wasn't making calls in the right way. When he did dial a headhunter or a personnel department, his tone was so negative and unappealing that he rarely got through the first screen. He was mailing out resumes, but just a handful each week, and he didn't even follow up on these. Jerry was scared and frightened of the search process, and the financial pressures made him so anxious that he wasn't able to do what he needed to do to land a job. Jerry became terrified by what he saw as his failure.

For Bob, the story is different. He has a job. It's not yet nine o'clock, but Bob is already complaining about what a lousy place this is to work. His boss is a moron—can you believe what he did last week? The pay is low, the benefits poor, and the cafeteria serves inedible garbage. He winds up with, "I've got to get out of here." You'd figure that good old Bob is mounting a huge job search campaign, and that he's got one foot out the door. You'd figure wrong. Bob's not going anywhere, at least not under his own steam.

He is frightened of making an effort, taking the plunge, and then finding that he can't make the grade. So, instead, he hides out in a dead-end job, with a going-nowhere company, letting his fears conquer the soul of his work life. Bob and Jerry have both allowed their fear to stall their job search.

For Bob and Jerry, or for you, if your job search is stalled, there is hope—if you are prepared to take very small but very important steps to change your work-life situation. One thing you should do is to write down all of your thoughts about yourself, your career, and your job situation. All of them. Just put it down on paper; don't edit anything. Then read them aloud. First to yourself, and then to a trusted friend or colleague. Ask for feedback. Ask the other person to tell you whether they agree and disagree with what you've written. Start to understand your negative thoughts and begin to discover who you *really* are.

When Failure Feels Like Forever

Fear of failure is so hateful to us, so threatening, that we'll do whatever we possibly can to avoid it. As bad as your job situation is right now, your fear of failure is even worse. So you stall, you procrastinate, and you point the finger of blame, but don't see the other three fingers pointing right back at you.

You can tell me that you are actually doing everything you can to get a job—everything you can imagine. You can be working like the devil on a search, but doing all of the wrong things. You might tell yourself and the world that, yes, you are trying to get a job. But in your heart of hearts, you may have doubts about the way you are going about it. Don't feel distraught; lots of people feel the same way. Job hunting and career management are not skills you were taught in school or anywhere else.

Evaluate your search. Are you being realistic? Are you working intelligently at your job search? Are you really doing all of the right things, or are you rationalizing doing what is comfortable? Or are you avoiding failure by making dumb decisions and then hiding behind them?

If your job search seems hopeless, try to understand what you get out of *not* doing what it takes to get a good job. How do you feel when that rejection letter comes? Do friends or relatives pester you by asking how the search is going, or whether you got the job? If you have to tell them that no, you didn't get the job, do you feel like a failure?

However, if you are stalling about getting your search in gear, think about what that will get you. What are you getting out of not looking for a job? Are you avoiding the rejection that is a big part of every job search? Are you escaping from the many *nos* you will have to hear before you hear *yes* from the lips of an employer?

If you are engaged in a genuine job hunt, I can guarantee that you will fail along the way. I hope that you will fail many, many times. If you don't, then you're not looking hard enough. Every job search involves failure and rejection. If you are networking, making phone calls, doing your research, sending out resumes, interviewing with prospective employers, and responding to ads, then you are creating hundreds of chances for rejection, hundreds of opportunities to hear the word *no*. This rejection must happen if you want to get out of your present situation! I can't tell you that it's a lot of fun to get rejection letters, or to have people hang up on you. It's never an enjoyable thing. It is a fact of life, and you can develop the ability you need to overcome rejection.

Lock and Load

Okay. You've been out of work for a while. You're low on ideas, and your gas tank reads "empty." You don't know which way to turn. The things you've done so far just haven't panned out. It's time to take it from the top.

Believe it or not, you can start over again, and you have certain advantages in doing so. At least some of the people who screened you out so many months ago have, in all likelihood, moved on to another place (hopefully a hot and fetid one in the hereafter). Sure, most of the jobs you applied for have been filled, but a whole new batch has now opened up. And, if there were ill economic winds blowing through an industry you took a fancy to, perhaps things are looking up for some of the companies on your list.

With a few adjustments here and there, and a bit more attention to a few points, you can rescue a faltering job search campaign, and get yourself back to work.

Getting Unstuck

If you are stuck, if your search is not working well, it's time to try things that may have seemed unnecessary or gimmicky earlier in your search. It's time to get unstuck—by any means necessary:

- Send copies of your job search activity schedule, including lists of companies to call, numbers of resumes to be sent out each week, etc., to two or three colleagues or friends. Have them call you on key dates to check up on you. Don't say you don't need supervision, and don't worry if it's embarrassing. Chances are, you do need help, and chances are, your friends would love to have a concrete way to help you. This is the time to put peer pressure and shame to work for you. If your friends can't help you, join a local job hunting group; your peers can help you, and you can help your peers.

- Reward yourself for progress in your search. Keep an account of your activities. When you reach a target (say 25 resumes sent out this week, and 25 follow-up calls made on the 25 resumes you sent out last week), then you can cash them in for a fun activity. At this point, that fun activity may be a morning of not having to do something you hate to do, like making follow-up calls on resumes.

- Don't get overwhelmed by irrelevant details. Create a personal "parking lot" for nonessential activities. A good meeting facilitator puts up a piece of paper in the front of the meeting room. When someone makes a comment that is off the topic, the facilitator writes it down on that paper, called the parking lot. If there's time, or if the topic comes up again, the idea is pulled out of the parking lot for general discussion. The meeting stays focused, and the person with the idea hasn't forgotten about it. Don't throw out your nonessential ideas. Don't rip up that encyclopedia-sized to-do list: Park it instead. When you have time, after you achieve your most essential objectives, visit the lot and take an old idea out for a spin.

- Break up major tasks into small steps. Don't write "find a job" on your to-do list. Instead, make a list of the many steps you need to find a job, using this book. As you complete each step, check it off. Save the checked-off list so that you can see yourself making progress toward your goal.

Sometimes, being a procrastinator is due to not knowing any better. There are many books and courses on priority management. They can help you give some order to your to-do list, and help you avoid the feeling of being overwhelmed. Managing priorities is a very learnable behavior!

Get a New Resume

White collar or blue collar, executive vice president or electrician, you should throw out whatever you've got and start over from scratch, because the current version obviously isn't working.

Write at least two new drafts. One should be in chronological format; the other should be in either functional or combination format. I recommend that you complete the detailed questionnaire in the first part of my book *Resumes That Knock 'em Dead*. This will help you evaluate exactly what you have to offer potential employers.

Don't pooh-pooh the idea of rewriting your resume by claiming that getting your foot in the door hasn't been the problem. It is entirely possible that your resume is strong enough to get you in the race, but doesn't pack enough punch to push you over the finish line. Your resume must get your foot in the door, set the tone for the interview, and, after all the interviewing is done, act as your last and most powerful advocate when the final hiring decision is being made. Build one from ground up that does this.

Rewrite Your Cover Letter

Adhering to a single, bland, "one-size-fits-all" cover letter is a common mistake. Remember, different circumstances require different letters.

I would advise you to make a commitment to send follow-up letters with religious zeal, if you are not already doing so. This may seem like a minor detail, but it is one of the most important—and easiest—ways for you to stand out from the competition.

When it comes to cover and follow-up letters, the whole really is greater than the sum of its parts. Employers maintain dossiers on every candidate during the selection process; your coordinated written campaign makes you stand out from the other contenders as someone who pays a little bit more attention to detail and who goes a little further to get the job done. Don't worry about sending your new resume to companies you've already contacted. A new resume means a new you.

Work As a Temporary

Get hold of a temporary employment directory or check the Yellow Pages for temporary agencies. Contact every appropriate temporary-help agency listed for your area, and offer your services.

There are two benefits to working with a temporary-help agency. First, while you can retain time to pursue a structured job hunt, you also get some work and a paycheck—thereby keeping your skills current and, just as important, the wolf from the door. Second, you may be able to upgrade that temporary job into a full-time position. (At the very least, you can expand your contact network.)

Today, there are temporary agencies that represent professionals at virtually all levels. Some even specialize solely in management people, and high-level ones at that, because companies are increasingly inclined to "test-drive" executives before making a permanent commitment to them. Interim Management Corporation (IMCOR) is typical of this new breed of temporary agency; almost 40 percent of its assignments result in full-time employment.

Check Your References and Credit Rating

Do it now. Don't let a mystery problem sabotage an offer at the last moment. You'd be surprised how many otherwise qualified candidates eventually learn that they were taken out of the running by flunking the "tie breaker" test. Two or more people are under final consideration; management decides to run a credit check and/or call references to help them decide who will get the job. If you have not attended to these areas, you should. Credit problems can undo months of preparation on your part; mediocre (or worse) references can be just as problematic.

Widen the Scope of Your Job Search

Under what other job titles could you work? Can you commute an extra twenty minutes for the right job? Consider relocation to another city, but bear in mind that, for most of us, this is an extremely costly proposition and that you should not depend on a firm's picking up your moving expenses. On the other hand, if you are single and can fit all your earthly possessions in the back seat of your Neon, some far-flung operation may be worth serious consideration.

Smokestack

This used to mean keeping an eye out for smokestacks over the course of the day, in order to find companies that might be hiring. Today, it more commonly means remembering to incorporate job hunting as part of your daily routine. Stop in and see what firms are in that office building you pass every morning. Perhaps there are opportunities there for you.

Of course, you are not going to get far by simply appearing at the reception desk and demanding an interview. Be a little more circumspect. Ask—politely—about the firm in question. What does it do? Who is in charge of hiring? Are there any circulars, advertisements, or company reports you can take home with you? After your initial visit, you can incorporate this information into a new research file for the company, and add the firm to your database of leads.

This, by the way, is the job hunting technique I personally loathe more than any other; but it was also the technique that landed the job that—22 years later—has obviously given me a buoyant career. The fact that you don't like a particular job hunting technique doesn't mean it won't work for you.

Body Check

If you find yourself running into brick walls on the job search front, it's a good idea to look at the most important points more thoroughly. Remember, one's personal friends often have trouble bringing up this subject; people in a position to hire simply move on to the next applicant.

If you do not brush and floss regularly, and have bad breath, this will not aid your candidacy. If you eat a lot of spicy foods (onions, garlic, cilantro), you may be aware of the importance of keeping your breath fresh after a pungent meal but this is not, alas, your only worry. These foods typically sour your sweat and taint your clothing. Change your diet and have your interview clothes cleaned before every wearing. (But note that polyester and other synthetic fabrics are notorious for retaining body odors even after cleaning—one of many reasons to avoid them.)

Have you put on a few pounds while looking for work? Many people use eating as a response to stress. Turn off the TV once a day and get some exercise; Nick at Nite will still be there after you work out. Couch potatoes don't make good candidates—period. Regular physical activity will improve your appearance *and* your mindset, so don't skip it.

These suggestions may be difficult for you to implement if they run counter to long-established patterns, but being in a permanent job search mode is, you must admit, a much more daunting prospect than change. If you need motivation, recall the statistical truth that overweight and malodorous people are always the last to get hired or promoted.

Prepare, Prepare, Prepare

It may seem obvious, but all too often, this is the step that people take for granted. When you walk into the interview, you should be ready to answer all the questions you could ever be asked, as well as all the ones you couldn't. *Don't* make the mistake of preparing only for the questions you want to hear!

Follow Up

I worked for some years as a headhunter and corporate personnel director. I can't count the number of times managers told me that there was really nothing to distinguish Candidate A (who got the job) from Candidate B (who didn't)—*except that Candidate A showed an unusual level of determination and attention to detail.* The way Candidate A conveyed this, of course, was usually through a dogged follow-up campaign.

Stepping Stone Jobs

Even though this has been touched on earlier in this book, it bears repeating in this context. If you have been unemployed for a significant period of time, you might find it fiscally prudent to accept that less-than-perfect job. That's okay. By the same token, there is a big difference between settling for less than your dreams and making the wrong job your life's work. If circumstances force you to take a temporary detour from your ultimate career goal, give an honest day's work for an honest day's pay, and continue to pursue other opportunities.

Remember: You're the Most Important Part of This

Maintain ongoing motivational input. Reading this book and its two companion books, *Knock 'em Dead* and *Resumes That Knock 'em Dead* is a good start. You should also consider going online or visiting the library to check out motivational tapes and related materials. You're worth it.

You are not a loser; you got blind-sided. The trick is to get back in the saddle. If you climb up and grip the reins, tomorrow you'll see all kinds of opportunities you didn't see before. You can get back on track, and you can get back to work.

APPENDIX B | Resources

HEALTH CARE

Publications

Hospital Phone Book
U.S. Directory Service, Miami, FL
Provides information on over 7,940
government and private hospitals
in the U.S.

*National Association of County Health
Officials Sustaining Membership Directory*
National Association of County Health
Officials, Washington, DC
Lists national health officials for almost
every county in the U.S. Published
annually. $10. Call 202-783-5550 for
more information.

National Jobs in Dietetics
Jobs in Dietetics, Santa Monica, CA
Lists jobs nationwide in the field of
dietetics. Published monthly; an annual
subscription is $84. Call 310-453-5375
for more information.

U.S. Medical Directory
U.S. Directory Service, Miami, FL
Over one thousand pages of information
on doctors, hospitals, nursing facilities,
medical laboratories, and medical
libraries.

Associations

HEALTH CARE ADMINISTRATION

American Association of Medical
Assistants
20 North Wacker Drive, Suite 1575
Chicago, IL 60606-2903;
tel: 312-899-1500

American College of Healthcare
Executives
1 North Franklin, Suite 1700
Chicago, IL 60606-3491; tel: 312-424-2800

American Health Information
Management Association
919 North Michigan Avenue
Chicago, IL 60611; tel: 312-787-2672

American Health Care Association
1201 L Street NW
Washington, DC 20005;
tel: 202-842-4444

American Medical Technologists
710 Higgins Road
Park Ridge, IL 60068; tel: 708-823-5169

Healthcare Financial Management
Association
Two Westbrook Corporate Center,
Suite 700
Westchester, IL 60154;
tel: 708-531-9600

National Association of Emergency
Medical Technicians
102 West Leake Street
Clinton, MS 39056; tel: 601-924-7747

Nuclear Medicine Technology Certification
Board
2970 Clairmont Road, Suite 610
Atlanta, GA 30329-1634;
tel: 404-315-1739

NURSING

American Association of Nurse
Anesthetists
222 South Prospect Avenue
Park Ridge, IL 60068-4001;
tel: 708-692-7050

American Association of Occupational
Health Nurses
50 Lenox Pointe
Atlanta, GA 30324; tel: 404-262-1162 or
800-241-8014

American Hospital Association
1 North Franklin
Chicago, IL 60606; tel: 312-422-3000

American Nurses Association
600 Maryland Avenue SW, Suite 100 W
Washington, DC 20024-2571;
tel: 202-651-7000

Medical Economics Publishing
5 Paragon Drive
Montvale, NJ 07645-1742;
tel: 201-358-7200

National Association for Home Care
519 C Street NE
Washington, DC 20002;
tel: 202-547-7424
(send SASE for general information)

National Association for Practical Nurse
Education and Service
1400 Spring Street, Suite 310
Silver Spring, MD 20910;
tel: 301-588-2491

National Association of Pediatric Nurse
Associates and Practitioners
1101 Kings Highway N, Suite 206
Cherry Hill, NJ 08034-1921;
tel: 609-667-1773

National Federation of Licensed Practical
Nurses
1418 Aversboro Road
Garner, NC 27529-4547;
tel: 919-779-0046

National League for Nursing
Communications Department
350 Hudson Street
New York, NY 10014;
tel: 212-989-9393

National Rehabilitation Association
633 South Washington Street
Alexandria, VA 22314;
tel: 703-836-0850

PHYSICAL HEALTH

Accreditation Council for Graduate
Medical Education
515 North State Street, Suite 2000
Chicago, IL 60610; tel: 312-464-4920

American Association for
Respiratory Care
11030 Ables Lane
Dallas, TX 75229-4593;
tel: 214-243-2272

American Association of Colleges of
Pediatric Medicine
1350 Piccard Drive, Suite 322
Rockville, MD 20850;
tel: 301-990-7400

American Board of Preventive Medicine
9950 West Lawrence Avenue, Suite 106
Schiller Park, IL 60176;
tel: 847-671-1750

American Medical Association
515 North State Street
Chicago, IL 60610; tel: 312-464-5000

American Occupational Therapy
Association
4720 Montgomery Lane, P.O. Box 31220
Bethesda, MD 20824-1220;
tel: 301-652-2682

American Physical Therapy Association
1111 North Fairfax Street
Alexandria, VA 22314;
tel: 703-684-2782 or 800-999-2782

American Podiatric Medical Association
9312 Old Georgetown Road
Bethesda, MD 20814-1621;
tel: 301-571-9200

American Society of Radiology
Technologists
15000 Central Avenue SE
Albuquerque, NM 87123-4605;
tel: 505-298-4500

Society of Diagnostic Medical
Sonographers
12770 Coit Road, Suite 508
Dallas, TX 75251; tel: 214-239-7367

DENTISTRY

American Association of Dental Assistants
203 North LaSalle Street, Suite 132
Chicago, IL 60601-1225;
tel: 312-541-1550

American Association of Dental Schools
1625 Massachusetts Avenue NW
Washington, DC 20036;
tel: 202-667-9433

American Association of Orthodontists
401 North Lindbergh Blvd.
St. Louis, MO 63141-7816;
tel: 314-993-1700

American Dental Association
211 East Chicago Avenue
Chicago, IL 60611; tel: 312-440-2500
(for Commission on Dental Accreditation,
direct correspondence to Suite 3400; for
SELECT Program, direct correspondence
to Department of Career Guidance,
Suite 1804)

American Dental Hygienists Association
Division of Professional Development
444 North Michigan Avenue, Suite 3400
Chicago, IL 60611; tel: 312-440-8900

National Association of Dental
Laboratories
555 East Braddock Road
Alexandria, VA 22305;
tel: 703-683-5263

National Board for Certification in Dental
Technology
555 East Braddock Road
Alexandria, VA 22305;
tel: 703-683-5263

MENTAL HEALTH

American Association for Counseling and
Development
5999 Stevenson Avenue
Alexandria, VA 22304; tel: 703-823-9800

American Association for Marriage and
Family Therapy
11331 5th Street NW, Suite 300
Washington, DC 20005;
tel: 202-452-0109

American Association of Mental
Retardation
444 North Capitol Street, NW, Suite 846
Washington, DC 20001-1512;
tel: 202-387-1968 or 800-424-3688

American Psychiatric Association
1400 K Street NW
Washington, DC 20005;
tel: 202-682-6000

American Psychological Association
750 First Street NE
Washington, DC 20002;
tel: 202-336-5500

National Board for Certified Counselors
3 Terrace Way, Suite D
Greensboro, NC 27403-3660;
tel: 910-547-0607

BIOTECHNOLOGY AND ENVIRONMENTAL TECHNOLOGY

Publications

Corporate Technology Directory
CorpTech, Woburn, MA
Lists over 35,000 businesses and
110,000 executives. Describes products
and services in such fields as automation,
biotechnology, chemicals, computers and
software, defense, energy, environment,
manufacturing equipment, advanced
materials, medical, pharmaceuticals,
photonics, subassemblies and
components, testing and measurements,
telecommunications, and transportation
and holding companies. Published
annually.

CorpTech Fast 5,000 Company Locator
CorpTech, Woburn, MA
Lists over five thousand of the fastest-
growing companies listed in the Corporate
Technology Directory, but includes
addresses and phone numbers, number
of employees, sales, and industries by
state. Published annually.

Directory of Environmental Information
Government Institutes, Rockville, MD
Lists federal and state government
resources, trade organizations, and
professional and scientific newsletters,
magazines, and databases. Published
every other year.

Environmental Telephone Directory
Governmental Institutes, Rockville, MD
Lists detailed information on
governmental agencies that deal with the
environment. The directory also identifies
the environmental aides of U.S. Senators
and Representatives. Published every
other year.

Sales Guide to High-Tech Companies
CorpTech, Woburn, MA
Covers over three thousand company
profiles and twelve thousand executive
contacts. Includes specific details on each
company's products and services.
Published quarterly; a yearly subscription
is $185. Call 617-932-3939 for more
information.

*Transportation Officials and Engineers
Directory*
American Road and Transportation
Builders Association, Washington, DC
Lists over four thousand state
transportation officials and engineers at
local, state, and federal levels. Published
annually.

Associations

Air and Waste Management Association
1 Gateway Center, 3rd Floor
Pittsburgh, PA 15222; tel: 412-232-3444

American Chemical Society
1155 16th Street NW
Washington, DC 20036;
tel: 202-872-4600 or 800-227-5558

American Institute of Biological Sciences
1444 Eye Street NW, Suite 200
Washington, DC 20005;
tel: 202-628-1500

American Institute of Chemists
501 Wythe Street
Alexandria, VA 22314-1917;
tel: 703-836-2090

American Institute of Physics
1 Physics Ellipse
College Park, MD 20740-3843;
tel: 301-209-3100

American Society for Biochemistry and
Molecular Biology
9650 Rockville Pike
Bethesda, MD 20814-3996;
tel: 301-530-7145

American Society for Microbiology
1325 Massachusetts Avenue NW
Washington, DC 20005;
tel: 202-737-3600

American Society of Biological Chemists
9650 Rockville Pike
Bethesda, MD 20814-3996;
tel: 301-530-7145

American Zoo and Aquarium Association
(AZA)
Office of Membership Service
Oglebay Park, Route 88
Wheeling, WV 26003;
tel: 304-242-2160

Association of American Geographers
1710 16th Street NW
Washington, DC 20009-3198;
tel: 202-234-1450

Botanical Society of America
1735 Nell Avenue
Columbus, OH 43210;
tel: 614-292-3519

Center for American Archeology
P.O. Box 366
Kampsville, IL 62053; tel: 618-653-4316

Department of Energy Headquarters
Operations Division
1000 Independence Avenue SW,
Room 4E-090
Washington, DC 20585; tel: 202-586-4333
(hotline for job vacancies, updated every
Friday)

Environmental Protection Agency
Recruitment Center
401 Main Street SW, Room 3634
Washington, DC 20460;
tel: 202-260-2090/3308

Federation of American Societies for
Experimental Biology
9650 Rockville Pike
Bethesda, MD 20814;
tel: 301-530-7000

Genetics Society of America
9650 Rockville Pike
Bethesda, MD 20814-3998;
tel: 301-571-1825

Geological Society of America
3300 Penrose Place, P.O. Box 9140
Boulder, CO 80301; tel: 303-447-2020

National Accrediting Agency for Clinical
Laboratory Sciences
8410 West Bryn Mawr Avenue, Suite 670
Chicago, IL 60631; tel: 312-714-8880

National Solid Wastes Management
Association
4301 Connecticut Avenue NW, Suite 300
Washington, DC 20008;
tel: 202-244-4700

Natural Resource Conservation Service,
Personnel Division
P.O. Box 2980
Washington, DC 20013;
tel: 202-720-4264

ENGINEERING

Associations

American Association of Engineering
Societies
1111 19th Street NW, Suite 608
Washington, DC 20034;
 tel: 202-296-2237

American Chemical Society
1155 16th Street NW
Washington, DC 20036;
tel: 202-872-4600 or 800-227-5558

American Institute of Chemical Engineers
345 East 47th Street
New York, NY 10017;
tel: 212-705-7338 or 800-242-4363

American Society for Engineering
Education
1818 N Street NW, Suite 600
Washington, DC 20036;
tel: 202-331-3500

American Society of Civil Engineers
1801 Alexander Bell Drive
Reston, VA 20191-4400;
tel: 800-548-ASCE

American Society of Mechanical
Engineers (ASME)
345 East 47th Street
New York, NY 10017; tel: 212-705-7722

Institute of Electrical and Electronics
Engineers
345 East 47th Street
New York, NY 10017; tel: 212-705-7900

Institute of Industrial Engineers
25 Technology Park
Atlanta, GA 30092-0460;
tel: 770-449-0460

Society of Manufacturing Engineers (SME)
1 SME Drive, P.O. Box 930
Dearborn, MI 48121; tel: 313-271-1500

INFORMATION TECHNOLOGY

Publications

Access
1900 West 47th Place, Suite 215
Shawnee Mission, KS 66205;
tel: 800-362-0681
(initial six-month nonmember listing,
$15; each additional three months, $15;
initial six-month listing for members of
the Data Processing Management
Association, $10)

AIIM Job Bank Bulletin
Association for Information and Image
Management
1100 Wayne Avenue, Suite 1100
Silver Spring, MD 20910;
tel: 301-587-8202
(four-month subscription: nonmember,
$100; member, $25; issued
semimonthly)

Associations

ASIS Jobline
American Society for Information Science
8720 Georgia Avenue, Suite 501
Silver Spring, MD 20910-3602;
tel: 301-495-0900
(free; monthly)

Association for Computing Machinery
1515 Broadway
New York, NY 10036; tel: 212-869-7440

Association for Systems Management
1433 West Bagley Road, P.O. Box 38370
Cleveland, OH 44138; tel: 216-243-6900

COMPUTERS

Publications

ComputerWorld
500 Old Connecticut Path
Framingham, MA 01701-9171; tel: 508-
879-0700 or 800-343-6474
(annual subscription: U.S., $39.95;
Canada, $110; issued weekly)

ComputerWorld, Campus Edition
500 Old Connecticut Path
Framingham, MA 01701-9171;
tel: 508-879-0700
(annual subscription, $5; free to students;
published each October)

High Technology Careers Magazine
4701 Patrick Henry Drive, Suite 1901
Santa Clara, CA 95054;
tel: 408-970-8800
(six issues per year, $29)

Technical Employment News
P.O. Box 1285
Cedar Park, TX 78613;
tel: 512-250-9023 or 800-678-9724
(weekly subscription, $55; annual
subscription, $88, U.S. and Canada)

Associations

IEEE Computer Society
1730 Massachusetts Avenue NW
Washington, DC 20036;
tel: 202-371-0101
(available to members only)

CU Career Connection
University of Colorado, Campus Box 133
Boulder, CO 80309-0133;
tel: 303-492-4727
(two-month fee for passcode to the job
hotline, $30)

Data Processing Management
Association
505 Busse Highway
Park Ridge, IL 60068; tel: 708-825-8124

Institute for Certification of Computing
Professionals
2200 East Devon Avenue, Suite 247
Des Plaines, IL 60018;
tel: 708-299-4227

Quality Assurance Institute
7575 Philips Boulevard, Suite 350
Orlando, Fl 32819; tel: 407-363-1111

Semiconductor Equipment and Materials
International
805 East Middlefield Road
Mountain View, CA 94043;
tel: 415-964-5111

BUSINESS AND PROFESSIONAL

Publications

The Almanac of American Employers
Corporate Jobs Outlook
Boeme, TX
Lists five hundred of the country's most
successful, large companies; profiles
salary ranges, benefits, financial stability,
and advancement opportunities.

Corporate Jobs Outlook
Corporate Jobs Outlook, Inc., Dallas, TX
Each issue reviews fifteen to twenty
major (five thousand employees or
more) firms. The report rates the firms
and provides information on salaries
and benefits, current and projected
development, where to apply for jobs,
potential layoffs, benefit plans, the
company's record for promoting women
or minorities to executive positions, and
college reimbursement packages. Also

includes personnel contact information for each firm. Published bimonthly; a yearly subscription is $159.99. Call (214) 824-3030. Note: This resource is also available online at www.vinnelljobcorps.org.

Directory of Corporate Affiliations
Reed Reference Publishing Company, New Providence, NJ
Lists key personnel in 4,700 parent companies and forty thousand divisions, subsidiaries, and affiliates. Includes addresses and phone numbers of key executives and decision makers. Published once a year, with quarterly updates. For more information, call 800-323-6772.

Directory of Leading Private Companies
National Register Publishing Company, Wilmette, IL
Profiles over seven thousand U.S. private companies in the service, manufacturing, distribution, retail, and construction fields. Includes companies in such areas as health care, high technology, entertainment, fast-food franchises, leasing, publishing, and communications. Published annually.

Encyclopedia of Associations
Gale Research, Inc., Detroit, MI
Published in three volumes. Volume 1 lists national organizations in the U.S. and includes over twenty-two thousand associations, including hundreds for government professions. Volume 2 provides geographic and executive indexes. Volume 3 features full entries on associations that are not listed in Volume 1. Note: This resource is also available

online through Dialog Information Services at www.dialog.com (or 800-334-2564). Call for more information.

International Directory of Corporate Affiliations
National Register Publishing Company, Wilmette, IL
Lists over fourteen hundred major foreign companies and their thirty thousand U.S. and foreign holdings. Published annually.

The JobBank Series
Adams Media Corporation, Holbrook, MA
A top-notch series of paperback local employment guides. The recent editions profile virtually every local company with over fifty employees in a given metro area. Company listings are arranged by industry for easy use; also included is a section on the region's economic outlook and contact information for local professional associations, executive search firms, and job placement agencies. The series covers twenty-nine major metropolitan areas, including Atlanta, Boston, the Carolinas, Chicago, Dallas/Ft. Worth, Denver, Detroit, Florida, Houston, Los Angeles, Minneapolis/St. Paul, Missouri, New York, Ohio, Philadelphia, Phoenix, San Francisco, Seattle, Tennessee, and Washington, DC. Many listings feature contact names, common positions hired for, educational backgrounds sought, benefits, fax numbers, internship information, staff size, and more. Available at most bookstores. Updated yearly.

National Trade and Professional Associations of the United States
Columbia Books, Washington, DC

Lists information on over sixty-five hundred trade and professional associations. Published annually.

Resume Bank
American Corporate Counsel Association
1225 Connecticut Avenue NW, Suite 302
Washington, DC 20036;
tel: 202-296-4522
(six-month registration: nonmembers, $65; members, $25; complete job-matching application, and five copies of resume free)

FINANCIAL SERVICES

Associations

BANKING

American Bankers Association
1120 Connecticut Avenue NW
Washington, DC 20036;
tel: 202-663-5000

American Institute of Banking
1213 Bakers Way
Manhattan, KS 66502; tel: 913-537-4750

Association of Master of Business
Administration Executives
AMBA Center
South Summit Place
Branford, CT 06405; tel: 203-315-5221

Banking Federation of the European
Economic Community (BFEC)
Federation Bancaire de la Communaute
Europeenne (FBCE)
c/o Umberto Burani
10, rue Montoyer, B-1040
Brussels, Belgium; tel: 32-2-5083711;
fax: 32-2-5112328

Banking Law Institute (BLI)
22 West 21st Street
New York, NY 10010;
tel: 212-645-7880 or 800-332-1105;
fax: 212-675-4883

BANKPAC
(formerly: Bankers Political Action
Committee; Banking Profession Political
Action Committee)
c/o Meg Bonitt
American Bankers Association
1120 Connecticut Avenue NW
Washington, DC 20036;
tel: 202-663-5115/5076
or fax: 202-663-7544

Electronic Banking Economics Society
(EBES)
P.O. Box 2331
New York, NY 10036; tel: 203-295-9788

Savings and Community Bankers of
America Educational Services
Center for Financial Studies
900 19th Street NW, Suite 400
Washington, DC 20006;
tel: 202-857-3100

U.S. Council on International Banking
(USCIB)
1 World Trade Center, Suite 1963
New York, NY 10048;
tel: 212-466-3352; fax: 212-432-0544

Women in Banking and Finance
55 Bourne Vale
Bromley, Kent BR2 7NW, England;
tel: 44-181-4623276

Women's World Banking—USA
8 West 40th Street
New York, NY 10018;
tel: 212-768-8513; fax: 212-768-8519

SECURITIES

Association of Securities and Exchange
Commission Alumni
West Tower, Suite 812
1100 New York Avenue NW
Washington, DC 20005;
tel: 202-408-7600; fax: 202-408-7614

International Securities Market
Association—England
7 Limeharbour
London E14 9NQ, England;
tel: 44-171-538-5656;
fax: 44-171-538-4902

National Association of Securities Dealers
(NASD)
1735 K Street NW
Washington, DC 20006-1506;
tel: 202-728-8000; fax: 202-293-6260

National Association of Securities
Professionals (NASP)
700 13th Street NW, Suite 950
Washington, DC 20005;
tel: 202-434-4535; fax: 202-434-8916

North American Securities Administrators
Association (NASAA)
1 Massachusetts Avenue NW, Suite 310
Washington, DC 20001;
tel: 202-737-0900; fax: 202-783-3571

Securities and Futures Authority
Cottons Centre, Cottons Lane
London SE I 2QB, England;
tel: 44-171-378-9000;
tel: 44-171-403-7569

Securities Industry Association (SIA)
120 Broadway
New York, NY 10271; tel: 212-608-1500;
fax: 212-608-1604

Securities Transfer Association (STA)
55 Exchange Place
New York, NY 10260-0001;
tel: 212-748-8000

Western Pennsylvania Securities
Industry Agency
1 Oxford Centre, 40th Floor
Pittsburgh, PA 15219;
tel: 412-731-7185

ACCOUNTING

Academy of Accounting Historians (AAH)
University of Arkansas, Department of
Accounting
Fayetteville, AR 72701; tel: 501-575-
6125; fax: 501-575-7687

Accounting Aid Society of Detroit (AASD)
719 Griswold, Suite 2026
Detroit, MI 48226; tel: 313-961-1840;
fax: 313-961-6257
E-mail: itpass@igc.apc.org

Affiliation of Independent Accountants
9200 South Dadeland Boulevard,
Suite 510
Miami, FL 33156; tel: 305-670-0580;
fax: 305-670-3818

American Accounting Association
5717 Bessie Drive
Sarasota, FL 34223; tel: 941-921-7747

American Institute of Certified Public
Accountants (AICPA)
1211 Avenue of the Americas
New York, NY 10036-8775;
tel: 212-596-6200 or 800-862-4272 or
fax: 212-596-6213

American Society of Tax Professionals
P.O. Box 1024
Sioux Falls, SD 57101;
tel: 605-335-1185

American Society of Women Accountants
1255 Lynnfield Road, Suite 257
Memphis, TN 38119;
tel: 901-680-0470

American Women's Society of Certified
Public Accountants
401 North Michigan Avenue,
Suite 2200
Chicago, IL 60611; tel: 312-644-6610

Associated Accounting Firms
International (AAFI)
(formerly: Association of Regional CPA
Firms)
1000 Connecticut Avenue, Suite 1006
Washington, DC 20036;
tel: 202-463-7900; fax: 202-296-0741

Associated Regional Accounting Firms
(ARAF)
3700 Crestwood Parkway, Suite 350
Duluth, GA 30136; tel: 770-279-4560;
fax: 770-279-4566

Association for Accounting Administration
(AAA)
136 South Keowee Street
Dayton, OH 45402; tel: 513-222-0030;
fax: 513-2212-5794

Association of Accounting Technicians
(AAT)
154 Clerkenwell Road
London EC I R 5AD, England;
tel: 44-171-837-8600/814-6999;
fax: 44-171-837-6970
E-mail: aatuk@pipex.com

Association of Government Accountants
2200 Mount Vernon Avenue
Alexandria, VA 22301; tel: 703-684-6931

EDP Auditors Association
3701 Algonquin Road, Suite 1010
Rolling Meadows, IL 60008;
tel: 708-253-1545

European Accounting Association (EAA)
European Institute for Advanced Studies
in Management
13 Rue d'Egmont, B-1050
Brussels, Belgium; tel: 32-2-511-9116;
fax: 32-2-512-1929
E-mail: vandyck@ciasm.be

Foundation for Accounting Education
(FAE)
530 Fifth Avenue, 5th Floor
New York, NY 10036; tel: 212-719-8300
or 800-537-3635

Governmental Accounting Standards
Board (GASB)
401 Merrit 7, P.O. Box 5116
Norwalk, CT 06856-5116;
tel: 203-847-0700; fax: 203-849-9714

Information Systems Audit and Control
Association
3701 Algonquin Road, Suite 1010
Rolling Meadows, IL 60008;
tel: 708-253-1545

Institute of Certified Management
Accountants (ICMA)
10 Paragon Drive
Montvale, NJ 07645; tel: 201-573-9000
or 800-638-4427; fax: 201-573-8438

Institute of Internal Auditors
249 Maitland Avenue
Altamonte Springs, FL 32701-4201;
tel: 407-830-7600

Institute of Management Accountants
10 Paragon Drive
Montvale, NJ 07645; tel: 201-573-9000;
fax: 201-573-9000

InterAmerican Accounting Association (IAA)
(formerly: InterAmerican Accounting
Conference)
275 Fontainebleau Boulevard, Suite 245
Miami, Fl 33172; tel: 305-225-1991;
fax: 305-225-2011

National Association of State Boards of
Accountancy
545 Fifth Avenue
New York, NY 10168-0002;
tel: 212-490-3868

National Society for Public Accountants
1010 North Fairfax Street
Alexandria, VA 22314; tel: 703-549-6400

INSURANCE

Publications

Insurance Field Directories
Insurance Field Company
P.O. Box 948
Northbrook, IL 60065; tel: 708-498-4010
($55; published each September)

Insurance Phone Book and Directory
US Directory Service
121 Chanlon Road
New Providence, NJ 07074;
tel: 908-464-6800
($67.95, plus $4.75 shipping)

Associations

ACFE Job Bank
Association of Certified Fraud Examiners
716 West Avenue
Austin, TX 78701; tel: 512-478-9070 or
800-245-3321
(membership fee $75; send two copies
of resume and cover letter indicating
salary requirements and where you are
willing to relocate)

Actual Training Program Directory Society
of Actuaries
475 North Martingale Road, Suite 800
Schaumburg, IL 60173-2226;
tel: 708-706-3500
(free; published each January)

American Academy of Actuaries
1100 17th Street NW, 7th Floor
Washington, DC 20036;
tel: 202-223-8196

American Agents & Brokers
330 North 4th Street
St. Louis, MO 63012;
tel: 314-421-5445

Best's Insurance Reports,
Property/Casualty Edition
A.M. Best Company
Ambest Road
Oldwick, NJ 08858-9988;
tel: 908-439-2200
(annual fee $70)

Independent Insurance Agents of
America
127 South Peyton
Alexandria, VA 22314;
tel: 703-683-4422 or 800-962-7950

Insurance Information Institute
110 William Street
New York, NY 10038;
tel: 212-669-9200

Insurance Institute of America
720 Providence Road
Malvern, PA 19355; tel: 610-644-2100

Life Insurance Marketing and Research
Association
P.O. Box 208
Hartford, CT 16141-0208;
tel: 203-777-7000

National Association of Life Underwriters
1922 F Street NW
Washington, DC 20006;
tel: 202-332-6000

National Association of Professional
Insurance Agents
400 North Washington Street
Alexandria, VA 22314; tel: 703-836-9340

Professional Insurance Agents
400 North Washington Street
Alexandria, VA 22314; tel: 703-836-9340

Society of Actuaries
475 North Martingale Road, Suite 800
Schaumburg, IL 60173-2226;
tel: 708-706-3500

FINANCIAL MANAGEMENT

Associations

American Education Finance Association
(AEFA)
5249 Cape Leyte Drive
Sarasota, FL 34242; tel: 941-349-7580;
fax: 941-349-7580
E-mail: gbabigianc@aol.com

American Finance Association (AFA)
Stern, 44 West 4th Street, Suite 9-190
New York, NY 10012; tel: 212-998-0370

Association of Commercial Finance
Attorneys (ACFA)
1 Corporate Center, 18th Floor MSN 712
Hartford, CT 06103; tel: 203-520-7094;
fax: 203-240-5077

Commercial Finance Association (CFA)
225 West 34th Street
New York, NY 10122; tel: 212-594-3490
or 212-564-6053

Financial Analysts Federation
P.O. Box 3726
Charlottesville, VA 22903;
tel: 804-977-8977

Financial Management Association
International
College of Business Administration
University of South Florida
Tampa, FL 33620-5500

Financial Management Service
Department of the Treasury
401 14th Street SW
Washington, DC 20227;
tel: 202-874-6750

Financial Managers Society
8 South Michigan Avenue, Suite 500
Chicago, IL 60603; tel: 312-578-1300

Government Finance Officers Association
of United States and Canada
ISO North Michigan Avenue, Suite 800
Chicago, IL 60601; tel: 312-977-9700;
fax: 312-977-4806

Institute of Certified Financial Planners
3801 East Florida Avenue, Suite 708
Denver, CO 80210; tel: 303-751-7600;
fax: 303-759-0749

Institute of Chartered Financial Analysts
P.O. Box 3668
Charlottesville, VA 22903;
tel: 804-977-6600

Institute of International Finance (IIF)
2000 Pennsylvania Avenue NW,
Suite 8500
Washington, DC 20006-1812; tel: 202-857-3600; fax: 202-775-1430

International Association for Financial
Planning
2 Concourse Parkway, Suite 800
Atlanta, GA 30328; tel: 404-395-1605

National Association of County
Treasurers and Finance Officers
c/o National Association of Counties
440 First Street NW, 8th Floor
Washington, DC 20001;
tel: 202-393-6226

National Society for Real Estate Finance
(NSREF)
2300 M Street NW, Suite 800
Washington, DC 20037;
tel: 202-973-2801

New York State Consumer Finance
Association (NYSCFA)
90 South Swan Street
Albany, NY 12210; tel: 518-449-7514;
fax: 518-426-0566

New York State Government Finance
Officers Association
119 Washington Avenue
Albany, NY 12210-2204;
tel: 518-465-1512; fax: 518-434-4640

North American Economics and Finance
Association (NAEFA)
Department of Finance
Syracuse University
Syracuse, NY 13244-2130;
tel: 315-443-2963; fax: 315-443-5389

Securities Industry Association
120 Broadway
New York, NY 10271;
tel: 212-608-1500

HUMAN RESOURCES

Publications

HR Magazine
606 North Washington Street
Alexandria, VA 22314; tel: 703-548-3440

Associations

American Society for Training and
Development
1640 King Street, Box 1443
Alexandria, VA 22313; tel: 703-683-8100

Employment Management Association
4101 Lake Boone Trail, Suite 201
Raleigh, NC 27607; tel: 919-787-6010

Institute of Management Consultants
521 Fifth Avenue, 35th Floor
New York, NY 10175; tel: 212-697-8262

International Personnel Management
Association
1617 Duke Street
Alexandria, VA 22314; tel: 703-549-7100

National Training Laboratory
1240 North Pitt Street
Alexandria, VA 22314; tel: 703-548-1500

Society for Human Resource
Management
606 North Washington Street
Alexandria, VA 22314; tel: 703-548-3440

LAW

Publications

ALA Management Connections
Association of Legal Administrators
175 E. Hawthorn Parkway, Suite 325
Vernon Hills, IL 60061-1428;
tel: 708-816-1212
(free; updated weekly)

Federal Careers for Attorneys
Federal Reports, Inc., Washington, DC
A guide to legal careers with over three hundred U.S. government general counsel and other legal offices in the U.S. Explains where to apply, the types of legal work common to each field, and information on special recruitment programs.

Judicial Staff Directory
Staff Directories, Ltd., Mt. Vernon, VA
Lists over eleven thousand individuals employed in the 207 federal courts, as well as thirteen thousand cities and their courts. The book also has information on court administration, U.S. marshals, U.S. attorneys, and the U.S. Department of Justice. Includes eighteen hundred biographies.

NDAA Membership Directory
National District Attorneys Association, Alexandria, VA
Lists all district attorneys' offices across the U.S.
$15 for nonmembers, $10 for members. Call 703-549-9222 for more information.

Paralegal's Guide to Government Jobs
Federal Reports, Inc., Washington, DC
Explains federal hiring procedures for both entry-level and experienced paralegals. The volume describes seventy law-related careers for which paralegals qualify and lists over one thousand federal agency personnel offices that hire the most paralegal talent. Also profiles special hiring programs.

Associations

American Association for Paralegal Education
P.O. Box 40244
Overland Park, KS 66204;
tel: 913-381-4458

American Bar Association Information Services
750 North Lake Shore Drive
Chicago, IL 60611; tel: 312-988-5000 or 800-621-6159

Internships for College Students Interested in Law, Medicine, and Politics
Graduate Group
86 Norwood Road
West Hartford, CT 06117;
tel: 203-236-5570 or 203-232-3100
($27.50, published annually)

National Association for Law Placement
1666 Connecticut Avenue, Suite 328
Washington, DC 20009;
tel: 202-667-1666

National Association of Legal Assistants
1516 South Boston Avenue, Suite 200
Tulsa, OK 74119; tel: 918-587-6828

National Federation of Paralegal Associations
P.O. Box 33108
Kansas City, MO 64114;
tel: 816-941-4000

National Paralegal Association
Box 406
Solebury, PA 18963; tel: 215-297-8333

NCRA Employment Referral Service
National Court Reporters Association
8224 Old Courthouse Road
Vienna, VA 22182; tel: 703-556-6272
(six-month registration: nonmembers,
$20; free to members)

Paralegal Placement Network Inc.
P.O. Box 406
Solebury, PA 18963; tel: 215-297-8333
(regular fee, $10; Nat. Paralegal
Association members, $15)

MEDIA/COMMUNICATION/
PUBLIC RELATIONS

Publications

P.R. Reporter
P.O. Box 6000
Exeter, NH 03833

Public Relations Consultants Directory
American Business Directories Inc.
5711 East 86th Circle
Omaha, NE 68127; tel: 402-331-7169

*SMPS Employment Referral Society for
Marketing Professional Services*
99 Canal Plaza, Suite 250
Alexandria, VA 22314;
tel: 703-549-6117 or 800-292-7677
(nonmembers, $100; members, $50;
five copies resume and SMPS
application—on file for three months)

Associations

American Society for Health Care
Marketing and Public Relations
American Hospital Association
1 North Franklin
Chicago, IL 60606; tel: 312-422-3737

American Society of Journalists and
Authors
1501 Broadway, Suite 302
New York, NY 10036; tel: 212-997-0947

Council of Sales Promotion Agencies
750 Summer Street
Stamford, CT 06901; tel: 203-325-3911

Dow Jones Newspaper Fund
P.O. Box 300
Princeton, NJ 08543-0300;
tel: 609-452-2820

Editorial Freelancers Association
71 West 23rd Street, Suite 1504
New York, NY 10010; tel: 212-929-5400

Institute for Public Relations Research
and Education (IPRRE)
University of Florida
P.O. Box 118400
Gainesville, FL 32611-8400;
tel: 904-392-0280

International Advertising Association
521 Fifth Avenue, Suite 1807
New York, NY 10175; tel: 212-557-1133

Investigative Reporters & Editors
University of Missouri
26A Walter Williams Hall
Columbia, MO 65211; tel: 314-882-2042

League of Advertising Agencies Directory
2 South End Avenue #4C
New York, NY 10280; tel: 212-945-4314

National School Public Relations
Association (NSPRA)
1501 Lee Highway, Suite 201
Arlington, VA 22209; tel: 703-528-5840

PR Newswire Job Bank
865 South Figueroa, Suite 2310
Los Angeles, CA 90017;
tel: 213-626-5500 or 800-321-8169
(send resume and cover letter)

Promotion Marketing Association of
America, Inc.
Executive Headquarters
257 Park Avenue South, 11th Floor
New York, NY 10001; tel: 212-420-1100

Public Relations Society of America
33 Irving Place, 3rd Floor
New York, NY 10003; tel: 212-995-2230

Public Relations Student Society of
America (PRSSA)
33 Irving Place, 3rd Floor
New York, NY 10003; tel: 212-460-1474

Society for Technical Communication
901 North Stuart Street, Suite 904
Arlington, VA 22203; tel: 703-522-4114

Writers Guild of America
555 West 57th Street
New York, NY 10019; tel: 212-767-7800

SALES AND MARKETING

Associations

TRAVEL

Adventure Travel Society
6551 South Revere Parkway, Suite 160
Englewood, CO 80111;
tel: 303-649-9016; fax: 303-649-9017

Air Transport Association of America
1301 Pennsylvania Avenue NW,
Suite 1100
Washington, DC 20004-7017;
tel: 202-626-4000

Airline Employees Association, Intl.
Job Opportunity Program
5600 South Central Avenue
Chicago, IL 60638-3797

American Travel Inns (ATI)
(formerly: American Travel Association)
36 South State Street, Suite 1200
Salt Lake City, UT 84111-1416;
tel: 801-521-0732; fax: 801-521-0732

Association of Flight Attendants
1625 Massachusetts Avenue NW
Washington, DC 20036;
tel: 202-328-5400

Association of Retail Travel Agents (ARTA)
845 Sir Thomas Court, Suite 3
Harrisburg, PA 17109;
tel: 717-545-9548 or 800-969-6069;
fax: 717-545-9613

American Society of Travel Agents (ASTA)
1101 King Street, Suite 200
Alexandria, VA 22314;
tel: 703-739-2782; fax: 703-684-8319

Cruise Lines International Association
500 Fifth Avenue, Suite 1407
New York, NY 10110; tel: 212-921-0066

Freighter Travel Club of America
3524 Harts Lake Road
Roy, WA 98580; tel: 360-458-4178

Future Aviation Professionals of America
4959 Massachusetts Boulevard
Atlanta, GA 30337; tel: 404-997-8097 or
800-JET-JOBS

Greater Independent Association of
National Travel Services (GIANTS)
2 Park Avenue, Suite 2205
New York, NY 10016;
tel: 212-545-7460 or 800-442-6871;
fax: 212-545-7428

Independent Travel Agencies of America
Association (ITAA)
5353 North Federal Highway, Suite 300
Fort Lauderdale, Fl 33308;
tel: 305-772-4660 or 800-950-5440;
fax: 305-772-5797

Institute of Certified Travel Agents (ICTA)
148 Linden Street, P.O. Box 812059
Wellesley, MA 02181-0012;
tel: 617-237-0280 or 800-542-4282;
fax: 617-237-3860

International Association for Air Travel
Couriers
P.O. Box 1349
Lake Worth, FL 33460;
tel: 407-582-8320; fax: 407-582-1581

International Association of Travel
Exhibitors (IATE)
P.O. Box 2309
Gulf Shores, AL 36547;
tel: 205-948-6690; fax: 205-948-6690

International Association of Travel
Journalists (IATJ)
P.O. Box D
Hurleyville, NY 12747; tel: 914-434-1529

International Federation of Women's
Travel Organizations (IFWTO)
13901 North 73rd Street, #210B
Scottsdale, AZ 85260-3125; tel: 602-596-
6640; fax: 602-596-6638

Travel Industry Association of America
1100 New York Avenue NW, Suite 450
Washington, DC 20005-3934;
tel: 202-408-8422

U.S. Travel Data Center
(affiliate of the Travel Industry Association
of America)
2 Lafayette Center
1100 New York Avenue NW, Suite 450
Washington, DC 20005;
tel: 202-408-1832

Yours in Travel Personnel Agency
12 West 37th Street
New York, NY 10018; tel: 212-697-7855

MARKETING/ADVERTISING

American Advertising Federation
Education Services Department
1101 Vermont Avenue NW, Suite 500
Washington, DC 20005;
tel: 202-898-0089

American Marketing Association
250 South Wacker Drive, Suite 200
Chicago, IL 60606-5819;
tel: 312-648-0536

The Convention Liaison Council
1575 Eye Street NW, Suite 1190
Washington, DC 20005;
tel: 202-626-2764

Direct Marketing Association
1120 Avenue of the Americas
New York, NY 10036-6700;
tel: 212-768-7277

Meeting Planners International
Informant Building, Suite 5018
1950 Stemmons Freeway
Dallas, TX 75207; tel: 214-712-7700

Retail Advertising and Marketing
Association
500 North Michigan Avenue, Suite 600
Chicago, IL 60611; tel: 312-251-7262

Sales and Marketing Executives
International
977 Statler Office Tower
Cleveland, OH 44115; tel: 216-771-6650

Sales and Marketing Management
355 Park Avenue South
New York, NY 10010; tel: 212-592-6300

FOOD SERVICES

Associations

Alaska Culinary Association
P.O. Box 140396
Anchorage, AK 99514;
tel: 907-265-7116

American Culinary Federation
10 San Bartola Road, P.O. Box 3466
St. Augustine, FL 32085-3466;
tel: 904-824-4468

Berks Lehigh Chef's Association
2012 Redwood Avenue
Wyomissing, PA 19610;
tel: 610-678-1217

National Food Broker Association
2100 Reston Parkway, Suite 400
Reston, VA 22091; tel: 703-758-7790

National Restaurant Association
1200 17th Street NW
Washington, DC 20036; tel: 202-331-5900

SUPPORT SERVICES

Associations

American Society of Corporate Secretaries
521 Fifth Avenue
New York, NY 10175-0003;
tel: 212-681-2000

California Federation of Legal Secretaries
2250 East 73rd Street, Suite 550
Tulsa, OK 74136; tel: 918-493-3540

National Association of Executive
Secretaries
900 S. Washington Street, No. G-13
Falls Church, VA 22046;
tel: 703-237-8616

PUBLIC SERVICES/SOCIAL SERVICES

Publications

*Directory of Legal Aid and Defender
Offices in the U.S. and Territories*
National Legal Aid and Defender
Association, Washington, DC
Lists legal aid and public defender offices
across the U.S. Published annually.

Associations

ACTION International
120 Beacon Street
Somerville, MA 02143;
tel: 617-492-4930

American Counseling Association
5999 Stevenson Avenue
Alexandria, VA 22304;
tel: 703-823-9800 or 800-347-6647

American Friends Service Committee
1501 Cherry Street
Philadelphia, PA 19102;
tel: 215-241-7000

American School Counselor Association
801 North Fairfax Street, Suite 301
Alexandria, VA 22314;
tel: 703-683-2722

American Vocational Association
1410 King Street
Alexandria, VA 22314;
tel: 703-683-3111 or 800-892-2274

Child Welfare League of America
440 First Street NW, Suite 310
Washington, DC 20001;
tel: 201-638-2952

Council for Standards in Human Service
Education
Northern Essex Community College
Haverhill, MA 01830;
tel: 508-374-5889

Council on Social Work Education
1600 Duke Street, Suite 300
Alexandria, VA 22314-3421;
tel: 703-683-8080
(send $10 for Directory of Accredited
BSW and MSW Programs)

Educators for Social Responsibility
23 Garden Street
Cambridge, MA 02138;
tel: 617-492-1764

Human Service Council
3191 Maguire Boulevard, Suite 1150
Orlando, FL 32803; tel: 407-897-6465

National Association of Social Workers
750 First Street NE, Suite 700
Washington, DC 20002-4241;
tel: 202-408-8600

National Center for Charitable Statistics
1828 L Street NW, Suite 1200B
Washington, DC 20036; tel: 202-223-8100

National Civic League
1445 Market Street, Suite 300
Denver, CO 80202-1728;
tel: 303-571-4343

National Exchange Club Foundation for
the Prevention of Child Abuse
3050 Central Avenue
Toledo, OH 43606; tel: 419-535-3232 or
800-760-3413

National Network for Social Work
Managers
1316 New Hampshire Avenue NW,
Suite 602
Washington, DC 20036;
tel: 202-785-2814

National Organization for Human Service
Education
Fitchburg State College, Box 6257
160 Pearl Street
Fitchburg, MA 01420; tel: 508-345-2151

Save the Children Federation
54 Wilton Road
Westport, CT 06880; tel: 203-221-4000

Social Service Association
6 Station Plaza
Ridgewood, NJ 07450;
tel: 201-444-2980

EDUCATION

Publications

*Who's Who in Special Libraries and
Information Centers*
Gale Research Inc., Detroit, MI
Lists special libraries alphabetically and
geographically. Published annually.

Associations

Academy for Educational Development
(AED)
1875 Connecticut Avenue NW
Washington, DC 20009;
tel: 202-884-8000; fax: 202-884-8400
E-mail: admind@aed-org

American Association of School
Administrators
1801 N Moore Street
Arlington, VA 22209-9988;
tel: 703-528-0700

American Association of School
Librarians
50 E. Huron Street
Chicago, IL 60611; tel: 312-944-6780

American Association of University
Administrators
1012 14th Street NW, Suite 500
Washington, DC 20005;
tel: 202-737-5900

American Association of University
Professors
1012 14th Street NW, Suite 500
Washington, DC 20005;
tel: 202-737-5900

American Educational Studies Association
(AESA)
University of Cincinnati
Graduate Studies and Research
Cincinnati, OH 45221; tel: 513-556-2256

American Federation of Teachers
555 New Jersey Avenue NW
Washington, DC 20001;
tel: 202-879-4400

American Library Association
50 East Huron Street
Chicago, IL 60611; tel: 312-944-6780

Association for Community Based
Education (ACBE)
1805 Florida Avenue NW
Washington, DC 20009;
tel: 202-462-6333 or 202-232-8044

Association for Educational
Communications and Technology (AECT)
1025 Vermont Avenue NW, Suite 820
Washington, DC 20005;
tel: 202-347-7834; fax: 202-347-7839

Center for Adult Learning and Educational
Credentials (CALEC)
1 Dupont Circle NW
Washington, DC 20036;
tel: 202-939-9475; fax: 202-775-8574

College and University Personnel
Association
1233 20th Street NW, Suite 301
Washington, DC 20036-1250;
tel: 202-429-0311

Council on International Educational
Exchange (CIEE)
205 East 42nd Street
New York, NY 10017;
tel: 212-661-1414; fax: 212-972-3231

Earthwatch
(formerly: Educational Expeditions
International)
680 Mount Auburn Street, Box 403
Watertown, MA 02272;
tel: 617-926-8200 or 800-776-0188;
fax: 617-926-8532
E-mail: info@earthwatch.org

Educational Research Service (ERS)
2000 Clarendon Blvd.
Arlington, VA 22201;
tel: 703-243-2100; fax: 703-243-1985

Federal Librarians Round Table
American Library Association,
Washington Office
1301 Pennsylvania Avenue NW, No. 403
Washington, DC 20004; tel: 202-608-8410

High/Scope Educational Research
Foundation
600 North River Street
Ypsilanti, MI 48198-2898;
tel: 313-485-2000 or 800-40-PRESS;
fax: 313-485-0704

Independent Educational Services (IES)
(formerly: Cooperative Bureau for
Teachers)
353 Nassau Street
Princeton, NJ 08540; tel: 609-921-6195
or 800-257-5102; fax: 609-921-0155

Institute for Educational Leadership (IEL)
1001 Connecticut Avenue NW, Suite 310
Washington, DC 20036;
tel: 202-822-8405; fax: 202-872-4050

Intercultural Development Research
Association (IDRA)
5835 Callaghan Road, Suite 350
San Antonio, TX 78228;
tel: 210-684-8180; fax: 210-684-5389

International Association for Educational
Assessment (IAEA)
P.O. Box 6665
Princeton, NJ 08541; tel: 609-921-9000;
fax: 609-520-1093

Madison Center for Educational Affairs
(MCEA)
455 15th Street NW, Suite 712
Washington, DC 20005;
tel: 202-833-1801; fax: 202-467-0006

National Association of Educational Office
Professionals (NAEOP)
P.O. Box 12619
Wichita, KS 67277; tel: 316-942-4822;
fax: 316-942-7100

National Association of Secondary School
Principals
1904 Association Drive
Reston, VA 22091; tel: 703-860-0200

National Association of Student
Personnel Administrators
1875 Connecticut Avenue NW, Suite 418
Washington, DC 20009;
tel: 202-265-7500

National Council for Accreditation of
Teacher Education
2010 Massachusetts Avenue NW,
Suite 500
Washington, DC 20036;
tel: 202-466-7496

National Council of Educational
Opportunity Associations (NCEOA)
1025 Vermont Avenue NW, Suite 1201
Washington, DC 20005;
tel: 202-347-7430

National Council on the Evaluation of
Foreign Educational Credentials
c/o AACRAO
1 Dupont Circle NW, Suite 330
Washington, DC 20036;
tel: 202-293-9161 or 202-872-8857
E-mail: aacrao@umdd

National Education Association
1201 16th Street NW
Washington, DC 20036;
tel: 202-833-4000

National Rural Education Association
(NREA)
Colorado State University
230 Education Building
Fort Collins, CO 80523-1588;
tel: 970-491-7022; fax: 970-491-1317

Special Libraries Association
1700 18th Street NW
Washington, DC 20009-2508;
tel: 202-234-4700; fax: 202-265-9317

University Council for Educational
Administration (UCEA)
Pennsylvania State University
212 Rackley Bldg.
University Park, PA 16802-3200;
tel: 814-863-7916/7917 or
fax: 814-863-7918

GOVERNMENT

Publications

The Capitol Source
National Journal, Inc., Washington, DC
Includes names, addresses, and phone
numbers for key figures in the District of
Columbia; also features information
about corporations, interest groups, think
tanks, labor unions, real estate
organizations, financial institutions, trade
and professional groups, law firms,
political consultants, advertising and
public relations firms, private clubs, and
the media. Published twice a year.

Congressional Yellow Book
Monitor Publishing Co., New York, NY
Gives detailed information on
congressional staff positions, committees
and subcommittees, and top staff in
congressional support agencies.
Published annually.

COSLA Directory
The Council of State Governments,
Lexington, KY
Provides information on state library
agencies, consultant and administrative
staff, plus ALANER numbers, electronic
mail letters, and fax numbers. Published
annually.

Directory of Federal Libraries
Includes library's administrator and
selected staff for three thousand special
and general, presidential and national
libraries, as well as library facilities in
technical centers, hospitals, and penal
institutions.

Federal Executive Directory
Carroll Publishing Co., Washington, DC
Profiles a broad range of agencies, both
executive and legislative, including cabinet
departments, federal administrative
agencies, and congressional committee
members and staff. The directory also
outlines areas of responsibility for legal
and administrative assistants. Published
six times a year; an annual subscription is
$178. Call 202-333-8620 for more
information.

Federal Organization Service: Military
Carroll Publishing Co., Washington, DC
Lists direct-dial phone numbers for
11,500 key individuals in fifteen hundred

military departments and offices.
Updated every six weeks; an annual
subscription is $625. Call 202-333-8620
for more information.

Washington Information Directory
Congressional Quarterly Inc.,
Washington, DC
Provides important information on the
federal government as a whole, and on
each federal department and agency. The
volume also provides details on regional
federal information sources,
nongovernmental organizations in the
Washington area, and congressional
committees and subcommittees.
Published annually.

Washington 2000
Columbia Books, New York, NY
Contains addresses, phone numbers,
and profiles of key institutions in the city.
Includes chapters on the federal
government, the media, business,
national associations, labor unions, law
firms, medicine and health, foundations
and philanthropic organizations, science
and policy research groups, and
educational, religious, and cultural
institutions. Published annually.

Associations

American Federation of State, County,
and Municipal Employees
1625 L Street NW
Washington, DC 20036;
tel: 202-429-1000

American Planning Association
122 South Michigan Avenue, Suite 1600
Chicago, IL 60603; tel: 312-431-9100

Civil Service Employees Association
P.O. Box 7125
Capitol State
Albany, NY 12210; tel: 518-434-0191 or
800-342-4146

Council of State Governments
P.O. Box 11910
3560 Iron Works Pike
Lexington, KY 40578; tel: 606-244-8000

International Association of Fire Fighters
1750 New York Avenue NW
Washington, DC 21006;
tel: 202-737-8484

International City/County Management
Association
777 North Capitol Street NE, Suite 500
Washington, DC 20002;
tel: 202-289-4262

National Association of Counties (NACO)
440 First Street NW, 8th Floor
Washington, DC 20001;
tel: 202-393-6226

National Association of Government
Communicators
669 South Washington Street
Alexandria, VA 22314;
tel: 703-519-3902

National Planning Association
1424 16th Street NW, Suite 700
Washington, DC 20036;
tel: 202-265-7685

New York State Professional Firefighters
Association
111 Washington Avenue, Suite 207
Albany, NY 12210; tel: 518-436-8827

State Services Organization (SSO)
444 North Capitol Street NW
Washington, DC 20001;
tel: 202-624-5470

DISABILITIES
ADA Regional Disabled and Business Assistance Centers

Connecticut, Maine, Massachusetts, Rhode Island, and Vermont:
New England Disability and Business
Technical Assistance Center
145 Newbury Street
Portland, ME 04101; tel: 207-874-6535
(voice/TDD)

New Jersey, New York, Puerto Rico, and Virgin Islands:
Northeast Disability and Business
Technical Assistance Center
354 South Broad Street
Trenton, NJ 08608; tel: 609-392-4004
(voice), 609-392-7044 (TDD)

Delaware, District of Columbia, Maryland, Pennsylvania, Virginia, and West Virginia:
Mid-Atlantic Disability and Business
Technical Assistance Center
2111 Wilson Boulevard, Suite 400
Arlington, VA 22201; tel: 703-525-3268
(voice/TDD)

Alabama, Florida, Georgia, Kentucky, Mississippi, North Carolina, South Carolina, and Tennessee:
Southeast Disability and Business
Technical Assistance Center
1776 Peachtree Street, Suite 310 North
Atlanta, GA 30309; tel: 404-888-0022
(voice/TDD)

Illinois, Indiana, Michigan, Minnesota, Ohio, and Wisconsin:
Great Lakes Disability and Business Technical Assistance Center
1640 West Roosevelt Road (M/C 627)
Chicago, IL 60608; tel: 312-413-1407 (voice/TDD)

Arkansas, Louisiana, New Mexico, Oklahoma, and Texas:
Southwest Disability and Business Technical Assistance Center
2323 South Shepherd Boulevard, Suite 1000
Houston, TX 77019; tel: 713-520-0232 (voice), 713-520-5136 (TDD)

Iowa, Kansas, Nebraska, and Missouri:
Great Plains Disability and Business Technical Assistance Center
4816 Santana Drive
Columbia, MO 65203;
tel: 314-882-3600 (voice/TDD)

Colorado, Montana, North Dakota, South Dakota, Utah, and Wyoming:
Rocky Mountain Disability and Business Technical Assistance Center
3630 Sinton Road, Suite 103
Colorado Springs, CO 80907-5072;
tel: 719-444-0252 (voice/TDD)

Arizona, California, Hawaii, and Nevada:
Pacific Coast Disability and Business Technical Assistance Center
440 Grand Avenue, Suite 500
Oakland, CA 94610; tel: 510-465-7884 (voice), 510-465-3167 (TDD)

Job Accommodation Network
P.O. Box 6123
809 Allen Hall
Morgantown, WV 26505-6123;
tel: 800-526-7234 (voice/TDD)

The President's Committee on Employment of People with Disabilities
1331 F Street NW
Washington, DC 20004;
tel: 202-376-6200 (voice),
202-376-6205 (TDD)

U.S. Department of Justice, Civil Rights Division
Office of the Americans with Disabilities Act
P.O. Box 66118
Washington, DC 20035-6118; tel: 800-514-0301 (voice), 800-514-0383 (TDD)

APPENDIX C | Professional Resume Writing Services

In the early stages of your job hunt, you might want to look into getting extra help from a professional resume writer. A professional in the field might be able to help you develop a more polished layout or present a particularly complex background more effectively.

The big question is, "Who should I use?" As in any other profession, there are practitioners at both ends of the performance spectrum. I am a strong believer in using the services of resume writers who belong to the field's professional associations. They tend to be more committed, have more field experience, and have an all-around higher standard of performance, partly because their membership demonstrates their commitment to the field and partly from the ongoing educational programs that these associations offer to their members.

Resume writers who are members of the appropriate professional associations are more likely to be able to help you fine-tune your resume into an effective marketing tool. Depending on the help you need, their services can range from $50 to $1000. (Don't gasp—the higher up the professional ladder you are aiming, the more important a polished and professional-looking resume becomes!)

Remember that a resume isn't just a piece of paper that gets your foot in the door. It also sits on every interviewer's desk as a road map to your professional background, giving them some guidance for the direction your interviews will take. It also works on your behalf long after you have left the interview, and it is probably the last document an employer will consider before making the final decision between candidates.

There are three dominant associations in the field: the Professional Association of Resume Writers (PARW, parw.com), the National Resume Writers Association (NRWA, nrwa.com) and Career Masters Institute (CMI).

Both PARW and NRWA have hundreds of members and provide ongoing opportunities for members to gain mentoring experience and additional training. Both offer resume-writing certification, and both operate e-mail list servers for members with access to e-mail. The professional training programs range from how to handle specific resume challenges to issues related to running a resume service. The associations build camaraderie between members and offer them access to the expertise of hundreds of other professional resume writers. Both organizations offer an annual convention with workshops on industry issues.

PARW offers training seminars several times a year throughout the country. NRWA offers its members a Web-based training program.

Members of the Career Masters Institute tend to be serious tenured professionals. Almost all (about 95 percent) are Certified Professional Resume Writers (CPRW), a distinction that sets them apart and clearly validates their capabilities. Many (approximately 30-40) have also earned their Job & Career Transition Coach (JCTC) certification. Several (about 10-15—and as a member, I'm one of them) are nationally published authors on resume writing, job search, coaching, and related career topics. Also important—most CMI members offer more than just resume writing services.

Although a powerful resume is the foundation for virtually every successful job search, CMI members also offer a host of career marketing services that can help their clients accelerate their campaigns. These services include Internet resume postings, e-mail campaigns to recruiters, direct-mail campaigns to growth companies, executive job lead reports, career coaching, counseling, and more.

Here are some of the members of these three estimable associations who have contributed resumes and valuable insights to the book (with a special thanks to Wendy Enelow and Gwen Harrison):

A CareerPro Inc.
201 North Federal Highway, Suite 108
Deerfield Beach, Florida 33441;
tel: (954) 428-4935; fax: (954) 428-0965
E-mail: careerpro@mindspring.com
Web: www.faxrecruiters.com/amme.html

Abilities Enhanced
PO Box 9667
Kansas City, MO 64134;
tel: (816) 767-1196
E-mail: M7125@aol.com
Web: www.abilitiesenhanced.com

Elizabeth J. Axnix, CPRW, IJCTC
Quality Word Processing
329 East Court Street
Iowa City, IA 52240-4914;
tel: (800) 359-7822 or (319) 354-7822;
fax: (319) 354-2220
E-mail: axnix@earthlink.net

Kathy Black
Career Recipes
P.O. Box 3686
Evergreen, CO 80437;
tel: (303) 679-1519; fax: (303) 670-4414
E-mail: kathyjane@earthlink.net
Web: www.careerrecipes.com

Tracy A. Bumpus, CPRW, JCTC
Executive Director
RezAMAZE.com
Austin, TX;
tel: (512) 291-1404 or (888) 277-4270;
fax: 208-247-2542
Web: www.rezamaze.com

Diane Burns, CPRW, IJCTC, CCM
President
Career Marketing Techniques
5219 Thunder Hill Road
Columbia, MD 21045;
tel: (410) 884-0213
E-mail: DianeCPRW@aol.com
Web: www.polishedresumes.com

Career Advantage
5536 Longview circle
El Paso, TX 79924;
tel: (915) 821-1036; fax: (915) 822-8146
E-mail: jmoore@dzn.com
CMI, CPPRW

Career Counsel
11 Hillside Place
Chappaqua, NY 10514;
tel: (914) 238-1065
E-mail: LinZlev@aol.com

Career Development Resources
1312 Walter Road
Yorktown Heights, NY 10598;
tel: (914) 962-1548; fax: (914) 962-0325
E-mail: cardev@aol.com
Contact: Mark Berkowitz
CMI, CPRW,NCCC, International Certified
Job & Career Transition Coach

Career Solutions, LLC
Trenton, MI 48183;
tel: (734) 676-9170 or (877) 777-7242;
fax: (734) 676-9487 or (877) 777-7307

Comprehensive Resume Services
5300 Spring Mountain Road, Suite 212-D
Las Vegas, NV 89102;
tel: (702) 222-9411

Deborah Wile Dib, NCRW, CPRW, JCTC
President
Advantage Resumes of New York;
tel: (631) 475-8513
Web: www.advantageresumes.com
Member, NRWA, PARW, AJST, CPADN, CMI

Jacqui Barrett Dodson, CPRW
7501 College Boulevard, Suite 175
Career Trend
Overland Park, KS 66210;
tel: (913) 451-1313; fax: (913) 451-3242
E-mail: dodson@careertrend.net
Web: www.careertrend.net

Wendy S. Enelow, CPRW, JCTC, CCM
President
Career Masters Institute
119 Old Stable Road
Lynchburg, VA 24503;
tel: (804) 386-3100
E-mail: wendyenelow@cminstitute.com
Web: www.cminstitute.com
Past President, The Advantage Executive
Resume & Career Marketing Service

Dayna Feist, CPRW, JCTC
Gatehouse Business Services
265 Charlotte Street
Asheville, NC 28801;
tel: (828) 254-7893; fax: (828) 254-7894
E-mail: Gatehous@aol.com
Member, Certification Board, PARW
Member, Career Masters Institute

Joyce Fortier, CCM
Create Your Own Career
23871 W. Lebost
Novi, MI 48375;
tel: (248) 478-5662; fax: (248) 426-9974
E-mail: careerist@aol.com
Web: www.careerist.com

Fox Resume & Career Resources
24242 S. Navajo Drive
Channahon, IL 60410;
tel: (815) 467-6153
E-mail: pfoxhr@aol.com
Contact: Patty Fox

Louise Garver, CMP, CPRW, JCTC
Principal
Career Directions
Connecticut office:
115 Elm Street, Suite 104
Enfield, CT 06082;
tel: (888) 222-3731 or (860) 623-9476;
fax: (860) 623-9473
Massachusetts office:
125 North Elm Street, Suite 301
Westfield, MA 01085;
tel: (413) 568-2356
E-mail: CAREERDIRS@aol.com
Web: www.resumeimpact.com

Wayne M. Gonyea, MS, CCM
President
Gonyea Career Marketing, Inc.
1810 Arturus Lane
New Port Richey, FL 34655;
tel: (727) 375-0489
E-mail: online@resumexpress.com
Web: www.resumexpress.com
Founding Member, Career Masters Institute

Gwen Harrison
Advanced Resumes
438 Shearwater Drive
Fortson, GA 31808;
tel: (877) 353-0025; fax: (888) 811-3241
Gwen@advancedresumes.com

Beverly Harvey, CPRW, JCTC, CCM
tel: (888) 775-0916 or (904) 749-3111
E-mail: beverly@harveycareers.com
Web: www.harveycareers.com
Certified Job & Career Transition Coach
Certified Professional Resume Writer
Charter Member Career Masters Institute
Member National Association of Resume
Writers
Member Professional Association of
Resume Writers

Contributor to PARW's Training Manual

Maria Hebda, CPRW
Career Solutions, LLC
tel: (877) 777-7242
E-mail: careers@writingresumes.com
Web: www.writingresumes.com

Nancy Karvonen, CPRW, IJCTC
Executive Director
A Better Word & Resume
Galt, CA;
tel: (209) 744-8203; fax: (209) 745-7114
Voice Mail/Pager: (888) 598-1995
E-mail: careers@aresumecoach.com
Web: www.aresumecoach.com
Certified Professional Resume Writer
(CPRW)
Internationally Certified Job and Career
Transition Coach (JCTC)
Member, Career Masters Institute
Member, PARW Certification Committee

Shanna Kemp
Kemp Career Services
2105 Via Del Norte
Carrollton, Texas 75006;
tel: (877) 367-5367 or (972) 416-9089;
fax: (972) 478-2890
E-mail: respro@aresumepro.com

Cindy Kraft, CPRW, JCTC
Executive Essentials
P.O. Box 336
Valrico, FL 33595;
tel: (813) 655-0658; fax: (813) 685-4287
Web: www.exec-essentials.com
Member: PARW and Career Masters
Institute

Louise Kursmark, CPRW, JCTC
Best Impression Career Services, Inc.
Cincinnati, Ohio;
tel: (513) 792-0030
Web: www.yourbestimpression.com

Lisa C. LeVerrier
President
Competitive Advantage Resumes &
Career Coaching
5523 N. Military Trail Suite #1212
Boca Raton, FL 33496
433 Plaza Real, Suite 275
Boca Raton, FL 33432;
tel: (561) 982-9573 or (800) 750-5690;
fax: (561) 982-7312
E-mail: gethired@earthlink.net OR
lisalev@earthlink.net
Web: www.jobcoaching.com

Christine Magnus
Business Services Plus;
tel: (718) 519-0477; fax: (718) 405-9894
E-mail: BizServ@aol.com
Member, PARW, Career Masters Institute

JoAnn Nix, CPRW
Beaumont Resume Service;
tel: (800) 265-6901; fax: (409) 924-0019
or (419) 781-2971
E-mail: info@agreatresume.com
Web: www.agreatresume.com

Debra O'Reilly, CPRW, JCTC
Resumewriter.com
16 Terryville Avenue
Bristol, CT 06010;
tel: 860-583-7500; fax: 860-585-9611
E-mail: debra@resumewriter.com
Web: www.resumewriter.com
Charter Member, Career Masters Institute

Member, Professional Association of
Resume Writers
Member, National Resume Writers
Association

Don Orlando, MBA, CPRW, JCTC
The McLean Group
640 South McDonough Street
Montgomery, Alabama 36104;
tel: (334) 264-2020; fax: (334) 264-9227
E-mail: yourcareercoach@aol.com
Certified Professional Resume Writer
Certified Job and Career Transition Coach
Master Team Member: Career Masters
Institute

Professional Resume Services
1214 East Fenway Avenue
Salt Lake City, Utah 84102;
tel: (801) 883-2011; fax: (801) 582-8862
E-mail: resumes@tacisp.com
Web: www.MyCareerResource.com
PARW, CMI, CPRW

Nadine Rubin
Adam-Bryce, Inc.
77 Maple Avenue
New City, NY 10956;
tel: (914) 634-1772 or (845) 634-1772;
fax: (914) 634-1772 or (845) 634-1772
Web: www.adambryce.com

Kelley Smith, CPRW
Advantage Resume Services
P.O. Box 391
Sugar Land, Texas 77487;
tel: (281) 494-3330 or (877) 478-4999;
fax: (281) 494-0173
E-mail: info@advantage-resume.com or
kands@concentric.net
Web: www.advantage-resume.com
Career Masters, PARW, NRWA

Rebecca Stokes, CPRW
President
The Advantage, Inc.
401 Mill Lane
Lynchburg, VA 24503;
tel: (800) 922-5353; fax: (804) 384-4700
E-mail: advresume@aol.com
Web: www.advantageresume.com

Gina Taylor, CPRW
Gina Taylor & Associates, Inc.
1111 W. 77th Terrace
Kansas City, Missouri 64114;
tel: (816) 523-9100
E-mail: ginaresume @aol.com

Jean West, CPRW, JCTC
Career Services,
207 10th Avenue
Indian Rocks Beach, FL 33785;
tel: (727) 596-2534; fax: (727) 593-7386
Web: www.impactresumes.com

Laura West
Agape Career Services;
tel: (888) 685-3507
E-mail: agape@centurytel.net
Web: www.AgapeCareerServices.com

Here are some other online resume services that have sterling reputations in the professional community:

1st Impressions Resumes and Careers
www.1st-imp.com

A+ Online Resumes
www.ol-resume.com

Affordable Resume
www.aaow.com/john_schwartz

Bakos Group
www.bakos.com

Career & Resume Management
www.crm21.com

Career Marketing-Resume service
www.careermarketing.com

Career Transitions
www.bfservs.com:80/bfserv.html

Careerpro
www.career_pro.com

eResumes
www.resumelink.com

Keyword Resume & Fax Service
www.ourworld.compuserve.com/homep
ages/deckerservices

North American Business Concepts
www.digimark.net/noam/

One-way Resume
www2.connectnet.com/users/blorincz

Protype
www.members.aol.com/criscito

Resume Publishing Company
www.csn.net

Resumes on the Web
www.resweb.com

Resumexpress
www.resumexpress.com

Superior Resumes
www.mindtrust.com

APPENDIX
D | Online Resources

A+ Online Resumes
www.ol-resume.com
E-mail: webmaster@ol-resume.com

Academe This Week
www.chronicle.merit.edu/.ads/.links.html

America's Employers Resume Bank
www.americasemployers.com/
resume.html

America's Job Bank
www.ajb.dni.us

Bilingual Jobs
www.bilingual-jobs.com

Brassring.com
www.brassring.com

Careerbabe
www.careerbabe.com

Careerbrain.com
www.careerbrain.com
E-mail: martin yate@careerbrain.com

Careerbuilder
www.careerbuilder.com

CareerCity
www.careercity.com

CAREERMagazine
www.careermagazine.com
E-mail: editor@careermag.com

Career Mosaic
www.careermosaic.com

CareerPath
www.careerpath.com
E-mail: webmaster@careerpath.com

CareerShop
www.careershop.com

CareerTips
www.careertips.com

CareerWeb
www.careerweb.com
E-mail: info@cweb.com

Check Your References
www.myreferences.com

Community Career Center
www.nonprofitjobs.org

Contract Employment Connection
www.ntes.com

Contract Executives
www.imcor.com

Cool Works
www.coolworks.com

Diversity
www.eop.com

DiversityLink
www.diversitylink.com

The Education Jobsite
www.edjobsite.com

Employment Spot
www.employmentspot.com

Exec.U.Net
www.execunet.com
E-mail: Canada@execunet.com

Executive Jobs
www.jobreports.net

FedWorld
www.fedworld.gov
E-mail: webmaster@Fedworld.gov

Fedworld Federal Job Announcements
www.fedworld.gov

Flipdog.com
www.flipdog.com

Getting a Job
www.americanexpress.com/student/

Global Careers
www.globalcareers.com

Gonyea Online Career Center
www.resumeexpress.com

Good Works
www.essential.org/goodworks/

Great Summer Jobs
www.gsj.pertersons.com

Headhunter.net
www.headhunter.net

Help Wanted USA
www.iccweb.com

Hoovers Online
www.hoovers.com

Hot Jobs
www.hotjobs.com

Industry Insite
www.industryinsite.com

International Jobs
www.internationaljobs.org

Internet Business Network
Interbiznet.com

Internet Sourcebook.com
www.internetsourcebook.com

Jaegers' Interactive
www.jaegerinc.com

JobDirect.com
www.jobdirect.com

JOBTRAK
www.jobtrak.com
E-mail: www.@jobtrak.com
tel: (800) 999-8725

Job Web
www.jobweb.org
E-mail: webmaster@jobweb.org

Kelly Services
www.kellyservices.com

Local Opportunities
www.Abracat.com

Manpower
www.manpower.com

Med Search America
www.medsearch.com

Minorities Job Bank
www.minoritiesjobbank.com

Monster Board
www.monster.com

Nationjob
www.nationjob.com

Newspage
www.newspage.com

Non Profit Jobs
www.philanthropy-journal.org

Penton Publishing
www.penton.com

Recruiters Online Network
www.ipa.com

Resumail Network
www.rsumail.com

Resumania Online
www.umn.edu/ohr/ecep/resume

Resume Express
www.resumexpress.com

Resume Link
www.resume-link.com

Resume Network
www.resumenetwork.com

Resumes on the Web
www.resweb.com
E-mail: sdas@ifu.net

Retail Jobs
www.retailjobnet.com

Shawn's Internet Resume Center
www.inpursuit.com/sirc/

Socrates Careers
www.socratescareers.com

Telecommuting Jobs
www.tjobs.com

Wall Street Journal
www.wsj.com

Yahoo Resume Bank
www.yahoo.com

Index

From the publishers of this book

CareerCity.com

Search *4 million* job openings at all the leading career sites with just one click!

Find all the great job openings without having to spend hours surfing from one career site to the next.

Now, with just one click you can simultaneously search all of the leading career sites . . . at CareerCity.com!

You can also have jobs come to you! Enter your job search criteria once and we automatically notify you of any new relevant job listings.

Plus! The most complete career center on the Web including . . .

- Descriptions and hot links to 27,000 U.S. companies
- Comprehensive salary surveys in all fields
- Expert advice on starting a job search, interviews, resumes and much more

You'll find more jobs at CareerCity.com!

Post your resume at CareerCity and have the job offers come to you!

It's fast, free, and easy to post your resume at CareerCity—and you'll get noticed by hundreds of leading employers in all fields.